THE LAST FLIGHT PLAN,

DESTINATION,

UNCERTAIN...

John L. Sparks

iUniverse, Inc.
Bloomington

The Last Flight Plan,
Destination, Uncertain...

iUniverse books may be ordered through booksellers or by contacting:

iUniverse
1663 Liberty Drive
Bloomington, IN 47403
www.iuniverse.com
1-800-Authors (1-800-288-4677)

Because of the dynamic nature of the Internet, any web addresses or links contained in this book may have changed since publication and may no longer be valid. The views expressed in this work are solely those of the author and do not necessarily reflect the views of the publisher, and the publisher hereby disclaims any responsibility for them.

Any people depicted in stock imagery provided by Thinkstock are models, and such images are being used for illustrative purposes only.

Certain stock imagery © Thinkstock.

ISBN: 978-1-4759-2922-5 (sc)
ISBN: 978-1-4759-2923-2 (e)

Printed in the United States of America

iUniverse rev. date: 5/31/2012

DEDICATION

This book would not be in your hands if it were not for
the only love of my life greater than aviation
—my wife Ellie.

This is a photo of Ellie early in our marriage.
Photos #55 & #56 depicts our more recent
years together. May all of you be as fortunate
and happy as we have been
John L. Sparks

Contents

A BRIEF NOTE ABOUT THIS BOOK   ix

Chapter 1 — In the Beginning ...   1

Chapter 2 — Which Way is Mexico, Amigo?   29

 Chapter 3 — Maybe Airplanes Would Be More Fun   58

Chapter 4 — Go East, Young Man, Go East   98

Chapter 5 — Dearly Beloved, We Are Gathered ...   123

Photo Section — 162–189

 Chapter 6 — Got a Job for a Pilot?   190

Chapter 7 — Gee, This Thing Is *BIG*!   218

Chapter 8 — The Crash, And Then the Crash   246

Chapter 9 — The "Mouse" Trap! In Italia ...   280

 Chapter 10 — Life in a Learjet   324

Chapter 11 — And Now a Word from our Sponsor   351

A LIST OF AVIATION FRIENDS AND CHARACTERS   373

A BRIEF NOTE ABOUT THIS BOOK

This book is not a work of fiction, although you may find that hard to believe at times while reading it, or is it my autobiography per se. I *have* based it entirely on my life and how I came to be in the airplane business and managed to survive. Due to the fact that just after WW II, a lot of ex-military pilots, mechanics and knowledgeable people who had served with all the military aviation branches during the war and were teaching young pilots how *they* did it, a heck of a lot of us are still around to talk about it, but, sadly, not for long.

There are possibly twenty-five or fifty-thousand or more of us old pilots who could write what I'm going to tell you. Yet again, there may be less than 20 per cent of that number. I know that the hundreds and hundreds of pilots I knew and worked with have dwindled to about twenty or thirty.

This book isn't about heroes and super pilots, although a few of these do show up briefly, rather it is some snapshots of learning a trade that was hard, dangerous, dirty and not too economically rewarding at the bottom rungs of the ladder.

After saying that, I have to admit that every pilot I knew and felt kinship with had pretty much the same feeling I did. This it wasn't just a job, but a career field that only a few got the opportunity to test themselves in.

I think the last word on this subject came from a trip I made with Calvin Rampton, the Governor of Utah, in 1963. I flew Governor and Mrs. Rampton from Salt Lake City to Moab to visit the new potash plant our company was building there.

The Ramptons were met by our project manager and his staff at the airport for the trip to the mine. As the Governor was about to get into the vehicle, he turned to me and said "John, I'm sorry we're making you fly on Sunday." Our project manager, Frank Tippie, a great man to work for, laughed and said "Governor Rampton, don't you know pilots are like baseball players? They'd do it even if they didn't get paid for it!"

I don't believe I ever heard a better description of the true pilot than that one.

The last two pages of this book are devoted to the names of aviation people that I worked with and learned from during my career. If my memory failed to remember someone who should be on the list, I do apologize.

All through this book you will see aircraft names and designations, stage and screen stars' names from the past, etc. I urge you to make use of a simple Internet search if these interest you. If you have an interest in pictures of all types of aircraft, cockpits and good aviation articles, I recommend that you try *Airliners.net* on Google or your search engine.

The purpose of writing this book is simple. I would like the new generation of student pilots and all pilots in general to see, by my example, that life is full of opportunities and pitfalls. Aviation was my platform to travel through life on. It served me very well. Each of us must find our own platform to make this journey, with a comfort zone that makes sense to us, and at the right price.

Believe me, everything has a price. *You will pay it*, willingly or unwillingly. Willingly is better.

Chapter 1 — In the Beginning ...

It is 11:40 PM local time—0640 GMT. People in London are starting the morning, with hot tea and biscuits probably; hoping the fog will lift and sunshine will bring some warmth into the chilly city air. In San Francisco the night life crowd is getting into full swing at the North Beach, Chinatown and Van Ness bar districts, with the fog slowly climbing the hills to deaden the clang of the trolley car's bell. Below me, people are sleeping or wishing they were, as they think of the thousand things that can make the night seem so long and sleep just a wish. Maybe they hear the soft engine sounds the airplane makes as I fly outbound in the holding pattern, level at 11,000 feet, watching the distance measuring dial coming up on 20 miles from the Omni station. When it clicks on 20, I start the left turn to bring me back to the holding radial. This I will fly inbound again to take me back to the VOR station. I will cross and turn left 180 degrees to the outbound heading. I will now fly to the 20 mile DME readout where I will turn left and intercept the inbound radial to the VOR. This is the sixth pattern I am making.

This is monotonous, almost like a dream. After a long day on this trip, the weather reports for our home airport had looked suitable to be able to make an easy instrument approach and landing. However, like many things in the aviation business, weather has a mind of its own. When it changed more than was anticipated and went below landing minimums, I was only a few minutes from the airport. The forecast indicated enough improvement within the next hour to have the airport above landing minimums, so I requested holding for the time being. It was either that or turning around and going to our alternate airport, 45 minutes away. There were three other airplanes also holding, two below me and one above me.

Fifteen minutes later the fog and light rain lifted to above minimums and I started the ballet that puts us into the approach sequence with the other aircraft; finally breaking out over the runway landing zone and touching down about an hour later than expected. I awakened the passengers as we started the approach. After we parked and as we deplaned at the hangar, they said thanks, see you next trip. I put in half an hour getting the plane taken care of, went home and slipped into bed carefully so as to not wake my wife, and looked at the clock on my nightstand. It said 1:55 AM. It had said 6:15 AM yesterday morning when my day started.

This was a standard trip in the life of a corporate pilot. Sometimes they get difficult, but most of the time it's business as usual. My initial advice to all the young pilots I have worked with is really simple and absolutely true.

Never miss an opportunity to take a nap, grab a sandwich, or hit the restroom. And above all, expect the unexpected on every trip. Train as much as you can toward being ready for anything, and study your trip routing for escape routes to any suitable airport along the route in case of an emergency. Really listen to the weather briefing and if it's not suitable, don't hesitate to tell the boss no. That's what they pay you to do. Any idiot can say its okay, but the skilled pilot knows there are definite limits and if you scare the you-know-what out of your passengers, they rarely forget it.

Find out everything you can about the problems that are unique in your home operational area, how to handle them, and do a great deal of listening when the old timers are talking. A lot of what you'll hear is how they got to be old timers. It may help you to become an old timer yourself. You cannot use what you do not know. You cannot teach what you do not know. If you don't understand something, ask a question or ask for a more detailed explanation. You will only look like an idiot if you don't do this and then damage a very expensive aircraft because you didn't.

So, this is what I did and have done to make my living for quite a while. Why was I doing it and how did this come to be? Funny you should ask. Here's the story ...

My name is John Lee Sparks, Jr. I was born in Ennis, Texas, on March 22, 1933. My mother and father separated a few years after my birth, so my early years were spent at my grandfather's place in Ennis. Growing up in the 1930's in the depression era in Ellis County, Texas, taught me a lot of hard lessons about work, even as a child. When I was seven years old, I helped pick my grandfather's cotton crop on his farm. The pay rate for all the pickers was 1¢ a pound, clean cotton, no stems or boles, and for 10 hours of work, I could pick about 18 to 20 pounds. Our field hands, black or white, could pick about 200-220 pounds in that time—sometimes a little more. Grandfather would always put me down for 25 pounds on the tally sheet just to make sure I had movie money on Saturday when we went to town. The field hands, black and white, got a little something extra if we had a good crop and they made good time picking.

My father had joined the army in 1937, and ended up in the Army Air Corps stationed in San Antonio. I was always told that my grandfather had paid off some gambling debts that my dad had incurred in Dallas or Louisiana. The gamblers were threatening to break all of Dad's fingers if he didn't pay up. Since my dad played piano in jazz bands at the roadhouses, with the big spangled balls in the ceilings, this threat, if real, would have ruined his whole future.

But, according to the story I was told, my grandfather had a provision attached to the payment—Dad had to enlist in the military service and be sworn in before

Grandfather would pay off the markers, as gambling debts were called in those days. True or not, Dad was in the Army Air Corps, and I got to go stay with him in San Antonio the summer of 1940, and again in 1941.

In 1940, Brooks, Kelly, and Randolph Army Air Corps fields were primary, basic and advanced training facilities for pilots and some navigators. Dad worked mainly at Randolph so I could go with him when his schedule was light, sometimes for half a day. I will never forget the first time we drove through the tall bronze gates with the M.P.s waving us through. We parked at the main administration building and walked around to the rear area to be able to see the flight line. All I could see was airplanes; row after row of silver bi-planes with the red, white and blue star roundels on the wings and fuselages. They had a round black engine and red, white and one blue stripe on the rudder. Dad told me these were the first airplanes the students would fly in with instructors. They were the Stearman PT-17s. *(Photo #54)*

We went into the big, stone administration building, and into a lobby with signs, flags, airplane pictures, and Air Corps insignias. This was mind-boggling for a seven year old. But the one thing I can still see, as if I had seen it only an hour ago, was a large photograph of the front of a building with a sign over the entrance that said "SWITLICK PARACHUTE CO." A smaller sign under this said, "We've never had a complaint." Dad had to explain the built-in joke to me. If you used it and it worked—no complaint. If it didn't work, well ... still no complaint.

Then he showed me a large plaque mounted next to the photo that had an open parachute canopy at the top of it and four or five columns of names with dates. Below the 'chute were the words "The Caterpillar Club." Again, Dad explained the significance of the plaque and the name on it. I think most aviators/pilots know this story, but for everyone else, here it is.

Parachutes date back to World War I, and were possibly even used in the Civil War by the U.S. Balloon Corps, as a means of escape from observation balloons when necessary. Before the time of discovery and utilization of synthetic fabrics such as nylon and Dacron, parachutes were made with the strands of silk spun by the silk caterpillar. Threads of materials such as linen, wool, cotton and others were utilized for the harness, shrouds and canopy reinforcement. But the canopy itself was made of the silk strands woven into a very thin lightweight material that formed the panels of the 'chute. So the term "To hit the silk" meant to bail out of an aircraft in trouble or just for fun. If you did this successfully, you were entitled to join "The Caterpillar Club," wear a small metal caterpillar on your collar and have your name and date of use put on the plaques at the factory. The military services had their own recognition plaques and what I saw was one of those.

Dad had a couple of friends who were instructors and he prevailed upon them to give me a tour of the flight line. I was allowed to sit in a cockpit, move the controls, run my hands over the fabric of the control surface and even put my arms around the shiny wood propeller.

I had always been told that you have to die before you can be in heaven. This day I found out that that was incorrect.

That summer visit really hooked me on aviation. The next year went by very slowly. I finally wheedled Mom into letting me go back to spend a month with Dad. The summer of 1941 was a time of uncertainty; a lot of unease about the war in Europe and Asia. The Battle of Britain brought home to us the reality of war. I read all that I could find and looked at all the pictures of airplanes being utilized by all the combatants. The Hawker Hurricane, Spitfire, ME-109, JU-88 Stuka Dive Bomber known as "Whistling Death" and others became everyday names in the war reports.,

I rode the train to San Antonio where Dad met me and the first thing I asked him was when are we going to the base? We went to Brooks Air Corps field the next two days, where I got to see the BT-13, a brand new basic trainer with a 450 HP engine. I was allowed to sit in it

[5]

and was bewildered by all the instruments, knobs, and switches. They had a line of brand new North American AT 6 "Texan" advanced trainers, but they were off limits, even to Dad.

The next morning, the phone woke us up just after dawn. Dad told me to get dressed. We had a quick breakfast and hustled out to Randolph Field. When we got inside the main gate, we could see a large crowd of people, seventy or eighty of them, crowded along the edge of the flight line. We ran out and joined the crowd. Dad asked a friend of his something. I had no idea what was happening. Suddenly, someone yelled "Here it comes, it's almost here." Then I began to hear a great roar of engines and looked up to see a bright shining glint in the early morning sun coming straight toward the runway.

The noise very quickly became louder and suddenly a huge airplane dropped down and flew over us at about 500 feet of altitude. It wheeled around and landed on the main runway, turned into the parking area and stopped right in front of this crowd.

This airplane had 4 engines and a tricycle landing gear like a DC-4. The ground crew brought out stands and equipment, opened the crew hatches, and the crew of about ten got out. We all eased forward and started to walk around it; walking under wings so high above us that nobody was able to jump up and touch the bottom of them. An officer addressed the crowd. "This is the Douglas B-19, the largest airplane ever built. It will be here a few days for servicing and then depart for Wright-Patterson Air Corps base for testing."

We all walked under every inch of this giant, awed by every feature of it. Dad and I went around it three times—the last time we stopped by the main gear tire. I was standing close to it and without thinking reached out my left hand, stretched up as high as I could, and put my palm on the side of the tire. My hand was still about 2 feet from the top of this tire, which we later found out was 8 feet tall. The B-19 remained the world's largest flying airplane until 1947, when Howard Hughes flew his huge flying boat the "Spruce Goose" for 60 seconds to claim that distinction. There was only this one B-19 built. It was scrapped at Wright-Patterson AFB in 1949.

One day in the late summer of 1940, my grandfather put me in our trusty old "Model A" and we went to the train station in Ennis. The Southern Pacific had streamliners that went through north and south several times a day. Beautiful and sleek, they were about the only real touch we had with the "Modern Marvels" of the 20th Century, so we kids really loved to see them. I thought we might be going to pick someone up at the station, but Grandpa said we were going to see someone there that he had always wanted to see.

When we got close to the station, we had to park a couple of blocks away. We couldn't get any closer. There were cars jamming the streets, people walking in groups, all headed toward the depot. Grandpa led me along until we were in front of the terminal. He hoisted me up on to a freight wagon that had several other kids already on it. He told me to stay there, as I would be able to see a lot better. People crowded all over the platform. Soon we heard the whistle of a steam engine, and into the station, rumbling and blowing steam out the sides of the locomotive, brakes squealing, there came a regular train with four or five passenger cars. The last car stopped with the back end about in the middle of the platform and the crowd.

The last car was different; it had a rounded end on it with a porch and an awning covering that. As soon as the train stopped, a pair of men came out and stepped to the bottom of the stairs on either side and looked the crowd over. The conductor came out and stood on the back platform, waving the crowd back from pushing in too close. The crowd got very quiet. One of the men on the stairs held up his hands and in a very strong, clear voice said "Ladies and gentlemen, the President of the United States, *Franklin Delano Roosevelt*."

The crowd froze. It was so silent that the only noise was the steam quietly hissing from the engine. There was a murmur from the crowd as a figure stepped out of shadows in the doorway into the light. Suddenly, the crowd broke into cheers, clapping, whistling, and waving as the President smiled and waved one hand high while the other clutched the railing of the little porch. You could see his face with white, gleaming teeth under the fedora hat he was wearing. He had a tan suit on and he looked so much like the pictures in the newspapers that it was almost as though we were watching the Movie Tone Newsreel at the Plaza Theater.

He held up his hand for a moment and the noise of the crowd dropped away to silence. I was about 80 or 90 feet away, so I didn't hear much of what was said. But to have the President, the most important man in the United States, speaking to us—I would guess he was asking for our support in the upcoming elections—was the experience of a lifetime for most of us.

It only lasted 5 or 6 minutes and then with a wave to the crowd, the conductor signaled, circled his cap around his head, and slowly the train pulled away headed north to Dallas. Nobody turned to leave until the smoke from the engine was all that could be seen in the distance. The biggest event and the biggest day for Ennis were over.

Mr. Roosevelt got his votes. Hard times stayed on in Texas. The English fought and barely won the aerial attack against them, which became known as "The Battle of Britain," and thereby, as it turned out, saving our bacon.

My grandfather told me on the way home that this was probably the one day I would tell my kids about and to be sure to remember it well. Neither he nor I had any idea that fate would so arrange my life that many more events similar to this one would occur.

And, as it turned out, I didn't have any kids to tell this to after all.

My grandfather passed away in June 1941. My mother and I moved to an apartment on South Main Street in Ennis, across the street from the Southern Pacific Railroad tracks. Mom worked as the office secretary and organist for the Tabernacle Baptist Church in downtown Ennis. She made $32.50 a week for six days work. I did little odd jobs when I could and sold *The Saturday Evening Post* every Saturday morning. I had a route in town of regular customers. They paid me 10¢ for the magazine, and I got to keep 5¢ of that; not bad. Most Saturdays I could clear $1.25 in the morning, and sometimes 25¢ or 50¢ more by helping ladies with their yard work, trash, or other small jobs; not bad at all. In Texas in those days, if you had a few coins clinking in your pocket, they said you were "living in tall cotton." I also carried ice from Roberson's Ice House, down by the city hall, to folks' homes, if it wasn't too far to carry 12 lb. or 25 lb. blocks. We used a 12 lb. block at home in the icebox in our apartment. Two blocks a week would keep us pretty well. I only had to carry them five city blocks. Life was pretty good.

One Sunday we went to church and, after services were over, we walked the nine blocks home and up the stairs to our apartment. Mom fixed dinner. In Texas, it was breakfast, dinner, and supper, unless you were one of the old "elite" families with servants perhaps. Then it was breakfast, lunch, and dinner. We sat down and started eating. Mom always had our little radio tuned to WFAA or KRLD in Dallas so we could listen to classical music while we ate.

Suddenly an announcer cut in and yelled "*FLASH*, the Japanese have attacked Pearl Harbor in the Hawaiian Islands! Ships are burning and sinking! Honolulu has fires raging, many people killed! Stay tuned for latest bulletins as we receive them." The classical music didn't come back on. Instead, patriotic music and military marches replaced them.

One of our neighbors rapped on our door and said, "Come on, we're going to the Daily News offices to read the bulletins as they come in." We all ran out to his old Plymouth and drove to the Ennis Daily News offices downtown. Already people were gathering at the big plate glass windows to read the bulletins from the teletype machine inside that had been taped to the windows outside. Soon there were hundreds of people gathered there—so many that they filled the sidewalk, the street and the sidewalk across the street. Someone had a great idea, and men with loud voices and pretty good diction started taking turns reading the bulletins as they came out. Everyone in the crowd was silent—a few people softly crying as the casualty figures started coming in; damage reports, eyewitness reports, deaths, wounded, missing, guesses as to whether the Japanese fleet would bring in an invasion force.

The afternoon lengthened into evening. A chill wind was blowing along the streets downtown, and still the crowd stood and listened. Some of the churches had been holding prayer meetings, open to all denominations, to ask for divine help for the people of Honolulu, and for our country in this uncertain turn in our history leading to—what? Slowly the crowd departed into the dark night of December 7, 1941, all of us knowing only that our lives had changed somehow beyond our understanding. The next day we sat by our radios and listened to the voice of the man who had visited our town so briefly less than two years ago, our President, as he committed our nation, the youth of the country, and each of us in some way, to begin a course of action with a very uncertain conclusion.

As you can imagine the war years started with quite a bit of confusion. And then it got worse, a lot worse. There were overnight regulations from Washington about setting up draft boards, food stuff boards, petrol boards, rationing for clothing, batteries, tires, building supplies, and so on.

The week after war was declared, the military enlistment centers were swamped with all age groups, from 65 to 16 (pretending to be 18). The men from Ennis went to Corsicana or Dallas. If they had a birth certificate and their bag with them, they could be on a bus that night to boot camp. In some cases, the family didn't know they were gone until they received a call from the recruiting office giving them an address to write to their sons or husbands.

By early1942, the draft board was running smoothly, ration boards were kicking into gear, and it was apparent that this was not going to be a one or two year struggle. Also, war bond drives were starting. School kids were engaged in collecting tin, copper, aluminum, iron, and lots of smaller items. And by late '42, the dreaded telegrams informing families of the wounding or death of their service husband, son, or other family member, were becoming more and more common. Homes had flags in the window to show a member in the service. A blue star flag was changed to a gold star if death had occurred.

1943 and 1944 continued the pattern. American defense industries were absorbing a majority of females, with many defense plants having 60-65% female workers. This was one of the reasons we could put a large number of combat troops into four major areas of combat, and have weapons, munitions, and supplies to support the large number of troops. We owe these ladies a lot.

June 6, 1944, brought the day everyone was waiting for—*D-DAY*, the invasion of Europe. We were told that now we would run along to Germany and get this war over with. A year later this did happen, but before that took place, we still had a hell of a fight on our hands. The Battle of the Bulge was the pivotal action that decided the fate of Europe. The American Army had 150,000 casualties in this bitter winter battle. The Allied forces continued on to Berlin after winning here, but the German Air Force came out with some weapons that demonstrated the future of combat, especially in the air. Jet aircraft, rocket aircraft, the first pulse-jet powered bomb with wings, the first true high altitude (65 *miles* high) rocket propelled weapon—the V-2.

1942 saw the opening of the Pacific campaign against the Japanese Empire. Our mighty naval fleet had been severely mauled at Pearl Harbor. If our four main fleet aircraft carriers had been there at anchor, the likely result would have been their destruction, or at best, major disabling damage to the point that they would have been unusable for a considerable period of time. This would allow the Japanese fleet to take control of the Eastern Pacific theatre. Australia and New Zealand would have been virtually defenseless. The Philippines were attacked the day after Pearl Harbor by a Japanese task force that would certainly prevail in a short period of time. This allowed the Japanese to take control of the Central Pacific area. Guam, Midway, Wake Island, and other American assets were rapidly overcome by their combined land and sea forces.

But the one piece of good fortune the U.S. Navy had on December 7th was that our carriers were at sea on practice maneuvers and suffered not a scratch. With this carrier fleet as the backbone of our naval strategy, we began making our moves against places with names almost never heard before in this country. We took back *Midway, Wake*, and *Guam* islands. My wife had an older brother in the Marine Corps. I was never to meet him as he was killed in action on Guam during that battle. Then the new names that the whole world would come to know: *GUADALCANAL—MAKIN ATOLL—NEW GEORGIA—BOUGAINVILLE—TARAWA—NEW BRITAIN—KWAJALEIN ATOLL—ENIWETOK ATOLL—SAIPAN—TINIAN—PELELIU—IWO JIMA—OKINAWA—*and finally, two names that no one of our generation will ever forget. The start of the atomic era that would change our world forevermore:

HIROSHIMA — NAGASAKI

The war had taken its toll on every city, town, and village in our vast country. We had put 16,000,000 (*sixteen million)* men and women in uniform during this global conflict. This does not count our war production labor force. From December 7th 1941, until August 17th 1945, our casualties were about 2,600,000, of which about 435,000 died in combat, prison camps, sickness, accident, etc. The rest were wounded or incapacitated in many different ways.

It has always been thought that the most heart-wrenching loss our country had to mourn was when word was received, in 1944, that the Sullivan brothers had been lost in action at sea. They were five young brothers who had enlisted in the Navy together, with their mother's approval. They trained together and then requested to serve their duty together. The Navy approved this, and they were assigned to the same combat warship. They all died together when this vessel was lost in action, with most of the rest of the crew also being lost. I believe the picture of their mother looking out her living room window with five gold star flags encircling her head ran in every newspaper in the country. The Navy immediately passed regulations which forbids more than two family members to serve aboard the same ship.

My hometown of Ennis, Texas, like all small towns, really suffered with our losses, much more so than Dallas, Houston, or other large cities. Every week or two our paper would print the reports of word being received of the death or wounding of someone from Ennis or Ellis County. Then, in March of 1945, we had to face our worst nightmare.

Among our young men who went to the military, four had gone to the Marine Corps. Three were classmates and graduates from Ennis High School in December 1942. They enlisted together, trained together, and then were split up and sent to different combat units. Their names were Wm. T. "Dooney" Pierce, Jr., James Wesley Goodwin, and Joe Riley Crow. The other marine had graduated several years earlier, gone to college, and wound up playing pro football for the New York Giants. In December 1941, after the Pearl Harbor attack, Jack Lummus resigned from the Giants and joined the Marines. By 1945, he was a Captain and had been in several island campaigns. Then the battle to re-take Iwo Jima occurred.

All four of these Ennis boys, each in different units, were in the Iwo Jima battle, one of the worst for the U.S. in the Pacific campaign. This 24 day fight from February 19th to March 14th, 1945, took the lives of 5,931 Marines. In addition, 17,272 were wounded. The Japanese lost about 59,000, with some 400 being captured.

None of the four Ennis Marines knew the others were there. Within the first 21 days of the battle, all four were killed in action. Captain Jack Lummus was awarded the Congressional Medal of Honor for his actions in leading his platoon after being severely wounded. Finally, in front of his attacking troops, he was mortally wounded by a land mine. This was the only Medal of Honor awarded to anyone from Ennis. When the news came to Ennis, the flag at the high school they had all attended could not be lowered to half-staff. It was already there, honoring the seventeen former students in all branches of the military who had been killed before the Iwo Jima battle.

One of my earliest memories as a young boy comes back to me as I write this chapter. I was five years old and I was at the July 4th 1938, parade with my grandfather, mother, and the rest of the family. We were standing on the really crowded Main Street in Ennis as the flags, bands, and parade passed by. We heard the clip-clop of hooves on the brick street and a big cotton wagon, with two white mules in harness pulling it, came rolling by. The two men on the driver's seat were old with faded blue uniforms and large brimmed campaign hats. Behind them, in the wagon box, were two old, old men with long white beards, old long gray coats, and little gray caps on their heads. They were sitting in big rocking chairs, waving at the crowd, and the crowd was clapping and whistling back.

My grandfather pointed at the wagon and said "John Lee, this is real history, and I want you to see it before it's gone for good. The two men driving the wagon are veterans of the Spanish-American War. The old fellows in the rocking chairs are the last two Confederate veterans of the Civil War who live in this part of Texas. Look closely, wave to them; they've come to more than ninety years. They may soon be gone." He was right. The next year only the Spanish-American War veterans were there, in the rocking chairs.

August 1945, the war was over. Everything slowed down or stopped. Women in defense industries got their final checks. Buses and trains were filled with veterans coming home to find there were very few jobs. The first new cars, since 1941, came off the assembly lines. Every car dealer had a six month to a year waiting list. Some of them sold cars on the black market to the highest bidder and made a killing. Sugar, coffee, meat, soap, tires, gasoline, shoes, and many other rationed goods during the last four years rapidly filled stores, stations and empty shelves. But alas, the young ladies of our country waited in vain for one of the most desired things in their lives—*nylon stockings*. Eventually they came, and life had meaning again. The school year of 1945-46 started as Japan surrendered. Several army and navy veterans who had dropped out to enlist, with one or two years remaining to graduate, came back to finish high school. They walked down the halls like teachers, tall and mature. It was said that they had to shave every other day! They were polite to us kids; still, they mostly grouped together. I cannot recall that they ever said a word about their time in the service.

The year went by quickly now and things seemed pretty normal. By late spring of 1946, a lot of our returned vets had left town, some with families, to find work if they could. This went on into 1947 and 1948. We were having trouble in Europe with the Russians. The Berlin airlift had started to supply the German civilians with enough food and coal to survive the Russian blockade around the city that allowed nothing to come in or out. In the summer of 1948, my mother let me go to San Antonio to visit Dad for a month. When he was discharged from the Air Force, he went to work in a business started by Colonel Ralph Lawrence, a friend from his Air Corps days, which had offices in the Fort Sam Houston grounds in South San Antonio.

Dad took me to work with him one morning. I met Colonel Lawrence and other staff members of the company. About ten o'clock, Dad said we were going to meet the president of the company. He said "Be very respectful when I introduce you." Now I was fifteen years old, would be a junior in high school in a couple of months, and I was thinking I was pretty hot stuff, as they used to say in that era. We entered an office with an anteroom. Dad knocked on a walnut set of double doors. A voice I could barely hear said to come in and I followed my father into a roomy, beautifully decorated office. Behind a large desk sat an older man with thin, white hair, very thin face, and a very kindly face and eyes. Dad brought me around to the side of the desk and said "Son, I want to introduce you to our president, General Jonathan M. Wainwright." He turned to place me beside him at the desk and said, "General, I want you to meet my son, John Lee Sparks, Jr. who will be here with me for a month."

General Wainwright pushed himself up out of his chair, held out his hand to me and said in a low voice, "I've heard about you from your father, John Lee. We're proud to have you visit here with us." I shook the thin, frail hand and could hardly speak. I don't remember much of what I said, but after a moment of chatter between the three of us, the General sat back down at his desk and said to Dad, "John, you go on with your work, and John, Jr. and I will get to know each other a little better."

I spent more than an hour sitting with the General, drinking a Grapette from his refrigerator and answering his questions about Ennis and school. I was pretty much in shock the first little while, but he had such a fine, homey manner that he put me at ease in a very few minutes.

I really don't remember this visit that well. During the next two weeks I visited with him three or four more times. He said he enjoyed visits from people because he had almost no real work to do, that they had needed a name people knew, and he needed something to do to get him out of his house.

On one of the later visits he said "Everybody seems to want to see the journal I kept in the prison camp. Let me show it to you." From a drawer in his desk he took a ragged stack of paper of all types and bound with string. I could see it was crammed with writing on every inch that was visible. The General told me his officers and men stole pieces of paper whenever possible from the Japanese offices. This was very dangerous; the penalty if caught doing this ranged from severe beatings, being locked in the "chicken coop" for days without food or water, or the most extreme punishment was execution by beheading. But his men wanted him to be able to keep a journal as he always had. He said even with almost no information, he reasoned that we would eventually win the pacific campaigns, invade Japan, with tremendous casualties, in about 1946, and subdue the Japanese home islands about 1948.

He laughed at this point and said, "Of course, if they had somehow gotten word to me about the atomic bomb, I could have refined the time scale and revised it down a year or so."

One day I was in his office, and while he was taking a phone call, I looked at a wall with many objects and items having to do with his military career that I hadn't yet had a chance to examine. There, in the center of the display and photos, was a beautiful wooden case with a glass cover. I moved near to it and read the citation below the medal in the case. It became apparent in a second or two that this was The Congressional Medal of Honor—the real thing—which is the highest award that can be given for military devotion and service above and beyond the call of duty. It had been awarded to Jack Lummus. I had never thought that I would be in the presence of the actual medal, much less have had the privilege of spending some time in the company of the holder of this award.

I left San Antonio a few weeks after this. Ralph Lawrence had taken Dad and me on two trips he made in his personal airplane, one to Houston, and one to Ft. Worth. I now know the airplane was a beautiful Stagger-wing Beechcraft. This was my first actual flying experience. I thought to myself after these trips, "I could learn to do this someday."

I took my first flight instruction in a Piper J-3 Cub at Redbird Airport in South Dallas, in the summer of 1950. It cost $6.50 an hour ($5 for the airplane, $1.50 for the instructor). After five hours of instruction, I had to quit because I became "stony" broke. People were right when they told me that flying was expensive.

General of the Army Jonathan M. Wainwright, holder of the Congressional Medal of Honor, hero of the battle of Corregidor, survivor of the Bataan death march, senior officer in the Japanese prison camp, who did everything in his power to keep every prisoner alive, if at all possible, and who sacrificed his health and welfare resisting the Japanese commanders at the peril of his own life—this kindly man passed away in September of 1953, aged sixty-three years. He was interred at Arlington National Cemetery outside Washington DC. He was buried beside his wife. His grave is one of the most visited in this huge monumental resting place for our American military forces, whether hero or simple G.I. from the ranks. He also gave a lot of inspiration to one young boy at a very impressionable time in his life.

In 1949, as a junior in Ennis High School, (*See Photo #1*) I had a good looking girlfriend and a 1934 Ford 4 door sedan with lousy brakes. They were the old mechanical pushrod type, always at about half-efficiency at best. One day in late summer, my girlfriend and I were coming to a stop sign on Highway 34 that ran through the town and continued west to Waxahachie. I was a little late getting on the brakes, slid past the stop sign, out into the intersection and just barely clipped the rear bumper of a beautiful brand new Ford "Woody" station wagon. I got stopped in the middle of the intersection, as did the Ford wagon. The door of it swung open and Robert Mitchum, the movie actor, jumped out. He ran around to the right rear and saw that there was only a minor scratch on the bumper (that's the way I saw it), and turned around as my girlfriend and I came hurrying up. He said "Kid, I drove my new car all the way from California to Florida, then halfway back, and now I have to meet a guy with no brakes in a little hick town in the middle of nowhere and he nearly tears my bumper off."

I'm apologizing as fast as I can, and I notice a very pretty woman, holding a child by the hand, standing by the open passenger door of the wagon. I tell Mr. Mitchum I'm especially sorry if I scared his family. He's standing there with his hands on his hips, wearing a skin tight t-shirt, and he looked a *lot* bigger than he did in his movies. He asked Nancy, my girlfriend, "Does this guy always drive this bad? If you promise to make him get them damn brakes fixed and drive slower, I'll let it go, but the next time he might really hurt somebody." She promised she would make sure I got them fixed right away. He didn't exactly smile, but he wasn't glowering at me anymore. "What the hell, we're all young and dumb once or twice. Now go get them brakes fixed." He turned to get back into the driver's seat, looked over his shoulder at me and said, "That's a cute kid you got with you. Take care of her, and don't ever get close to my car again". He slid in, fired up, and rolled off to the west—off to California. A few people had stopped along the sidewalk to watch, even though this whole thing had hardly taken three or four minutes.

I didn't get the brakes fixed right away, but it didn't matter much, as I got grounded because the City Police Patrol had noticed my license plate had expired. That solved the problem until I could save up enough money for brakes and plates.

It was 1950. I had graduated from high school. War was looming again. The Chinese Communist Army was expanding southeast into Korea. Russia was tightening its grip on Central Europe. The U.S., through NATO commitments, was insisting that the U.N. Assembly take action to stop aggression in these and other hot spots. Unrest, uneasiness, trepidation of coming events filled our lives. The draft boards started giving notices that the military draft was not over, but would be increased to keep us prepared for whatever might be coming.

I was working in Dallas, still broke, trying to save money for more flying lessons. That proved hard to do. There were too many pretty girls around and too many parties out by SMU. I met several of the SMU football team at these parties, played shuffleboard and snooker with them at the bars on Lovers Lane, Mockingbird Lane and other beer bars around. Some of the jocks on the Mustang team had been big news last season, and the upcoming season polls had SMU high up in the predictions. I couldn't know that Doak Walker, Kyle Rote, "Chicken" Roberts, "Big" Dick McKissick, and several others would dominate the Southwest Conference. All I had learned was *don't* play shuffleboard with them for money or beer. These guys were sharks! *No Mercy*!

I also heard that my draft board was calling up a larger number of 1-A inductees for the first quarter of 1951. I looked at my draft card. Uh-oh. *1-A*.

I worked at Procter & Gamble with a guy who kept talking about enlisting in the Navy before he got called up for the Army. I drove him down to the recruiting offices in downtown Dallas. We walked back and forth looking at the posters; Army, Navy, Coast Guard, Air Force, and Marine Corps. Each one looked great; sharp uniforms, learn a trade, see the World and serve your country. The one I liked said "The Marines are looking for a few good men!" I thought of Jack Lummus, Dooney Pierce, James Goodwin, and Joe Crow. My mother was good friends with all of their families. They had all been Marines.

I went in and my buddy headed down to the Navy office. I talked to the recruiting Sergeant, he explained things, but he said since I was only seventeen, my mother would have to sign a consent form. I got all the papers and went home to Ennis. My mom listened to me. She nodded her head, picked up the consent form and signed it. She looked at me, handed over the paper and said, "Now I know what it's like to have a grown son, instead of a boy without a father". I told her I wouldn't go if she felt badly about it. She put her arms around me and said "No, I'll be right glad to have a man in the family. You have to find your own way from here out. Just remember, I'll always be here when you need me."

And she always was. That day was December 7th 1950. On December 9th, she went to Dallas and watched me being sworn in as a recruit in the Marine Corps. That afternoon she waved goodbye to me as a train full of recruits of all the different services pulled out of Union Station, headed for California and a new era of life for us all.

My mother told all our relatives and friends that she hoped I had found what I wanted, but no matter how it came out, I was a son she would always be proud of. I wrote Mom after a couple of weeks of boot camp and told her how great it was and how much I was enjoying it.

If there is a reckoning in an afterlife, I hope I will be forgiven for telling a lie to my mother of that magnitude. I just couldn't bring myself to tell her that I had stumbled into a dark hole and fallen straight into *Hell*! Boot camp didn't look so bad in all the John Wayne movies I had seen. It looked like a big Boy Scout Jamboree or maybe football camp. But the first ten minutes off the bus at MCRD in San Diego set the tone for the next nine weeks of Marine Boot Camp. Two drill instructors, who would make Burt Lancaster look like the skinny kid at the beach who gets sand kicked in his face, took us, all eighty-seven of us, in hand, and one said, "You have another 60 seconds to be civilians. Better enjoy them!"

I'm going to make this chapter as short as I can get away with. We lost twelve recruits in the first four weeks. Some were sent to NTC, (the naval training center right next to MCRD) to train as sailors. Others were given C.O.G. (convenience of the government) discharges because of physical or mental problems that developed pretty rapidly during the intense training. One escaped to Mexico, it was rumored, and was listed as AWOL, (absent without leave). The training program was designed to put us under enough stress to bring out any defects in us before we got into actual combat situations. Believe me, it worked! It was severe, but not brutal or overly harsh. This training developed strengths in us we had never known before. We found that the bonding with fellow Marines had nothing to do with how we felt about them personally. When you're links in a chain, you have to take the pressure evenly without breaking. If you break, the whole chain can go down.

The reason most of us made it was named Sgt. Warner, the lead D.I. (drill instructor) for our recruit platoon. Almost every one of us were younger, taller and heavier built than this 5'10" mild looking marine who was always standing in front of our tents at 5:00 AM, when we fell out, looking like a recruiting poster. You could cut yourself on the creases of his shirt and trousers with his hat squared away and his shoes standing on top of the sand with a flawless shine. And this was on his *bad* days!

We quickly learned from the two junior D.I.s, that this marine had fought in a number of the hardest battles in the Pacific Theater in WW II. He was a Para-marine and had many combat parachute jumps. He had quite a few combat awards and citations, none of which he ever said a word about while he led our platoon. When he spoke it was quietly, with authority. He gave orders, his assistant D.I.s implemented them and we learned, if not the first time, then the tenth or the twentieth. We found out the real scuttlebutt about this older marine (he had to be at least thirty!) on the first 5 mile run he took us on. The truth was ... he could run faster backward than we could forward!

Time passed. Hell had turned into only purgatory once we started to "Get with the program." After all this effort and sweat, physically demanding procedures, classes, seven day weeks, it started to make some sort of sense. And then it changed. We were stunned. Out of nowhere, Sgt. Warner announced that this coming Sunday we would have the entire afternoon *OFF*! We were dazed. We could catch up on letter writing, sleep, have a card game, walk around the base *not in_formation.* And then the topper;

the middle of next week we would be going to Camp Matthews, up in the hills northeast of MCRD, for our rifle training and qualification.

The rifle range was the best part of boot camp for me by far. I had hunted with a .22 rifle and a 12 gauge shotgun with my uncles for years, and shot at targets with a 30-30 several times. I had very sharp vision, it had tested at 20-15 on my physical, and I had no sense of danger handling firearms.

In short, I "Aced" this training and shot expert with the Garand .30 cal. Service rifle and the M-1 carbine. We also fired the Colt Model 1911 .45 cal. pistol, the Tompson .45 cal. submachine gun and the Browning automatic rifle, .30 cal., known as the "BAR", for familiarization. We fired rifle grenades with the Garand, threw hand grenades and observed mortar crews firing portable infantry mortars of various sizes.

The platoon returned to MCRD and received high praise from Sgt. Warner. "Well, at least none of you shot anybody else in your squad." We were short four recruits who were kept over to try to qualify again—no qualification, no future in the Marines. Every marine, one stripe or one star, has a basic MOS (Military Operational Specialty) number of 001 to start out with and goes on from there, depending on what they become trained to do. This basic number defines a "Mark 1 gravel agitator," short for an infantryman. The saying was, "If you can't shoot, you can't stay." Three of the four qualified. The last one changed Marine green for Navy blue.

Finally, graduation; we washed and ironed, spit shined our boondockers, trimmed hair, close shaved, put our tents in order, stacked our rifles, and stood our final D.I. inspection by Sgt. Warner. This time he had his ribbons lined up on his chest, three rows of them. As he walked down the ranks, we snapped to attention from parade rest as he came abreast of us. Once or twice he adjusted some detail on our greens. When he was through, he and his two assistants stood in front of us. Sgt. Warner looked back and forth at us in the ranks, shook his head and said to the corporals beside him "Well, I guess we lucked out. Maybe we won't have to do it all over again, a few of 'em almost look like jarheads."

At the graduation ceremony on the main parade ground, the Captain congratulated us on our first achievement in the Corps. He then called the roll, and each man came forward as his name was called, shook hands with the Captain. The Lieutenant beside him handed the new marine his orders. "Camp Pendleton, Camp Pendleton, Camp Pendleton," and we all froze as this next poor bastard heard his assignment. "*SEA SCHOOL!*" How we pitied this poor grunt. Sea School was based across the parade ground from the Admin. Building at MCRD. We had seen the Sea School guys; standing at attention or parade rest for hours in their wool dress blues, white flat hats on, white gloves, finally marching off doing a fancy rifle drill, sharp slaps on the rifles in perfect unison. We had heard about the snap inspections; "junk on the bunk"—you don't want to know—bounce-a-quarter-on-the-bunk and latrine scrub downs with tooth brushes. There were never more than twenty-four or thirty in Sea School at any one time, but when they did those close order rifle drills with the fancy twists and rolls, passing the rifles around, passing through ranks in different directions, it sure looked like a lot more. Nobody wanted Sea School, but somehow they chose four out of every class to go. If you busted out of there, you wound up at Camp Pendleton in a platoon of strangers. It was said that that was no fun either.

Two had already gotten orders to Sea School. There were about thirty of us left; then the call "Private First Class John L. Sparks." I marched smartly up to the Captain, shook his hand as he said congratulations, and turned to receive my orders. The lieutenant handed them to me and said "*SEA SCHOOL!*" And so it was done.

At the end of the ceremony, we stood at attention and saluted the officers, our first salute in the Marine Corps. The four of us going to Sea School were instructed to pack up and move our gear to their barracks before signing out and receiving our eight day boot leave orders.

Sgt. Warner came in to say goodbye to us before a jeep ran us and our gear over to the barracks.

I asked him how they had picked us four out for Sea School, and he said, "You picked yourselves, you four were the top finishers in the platoon." We all said, almost in unison, "They didn't say anything about this when we signed up!"

All three D.I.s laughed and said "Of course not. If they had, all of you recruits would dog it as much as you could. We would never get you broke in." Sgt. Warner said "Give it a chance. Most guys like it once they get out into the fleet." Then he said "I always hoped to go sea going, but they never asked me. I got a job, you got a job. Do me proud. Make 'em say "That's one of Warner's boys." We all four swore we would.

I hope we did.

We came back from boot leaves. I had six days with my mother and the aunts, uncles, and cousins. I dressed in greens for mom. It was pretty cool in March and when we went visiting at her friends, she wanted to show me off, her only child. I owed it to her. The other two days were spent traveling.

Sea School was everything I had heard about it, and more. The word "intense" would describe an average training day. Evenings we got to relax and steam press the pleats in our shirts and trousers, spit shine our shoes, polish all our brass, clean our rifles, read the lesson plan for the next day's classes, write letters home and clean the "head," as the toilet was now called. After that we had the rest of the evening off.

We lived as teams in the barracks, six men to a team. We learned to work as a unit, to take credit as a unit, but especially to suffer discipline as a unit. If one of us really screwed up, the rest of us had to straighten him out. If we couldn't or wouldn't do it, we *all* got restricted to base for the weekend. This will get your attention in very short order.

We learned many new things; shipboard etiquette, naval terminology, Naval vs. Marine regulations, keeping naval prisons, (brigs), standing watch aboard naval vessels, etc. Some courses detailed aspects of Embassy duty, detached duty in foreign nations, etc. It was a lot to learn, but it wasn't dull. The water survival course consisted of swimming under burning oil, rescuing a swimmer in trouble and especially, leaving a sinking ship, etc. We had a controlled jump from a 60 foot high platform into the deep end of the swimming pool—required! This was the hardest thing I had ever done in my life. But if you refused, it was off to Camp Pendleton. I somehow made myself do it. I now knew what real fear was, but also that it could be controlled.

We graduated. Everybody made it. I was posted to the Marine detachment at North Island Naval Air Station across the bay in San Diego, to work there while awaiting orders to catch a ship assignment. This came in a few weeks—travel up to Treasure Island in San Francisco Bay, catch a flight out of Travis Air Force base on a Navy RD-4 transport plane with ninety marines and sailors with stops in Hawaii, Midway Island and then Japan—Tokyo, then Yokosuka on the east coast to join the Marine ship's company on the Essex class aircraft carrier, CV47, the *USS Philippine Sea.*

Five days later I landed at Haneda Airport in Tokyo and was transported to Yokosuka to join the carrier. There were three marines and possibly twenty or thirty sailors in our group. We went aboard the carrier by proper naval protocol and respect; Permission to come aboard; Granted; Salute the officer of the deck and turn and salute the flag—everything in measured steps aboard a naval vessel.

Within 48 hours, we were moving out of the harbor. Our destination, along with about twenty supply vessels, and about eight or nine screening war ships, destroyers, and one heavy cruiser, was a battle group in the Sea of Japan designated Carrier Group 2. This group had two other carriers and with many other types of capital vessels was operating off the east coast of South Korea.

The total number of ships ranged between forty and fifty, as they came and went on various missions.

For four months or more, we sailed an oval pattern to keep within the combat range of all our aircraft—the F4UF Corsair, the "bent wing bird" from WW II; the Douglas A1-D Skyraider, a multi-purpose low level attack bomber that could carry anything you could hang on it; then our jet fighter, the first good operational carrier jet, the Grumman F-9 Panther, small but very quick and deadly. Our planes from all the carriers flew almost daily combat missions into the Yalu River basin, and the mountains surrounding it, to try and help the U.N. forces stem the rush of the million man Chinese army coming in from North Korea. We had a lot of shot up, damaged planes come back. Sadly, we also had too many not come back.

Our fighters shot down a Russian amphibian type torpedo plane about thirty miles from our carrier. A destroyer picked up the two man crew and put them aboard the Phil Sea. I remember one of the crew had stainless steel dentures. They were from the Russian base at Vladivostok and were trying to defect to the U.S. side. Our planes made warning passes trying to turn them away from the task force, but they kept on coming in spite of warning shots across their nose. Finally, they went down low to the water, and a F4UF Corsair shot them down upon orders issued from fire control aboard the Phil Sea. After a few days on board the carrier, the crew was flown back to Japan on a courier plane trip. We never found out what happened to them.

I could write a complete book on just this carrier operation. I loved being around the aircraft, watching them work, seeing how the pilots—almost all but the jet pilots were WW II retreads who were in reserve Naval squadrons called back into action—just went out and did the job every day. There were no stars and no super pilots. They were just Naval Aviators—the best in the world.

We went back to Yokosuka after five months on station. Scuttlebutt had it that we were going back to

San Francisco to refit at Hunters Point shipyard. For once scuttlebutt had it right. We ran through a small typhoon northeast of Japan on the great circle route to the States. If you've ever wondered if a carrier could have a wave break over the bow and put half the flight deck under water, the answer is yes. The Navy had Chief Petty Officers so seasick they had them strapped into their bunks like mummies.

We Marines just toughed it out.

Chapter 2 — Which Way is Mexico, Amigo?

I wish I had kept a picture of the Philippine Sea coming into San Francisco Bay, with the Golden Gate Bridge behind us. All the crew who were not on watch came out to get in the picture. I was standing just in front of the island with some Navy pilots. They were all in favor of borrowing the Captain's gig and running over to Fisherman's Wharf for some lobster and a few cold ones. I could imagine Captain Ira Hobbs saying, "Sure, boys, here's the keys. Be sure you fill it up before you bring it back." Captain Hobbs was a heck of a nice guy to work for, but there were limits, even for the pilots.

We off-loaded all the live ammo on barges out in the middle of the bay, and then tugs pulled us into a dry dock at Hunters Point naval shipyard. That afternoon, the daughter of Earl Warren, the Governor of California, known as Nina "Honey Bear" Warren, came aboard to inspect "her carrier." We had raised more than $9,200 for the 1951 March of Dimes, and we had named Nina "Miss Philippine Sea." Nina was stricken with polio last November 27th and now she was able to walk without crutches. We were going to have a ship's company party in her honor that night at the Scottish Rite Auditorium in San Francisco. Being part of the honor guard, I got to dance with her for about 10 seconds that night at the party. She was a living doll and won the hearts of everybody on the ship, especially Capt. Ira Hobbs. About thirty of us got a very brief turn on the dance floor with her, but she tired very quickly. Four of us "Dress Blues" Marines and about twenty-five Navy Pilots were her Honor Escort for the night. (*Photo #2*)

The next day we cleaned our quarters and received duty assignments for the time we would be in dry dock. As soon as we were secure, liberty started for the watch not pulling duty for the next 12 hours. Life quickly settled down to a work routine for some of the Navy; working with the shipyard men on the hull, propellers, updating and repairing. Looking from the edge of the flight deck some 140 feet to the bottom of the dry dock was a one-time experience for most of us. We were told that this work would take about six months to complete.

The marines settled into a security, watch standing, brig watch, off duty, liberty schedule. Some took their leave time and others were replaced. The liberty we had took us down to the bars, pool halls, dance halls—places you wouldn't take your mother for sure. As the weeks went on, it started trouble for some of the ship's company, Navy and Marines alike. About six weeks into this period, I was having trouble staying sober for most of the night. I was getting into trouble at many of the bars we went into, with pushing, shoving, fights, torn uniforms and civvies. The Sarge told me I was getting on thin ice and if I was smart I'd shape up.

One afternoon one of the workers at the shipyard—we had gotten to know several of the younger ones and they gave us rides into the bar district and did some drinking with us—saw me and another marine buddy of mine coming out of the liberty gate. He yelled at us to get in his car as he was going bar hopping and we were welcome to go along, and we did.

The memory of us getting into that car is the last one I have of my life in the Marine Corps as a Seagoing Marine.

The new life I now had to start living began with pain, confusion, disorientation, much activity by many people, other things I couldn't understand and little that I can remember now. I can't put into words the sensations, images and noise. I faded in and out of consciousness. I now only remember bits and pieces. The psych doctor told me later that this is sometime called a dream state or something like that. The first clear memory I can come up with is people turning me over, lifting me, with pain, dull, not sharp and a pounding in my head. I tried to open my eyes. Nothing happened. I tried to speak, but couldn't.

I came around in about four days. The doctor said I was possibly in a car wreck, but more likely was hit several times on the head with something like a pipe. There were long, deep bruises on my body, my left arm was injured in the shoulder joint, but the major injury was along a portion of the right skull hemisphere. This caused a dangerous swelling of the brain and dura mater, but I was lucky. There was no skull fracture as such. I was having severe headaches, so bad I was unable to walk or operate on my own for several weeks. My vision was blurred and I couldn't stand to look into any bright lights.

The doctors and psychiatrists worked with me for almost five months. I was treated, rehabilitated in depth, and the pain of the headaches finally receded to a point that I could become ambulatory with care. At one point I was given lots of drugs to control the pain of the migraine type headaches, one of these being a drug called Demerol. I received a shot of it to control a terrific head pain one afternoon, and it really did help a lot. The pain left me, I began to feel so much better that I decided to get up and walk around the ward and visit for a while. I did this and after going up and down the ward for a time, I walked past my bed. I looked over at it, and there I was, stretched out like a log under the covers with a white towel over my eyes. I ran over and started yelling at me to get up, get up—then, nothing, just nothing. When I did open my eyes, a corpsman and the ward duty doctor were holding me down. They were saying things like "its okay, you're alright, wake up, wake up" ....

This is the only out-of-body experience I have ever had. It scared me so badly and it was so vivid, so real, that I refused to take Demerol anymore. They found another drug, which was not psycho-tropic, to replace it. The new drug wasn't as effective at relieving the pain, but I didn't care. One of those episodes was a life-time supply as far as I was concerned.

I was given an "in depth" physical and mental exam, and was found to not meet the required standards of the Marine Corps. I was released with an Honorable discharge in December 1951, with full benefits except that because my injuries were non-service connected, I received no compensation for disability.

I told the Board that I wanted to finish out my hitch. They said "Rules are rules. Thanks, goodbye, and good luck."

I felt like a quitter, or maybe a deserter would be a more apt description. The head doctors told me I might feel this way for a long time unless I came to realize that I hadn't made this choice myself. Ernest K. Gann said it best, I guess. "Fate is the hunter. You are the quarry." I still have this feeling somewhat, though, even now sixty years later.

I had severe headaches for years, but they gradually faded into an occasional miserable one, rather like a hangover. However, in 1953, I passed a 2nd class flight physical. I told the doctor I had occasional bad headaches. He advised me not to fly if I had one or thought I might have one coming on.

The headaches continued to fade over the years. My flying was never affected, but I never got over the feeling that I messed up my Marine life. I had come to like the Corps. I don't think I would have done twenty years, but who knows?

I got a letter from my Dad telling me he was going to be living in a little town in Southern California called San Clemente, between L.A. and San Diego. He would be there for a year or two working for the Service Life Insurance Co. out of San Antonio. He said to come and visit when I could. When they told me I was getting a medical discharge in a week's time, I had a place to go that wasn't too far away. His third wife, Florence, was with him and I had an idea that it might be a very short visit, depending on how her mental health was. She and I had never gotten along well, as she was convinced that I was trying to break up their marriage. I was told that she had a mild form of paranoia, and delusions of persecution and danger were part of her everyday life. I know that it was severe enough that she wouldn't even take an aspirin if it came from a bottle that had the seal broken—even if Dad had just brought it home for her. However, any port in a storm. It sounded as though it would be okay for a week or so.

San Clemente turned out to be a beautiful little coastal town. The houses were mostly white stucco with red tiled roofs, at least in the central part of town surrounding the business district with nice hotels, open bars with patios just off the street level, just a few blocks from the beach and a lazy, laid back way of life. It was probably about twelve to fifteen thousand population at the end of 1951, and although a little pricey, many people were retiring there. My Dad was renting a home about four blocks south of downtown and about the same distance to the beach.

I dumped my stuff at the house and decided that a swim in the Pacific was the best thing to start my vacation with. I got into beach togs, trunks, t-shirt, ball cap, and took a towel and walked the three blocks to the beach thinking that I should have had some lunch before starting out. Oh well, not to worry, I could get a hot dog and a beer or coke at the beach. I came over a little sand ridge, and there was the beach, stretching far to the south and far to the north. About a half a mile to the north, I saw some people running around, dashing in and out of the light surf and that was it; no pier, no snack shacks, no buildings—just beach and more beach.

Oh well, at least there are people up to the north, so after about a 15 minute slog through the sand, I arrived at the movie set of *Beach Blanket Bingo.* Well, not really, but every surf flick I ever saw after that looked like it had been filmed on this exact spot. There was music playing out of a battery powered radio, blankets spread out, washtubs with bottles stuck in ice, girls in racy looking one piece swim suits—they were sure racy for those days—guys in trunks playing volleyball, with a few girls dashing in and out of the action. Here I stood with a towel in my hand and not a clue as to what to do next.

All these kids were as bronze as South Sea Islanders; hair bleached almost white, dark, dark sunglasses, and no one looking older than twenty-two or twenty-three. And here I am, looking like I haven't been out in the sun for ten years, squinting with eyes barely open, no sunglasses and the only one with a ball cap on. People are splashing in and out of the surf, laughing and singing along with the radio. A couple of the girls point at me and waved. I waved back. They motioned me to come on over, so the problem solved itself. I tramped the 40 yards through the sand and, to my surprise, a guy walked up as I got to the girls and handed me a beer, saying "Here, you sure look like you could use one of these." I thanked him and asked if I was barging into a private party of some sort. "Hell no," he said, "this party's been running for nearly three years, and it just happens to be here today."

To make a very pleasant long story short, I had stumbled onto "The Beach Bums," the group of young Californians who pretty much started the beach culture that is still alive, but not nearly as well, as it was in the '50s to the late '80s. This loose confederation of kids who wouldn't settle for the American dream the way it was laid out for their parents, had decided a hedonistic way of life could be their reality. They were amoral, non-goal oriented, irreligious, and satisfied with a pagan lifestyle, for want of a better definition, regardless of what their parents' generation and preceding generations had mandated.

They were not hippies or flower children, although they opened the way to that type of thinking, by showing society that non-conformist thinking and dreaming was still allowed under the structure of our Constitution and canons of law. Many of these adherents to the beach culture did grow out of it and became very useful citizens. I was offered one hit on a joint of marijuana in the entire five months I was involved with the Bums and after telling this particular guy to take a hike, nobody offered me as much as a warm beer—always cold.

The one thing the Beach Bums were into that I did get hooked on and which gave me much pleasure in my life, was an early experience with scuba diving. Some of them had come up with a couple of the early Cousteau aqualungs and using iron window sash weights tied around our waists with heavy cord, we took turns swimming out in the surf to deeper water, or off some of the piers up and down the beach. No one in the bunch I did this with was ever seriously injured, but there were a number of very serious and fatal injuries in California before better equipment, training, and finally, licensing made it a sport with reasonable safety. I went on in later years to complete my training and did become certified as open water, deep certification, 210 feet depth, scuba diver. My dives in the Bahamas, Jamaica, the Cayman Islands, and Florida provided me with the same type of wonder and pleasure that flying has. These experiences, along with a wonderful wife, have brought a fulfillment to living that I was never promised and very likely do not deserve.

Meanwhile, back in San Clemente, I worked at various jobs in the community to finance my wild lifestyle. I worked hard to keep my stepmother appeased and tried to establish a better relationship with my father. This worked with varying degrees of success; better, worse, and not at all. I started spending more evenings at the big hotel in the downtown area, to try to keep the pressure off at home. One late afternoon, I watched an older guy in a wild flowered shirt banging a portable typewriter on one of the patio tables at this hotel. He was paying no attention to anything or anyone until he finished his drink, looked all around, saw me standing a few feet away, handed me his glass and said "Get me another one, and get yourself something." I figured the bartender would know what he was drinking, so I went in, told him what I wanted, plus a draft beer for me. He whipped it out with the nonchalance that the true pro has in his work, made a note on a tab, and shoved them over to me.

When I set the drink on the table, he grabbed it, took a deep swallow, looked up at me and pointed to the chair at the side of the table. I sat down because I was killing time anyway and a free beer was not to be sneezed at in my financial situation. He typed until the page was finished, pulled it out of the little Royal portable, and said "What time is it, kid?" I looked at my watch and said "5:25." He groaned and said "The hell with it. I can finish it tomorrow." He started packing the papers and notes into a briefcase. Then he leaned back and looked down toward the beach, where some bungalows were scattered in the palm trees. A guy with a lot of hair hanging down over one eye was just coming up the patio steps from that direction. He stepped onto the patio and headed to our table.

In an easy, mellow voice he said, "Fred, I thought you said you were going to come get me for cocktails before we ate. And here you are, wasting your time visiting instead of working." He pulled out the chair on the other side of the table, looked across at me as he was sitting down, and said, "And who might you be?" I stood up and said, "Oh, I'm just a fill-in waiter, waiting for his tip." The older man at the table said, "Well, tell us both who you might be."

It took a minute or so to tell them my story and what I was doing here, etc. When I got through, I said "Well, thanks for the beer. Can I get you something else before I go? This time, no tip involved." I wound up getting two drinks and another beer. The bartender wrote on the tab and the drinks were delivered.

The older man said, "What's your name, boy?" I told him John Sparks, just visiting in town before heading home to Texas. The older man said "Well, you might as well meet this fellow here since you're neighbors. Say hello to Will Rogers, Jr., from Oklahoma, I believe." I knew the younger man looked rather familiar, and now I could see that he did resemble Will Rogers quite a bit. I thought they were probably pulling my leg, but I could go along with the joke.

"Well, isn't that a coincidence. I'm the grandson of Tex Ritter and he always claimed that he had written most of your father's jokes for him."

Will Rogers, Jr. made a grimace, shook his head, and said laconically "Damn that Ritter, he never could keep his mouth shut." We were smiling and then Will, Jr. pointed to the older gentleman and said "Now, it's his turn. Meet the worst detective story writer ever thrown out of Hollywood for being too subtle. This is a guy I know you've never heard of by the name of Fred Brown."

"Could that be Fredrick Brown, the one who started a story with, "It was a hot, sultry night when the mob hit town." I asked? "If so, I've been reading his books since high school and never understood a single one of them."

That was a very deliberate lie, even while joking, as Fredrick Brown had been a great favorite of mine, along with Damon Runyon and others of that era. We visited that afternoon for 30 minutes or so. During the next two months, I had the chance to occasionally visit with Will Rogers, Jr., as he was writing "The Will Rogers Story " screen play, and preparing to play the role of his father in it. I never had the chance to see Frederick Brown again, but I kept reading his works as they came out. When he died in 1972, I thought about the 30 minutes our lives had intersected. Two of his many works, *The Fabulous Clip Joint* and *Arena,* have been brought to television and were awarded high praise. He remains one of my favorite authors.

When the news of Will Rogers, Jr.'s suicide was reported in 1993, it again brought back these memories. I have just recently seen "The Will Rogers Story" on the American Movie Channel and it too leads to distant, dimming thoughts of my youth.

But that time and that place were not done with me. San Clemente had one final trick up her "figurative" sleeve, and it was the topper from my point of view. The big hotel downtown had a great bar and restaurant on the main floor with a shining, polished dance floor. It was a Saturday night and my buddy, one of the beach bums, wanted me to go out with him to this fancy bar in the hotel. I told him okay as long as we went casual, since I didn't have any dress-up clothes, and also that we didn't get into spending a lot of money, which I also didn't have. He told me not to worry that he would lend me $5 if I ran short.

We got there about 7:00 PM. The place was about half full. They had a stag section for guys who wanted to have a few drinks and didn't have dates. We could drink beer for 50¢ a bottle and get a hamburger and fries for only $1.25, so it wasn't as bad as some fancy joints I'd been in. They had a guy playing the piano. He was pretty good and nice to dance to. About 8:30 PM, a group of people swept into the place. Everybody jumped up and started clapping and yelling. I could see quite well as it wasn't really dark, but it wasn't bright either. A big guy comes walking across the floor, waving and smiling, and I realized it was Frankie Laine, the singer. A great looking brunette in a slinky gown was on his arm. It was Ann Miller, the dancer. The guy following them walked around to the piano, shook hands with the piano player, and then sat down on the bench and ran off some riffs and chords while people were still coming in. Then, in came Howard Duff, dressed in a great suit, with a pretty girl on his arm that I sort of recognized, but couldn't come up with a name for. I asked my buddy if he knew who it was. He said he thought it was Ida Lupino, as he had heard she and Howard Duff were married a few months ago. When he said Ida Lupino, I recalled seeing her in a movie when I was in high school. She looked older now and just like a movie star should look.

We watched the dancing for a while, and then the guy at the piano says into the mike "Well, since we got 'em in here, we might as well put 'em to work. Give a hand for our surprise entertainment for tonight, straight from Hollywood, the best singer, the best dancer, and, next to me, the best piano player in California. Here's Frankie Laine, Ann Miller and Carl Fischer!"

The place went wild, clapping shouting and whistling, as the three walked out to the center of the dance floor. Frankie Laine waved both hands while Ann Miller and Carl Fischer walked to the little dance stand. The bar piano player brought a mike on a long cable to Frankie, and he yelled "Thanks, thank you, thanks." Then he turned and waved to Carl, who crashed a couple of chords on the piano, played a big riff from end to end on the keyboard and they were off!

Frankie sang three or four songs, each one pretty short, and then bowed and said, "Here's who you really want to see. C'mon out, Ann. Folks, the best looking pair of legs in Hollywood, and everything that goes with 'em, Miss Ann Miller!"

That nearly brought the house down as she ran out to Frankie, did a sliding split, and popped up right in his arms. He whirled her around in a circle and spun her out in a circle. The piano was playing a bluesy number and she was just shadows, swirling skirt with some fast tapping from one side of the room to the other. It seemed as if she had no weight—she floated when she wanted to and she came down when she wanted to. Carl Fischer and the piano were in perfect harmony with her, changing the rhythm with some Gershwin, a little Cole Porter, some Harry James, all in and out, and Ann Miller just stepping on the notes, the chords, or the high riffs as though they were flower petals on a shimmering pond. It wasn't magical, it was more than that. It was ethereal.

Seven or eight minutes probably went by and with a great, ripping, pealing set of chords, it was over. The dancer had sunk to the floor, her head embraced in her arms, those long, graceful legs disappeared under the swirled out skirt on the dance floor. We waited. She raised her arms, shook out that beautiful, black hair, rose in one motion into a bow, and the place erupted. The noise was palpable, you could feel it in the surface of the table and chair. We were all standing, about one-hundred twenty people, celebrating the thing called beauty that had casually walked into our lives this night.

It was almost an anti-climax when Frankie came back a little later and did several more numbers. He and Carl finished the set, and the evening, by doing a song they had created, and singing together what has become one of the great standards of this era, or any other. *We'll be together again.*

I managed to slip through the crowd later on and catch Howard Duff at the table their group had. When I got the chance, I tapped him on the shoulder and said, "Excuse me, Mr. Duff, but I had to come over and say "Hello," and apologize again for my rude behavior in the entrance of the Coronado Hotel last spring." I had been on liberty one night in San Diego before shipping out to catch the carrier, and had bumped into a man in the entrance doorway of the Coronado Hotel. We both went down on our butts. I helped him up, and it turned out to be Howard Duff. I had apologized, told him I was a Marine on liberty, and he said forget it, just be more careful.

He stood up, looked at me, and said "Yeah, the kid on liberty. I never forget the faces of people who assault me."

He turned and said to Ida Lupino "Honey, this guy knocked me on my can a while back, and I didn't even call a cop." He looked back at me and asked what I was doing in San Clemente. I told him I was out of the Marines, and staying with my father here until I got feeling good enough to go back home to Texas.

Mr. Duff introduced me to Ida Lupino, Ann Miller and Carl Fischer. Mr. Laine was gone visiting somewhere else. I told everyone how much my friend and I had enjoyed the performance. I mentioned that my mother was a piano teacher and church organist and that my father was a professional piano player before the war, playing with jazz bands at roadhouses in Louisiana, Florida, Alabama, and East Texas. Carl Fischer and I talked a little about music. He said he would like to hear my father play sometime. I told him that my dad played by ear for the most part, and he had never learned to read music beyond the elementary basics. Carl said most of the good jazz musicians played the same way. He was a very interesting man to visit with. He told me that he was a little more than one-half Cherokee Indian. He didn't look it. He had a little black, pencil thin moustache and sharp Hollywood type clothes. He said that he was raised in California, but had traveled across some Apache, Navajo and Cherokee reservations because he was interested in his native background. He was hoping to complete a work using Indian themes in a concerto, or tone poem of some form, but he'd been working on it several years and it wouldn't seem to come together.

Neither of us could have known that less than two years from that evening, Carl Fischer would be dead, but his tone poem was finished very shortly before his death. Frankie Laine was the factor that saved his final project, which was recorded under the title "*Reflections of An Indian Boy.*" It was released two or three years after his untimely demise. I have a copy of the original release. It is the only tangible link I have to all my experiences in San Clemente. I never thought to ask a single one of the notables I came in contact with for an autograph.

As the years passed, so did this group of people that I spent one magical evening with. I asked them if they were booked here often, and they said they were escapees from Hollywood when their schedules permitted. Sometimes there might be eight or ten stars, semi stars, studio friends (wardrobe, hairdressers, stunt men, etc.), and they would skip town and go to Laguna beach, Palm Springs, San Clemente, Huntington Beach, Newport Beach and a few other places. The hotels had deals with them. They entertain while they're there and it's on the house for their tabs and rooms.

I was flying out of Denver in 1990, when I read in the Denver Post of the death of Howard Duff at the age of seventy-three. In 1990, I also read of the death of Ida Lupino. In 2004, it was Ann Miller who left the stage. And finally, five years ago in 2007, the kingpin of the group that came from Hollywood that night—the one I didn't meet in person, the one who had a terrific career in the entertainment community after starting from nowhere with nearly nothing, left us. There was only one Frankie Laine. If there is such a thing as a "Class Act," I got to see it in San Clemente that night.

In April 1952, I had been in San Clemente nearly four months. As I got my strength back, and the headaches had become less numerous and easier to cope with, the situation in my dad's house had become very stressful. My stepmother was less in touch with reality every month. She now contended that Shriners from San Antonio, TX, were slipping into her bedroom in the middle of the night and taking some of her lingerie back to San Antonio. This was about as extreme as it got, but I knew it was time to think about getting out of this environment and getting on with my life. The trouble was I had not a clue what the next step should be.

I had managed to squirrel away about 50 bucks, and I thought I could pick up another 10 or 20 by the end of the month. This would get me and my '40 Chevy coupe back to Ennis and then I would spend some time with my mom, Ella Fern Sparks, and try to come up with a plan. I told my friends, the Beach Bums, that I was going home and I sure hated to leave them. They threw me a going-away bash. It was just another good excuse for a beach party, as if they needed an excuse.

They bought me a tank of gas as a going away present—gas was up to 32¢ a gallon—and that really helped. I thought about swinging up through Nevada and hitting this neat small city called Las Vegas. A bunch of us from the Naval Hospital had gone there on a weekend liberty once and had a great time for two days, at the end of which we all had hangovers, were stony broke, and had learned that those Casinos might give away some things, but money wasn't one of them.

I decided going the shortest route would be the smarter move. I planned to go by the cut-off to Yuma, Tucson, El Paso, and zigzag across West Texas to Ennis. I told Dad and Florence I was leaving the next morning and that I really appreciated them letting me stay at their house. I knew they were relieved and so was I. I just hadn't understood how real mental illness is, but a little later in life I did come to realize that my stepmother was doing the very best she was capable of with her impaired abilities. She hadn't asked or desired to be the way she was. Since the time I came to this understanding, I have made my best efforts to interact with all persons I come in contact with, regardless of any handicap—mental or physical—as if it were myself who was forced to be in their position. I don't know if I've been very good at doing this, but it's as much as I seem to be capable of.

About ten miles west of Yuma, early afternoon, I heard a soft rapping noise coming from the engine compartment. I looked at the oil pressure gauge; it was showing about 15# (pounds), when it should have been about 30#. I knew from experience that the main rod bearing caps, six of them lined with babbitt metal, were worn down and had to be adjusted, and soon. I pulled into the first filling station/garage I came to on the outskirts of Yuma and shut off the engine. The place was rundown and dowdy looking with some junker autos in the back of the two stall shop, two lift pump gas pumps and an office hooked onto the shop that looked like it had been built about 1930. There was nothing further down the road that looked even this good.

An older guy with grey hair under his cap, grey stubble whiskers, in greasy coveralls, wiping his hands with a big, greasy, red rag, came out of the shop and nodded at me.

"I heard you coming" he said. "Sounds like rod bearings to me." I nodded in agreement. "Me too" I said. "I can shim them up if the babbitts okay, but I don't have any tools. Would you have a jack and some wrenches I could rent for a few hours?"

He did and when he saw my dog tags after I took my shirt off, he told me to pull it up into the shade—it was about 103 degrees—and he fixed me up with a jack and all the tools I would need, along with a creeper to get under the car. In an hour I had drained the oil and taken the pan off. When I got the first rod cap off, I knew I was in trouble. The babbitt was worn almost down to the steel of the rod cap. I pulled the rest of them off, there are six of them, and found they were all about the same. It was about six o'clock and I went in and told E.J.—he told me to call him that when he got the tools—that they were done for. He looked at them and said that I sure wasn't going far with this bunch.

I asked if he might have some. He said no and that he got all his parts from a store in town, or at a nearby wrecking yard. He called the wrecking yard and learned they had some very good used caps and shims and the gaskets I would need, but they couldn't get them ready this late in the day. It would be about noon tomorrow before we could get them. The price was about one-third of new parts, so I told E.J. to fix it up. He did and told me the cost would be about $17.50 which I could pay, but it was going to take most of my reserve.

E.J. happened to own this little business and he lived on the place. He told me I was welcome to stay the night and could sleep on the floor of the back room on a pallet, instead of being folded up in my coupe. He took me down the road a mile or so to a little café that served good, plain food at cheap prices. He said he lived "close to the bone," and I said I was very familiar with that kind of life, being from Texas.

To make this short: we got the parts at noon, I worked all afternoon getting the job done; it's a touchy procedure, but I'd done it before. E.J. wouldn't let me put the old oil back in, it was black and gritty for sure. He pumped out new oil and put it in, we cleaned and checked the plugs and points and just as it was getting dark, we fired it up and it ran like a Singer Sewing Machine. E. J. insisted on me staying the night again.

The next morning, I got out my wallet and counted my money. I had $46 and some change. I owed E.J. $18.20 for the parts, $1.40 for oil, $4.65 for gas, and I figured about $5 for renting his tools, using his shop equipment, his labor, and a few odds and ends. That totaled $29.25. That left me $17 to get to Texas on.

E.J. held the $29.25 in his hand. By now in the evenings after supper sitting in the dark, under the stars in the cool air, we'd told each other about our lives. He knew I was a young ex-Marine headed home. I knew he had kicked around all over Arizona and New Mexico, had been married for twenty-seven years until his wife passed away, and had two kids. He had a daughter who was married with one child and lived in Bisbee, AZ. His son was in the Army in WW II, was working now in Farmington, NM, and was separated from his wife.

E.J. asked me how much I had left. I told him $17, but that would be enough I thought and if it wasn't, I'd stop and work for a while. He said "You're stopped now. Work a week or so for me getting this place cleaned up, gas cars when they come in and help me finish the work on those two cars in the shop. I'll pay you a dollar an hour for a week, then stay or go as you please."

I told him I'd stay until the shop work was done, the station was cleaned up and the front repainted, but five days was the longest I would hang around. Six days later, I pocketed the money he paid me. I would only take $38; I figured that was all I really worked. It also helped square us for the coffee and breakfasts he had fed me. When I shook his hand and said goodbye, I gave him a sack with one of my Marine Corps khaki shirts in it and said "In case you want to dress up and go to town some Saturday night." I told him to call his kids and to go see them if he found the time. As I drove out onto the old highway, I could see him standing by the pumps in the rear view mirror. He was everyman. I was the wanderer.

Nine years later I flew into Yuma on my way to Queretaro in Central Mexico. My passengers were two of Charley Steen's mining engineers who were involved with reworking an old silver mine there. They needed some paperwork from a firm in Yuma. They had a meeting set up at the airport on our way south to our destination.

Out of my side cockpit window, I could see the area where the old highway had been. It was gone. A modern interstate had been built north of town, cutting off Yuma except for the on/off ramps. Where it had been all desert around the little gas station/garage, there were now houses, buildings, streets, new style gas stations and traffic ... the desert had bloomed.

I wondered if it had benefited E.J. or made a wanderer out of him too.

That early morning I drove east with the little Chevy 6 cylinder engine purring like a whisper of wind through the pecan trees down on the Trinity River at home. I drove through Tucson, Deming, Las Cruces and, in the dead of night, El Paso.

The next day, as the sun was lowering toward sunset behind me, I was about 230 miles past El Paso. As I topped a small rise and started down a slight hill, I was dazzled by sunlight being reflected off of thousands of aircraft hulls and wings. To the east and south of the highway, as far as I could see, row after row of large aircraft were parked wingtip to wingtip. I recognized our bomber fleet from WW II, some mothballed, others being dismantled and stripped. There were B-29's, B-24's, B-17's, A-26's, B-26's, and smaller models of our fighters and trainers. There were quite literally thousands of aircraft, and in the middle of this array, there were tall furnaces set up called the "cookers," to melt the aluminum and cast it into ingots.

This was Pyote Air Force Base, a bomber training airfield during the World War II era, and now a storage and disposal center. There were rows of engines, landing gear with tires still attached, control surfaces, propellers, and stacks of other spare parts to support many of these models flying now in the Korean War.

All the traffic on both sides of the highway was slowed to about half speed, their occupants gazing at these skeletons of our air armada, hundreds of millions of dollars in materials, labor, maintenance, training, all now waiting patiently to be sacrificed in their turn.

Even though I wasn't a pilot yet, it still brought an intense feeling of sadness and loss, to see this end for such beautiful, modern technological marvels. Although their entire reason for being was to bring death and destruction to other human beings, the ultimate purpose of these tools of warfare was to help destroy tyranny, and return our world to a state of freedom that would allow all peoples to choose their own destiny without fear. This they had done. Now for much of this technology, the "swords into plowshares" dictum brought their creation and employment full circle.

As I drove past the last of the lines, glinting in the rays of the failing, reddened, sunlight, I thought of the times I had seen horses with a broken leg or suffering from other serious injuries, and being "put down." They had had no future.

A certain reserve of our military aircraft must be preserved in order to be ready for immediate use and training. For the rest, the majority of the "old technology" types had to go. They had no future.

I pulled into Ennis about ten o'clock in the morning, swung by Mom's office at the church, caught up on most of the family gossip, found out that the railroad was laying off employees, as was Ennis tag factory, and the cotton gins. People were moving to Dallas or Corsicana, Waco, Waxahachie and other places to find work. It had been dry and it looked as though the cotton crop would be about half picked soon and was not producing very well, etc.

That afternoon late, after mom got off work, I took her to Hoover's Café in downtown Ennis for supper. Hoover's put out a Chicken Fried Steak plate with white gravy, biscuits, greens, buttermilk or sweet tea, a square of Lemon Mousse or peach cobbler, and they were always packed. People came from all over the county and other close counties to eat here. It wasn't cheap; it would cost about 75¢, but it would be the best 75¢ worth of food you could find in Ellis County. Now I knew I was home.

Mom asked me what I was going to do now. I told her that after I rested up a few days, I was going to Houston to meet with one of my old classmates who said he could get me a job making good money working around the docks in the harbor. She was disappointed. She'd hoped I would stay in Ennis awhile. I told her it looked like there was no work here, so I'd go find some, but I'd get back home as often as possible.

I hung around Ennis for a few days, and ran into a great car deal at one of the dealers in town. He had a blue 1947 Chevy convertible, white top, lots of miles for those days, 63,000. The top had a split that had been repaired with white tape sewed on it, the radio didn't work, but the heater did. The tires looked okay—about half worn down. It was a trade-in on a new car, but used cars weren't selling well with there being no work in the county, so it was marked down to $150. I showed him my '40 Chevy coupe, grey lacquer prime paint job California style, good looking plastic seat covers and an average mileage of 33,600, ran great and drove well. We made a deal, my car and $45 cash. I went to the bank and got my two U.S. Govt. War Bonds; $25 each, cashed them in at the post office, filled out the paperwork, switched my Texas plates over to the convertible, and drove home to show Mom. She said it was nice, but she had kinda wanted the coupe, but hadn't got around to talking to me about it.

I went back to the dealer and asked him how much he would sell the car for if my mom wanted to buy it. It so happened that he was a member of the Tabernacle Baptist Church, the one Mom was the organist and secretary for. He said if she wanted it, she could pay him $75 for it, and pay that off however she wanted to, say at $5 a month.

Mom jumped at the deal and in one day we became a two car family. I fixed up everything on both of them in a couple of days and even got my radio to work most of the time. Now I was going to Houston in style; almost broke, but in style. That counted for a lot in those days when draggin' Main was the highlight of the day.

A few days later I kissed Mom, told her to be careful with her driving, threw what little I owned into the open convertible and headed south 190 miles to Houston. When I got there I called my buddy and got directions to where he was living. It was in the basement of his sister's house and I could stay there until I found my own place. He graduated from Ennis High a couple of years before I did. He had a good job on the docks and had friends there that could get me work with the stevedore hiring hall bosses. The way it worked was that I had to give back about 8 per cent of what I made, but I would be making quite a bit more per hour than any other job I could find.

We had to be at the "shape up" at the Union Hall at Harrisburg and 75th street at 5:30 AM every morning to get hired by the union labor gang foremen for that day. They would pick the union old timers they knew first, and then fill in with other husky guys to make up the crew for a particular ship for that day. If you did good work, they would pick you up each day until that ship was finished loading. If you gave them any trouble, they would spread it around to the other foremen, and you couldn't get the time of day out of them anymore. You were pretty much under their thumbs.

For three months, five or six, sometimes seven days in a row, we sweated our butts off in the holds of ships, from as little as three hours to as much as twelve occasionally, loading or unloading all sorts of cargo. Loading export cotton bales was about the hardest. They were full weight bales crushed down to about two-thirds the size of a regular bale and were stacked horizontally about five high. It took five guys to get the last bale on top.

We made pretty good money even with the union taking a slice off the top. There were plenty of bars and juke joints in the waterfront area to help redistribute the rest of it. I mailed some home to Mom to keep for me. That's about the only smart thing I did do during this period. The drinks were cheap, but the girls weren't.

One weekend in late summer, I got an invitation from the jocks at Sam Houston State Teachers College in Huntsville to come up to a "mid-summer's pre-football training camp party." I drove up and met the guys at the athletic dorm and we were soon piling into a neat little roadhouse bar off the campus. During the general melee these things usually are, one of the guys I had played against in high school told me that eight or nine of the athletes from the small colleges in the area were going to Mexico City with scholarships to play football for Mexico City College, an American college there run by Americans for both Mexicans and Americans. Marvin Gray, who had played at Sam Houston, was the new coach and wanted a bunch of gringos to come down and play for them. He asked me "Why don't you come down with us?" I said, as I drank my 5th or 6th beer, "If Marvin says its okay with him, hell yes, I'll go with you."

The next day they called Marvin in Mexico City, told him they had three more who wanted in, and he okay'd us all for a scholarship. So, along with my hangover, I get word that I have to be in Mexico City in two weeks to get ready for training camp.

A week later, I kissed Mom goodbye, jumped in my Chevy convertible and, like a guy who knows exactly what he's doing, headed south for Mexico City via Laredo and the Pan American Highway. At Nuevo Laredo the border guards said I couldn't get a tourist visa and entry papers for my car until I had driven 50 kilometers south. So that's what I did and finally convinced the immigration and customs officials that I did indeed own this car, paid fees for the car permit and my tourist visa, good for six months, got a map, and headed down the Pan American Highway all the way to Mexico City. I had changed most of my dollars into pesos, so then it was just enjoy the drive.

And I did right up to the point that the Pan American Highway turned into the Pan American Gravel Pit; then later into the Pan American Buffalo Wallow, the Pan American Rock Quarry and the Pan American Desert Sand Dune Park. I occasionally ran across a small village and could go into a cantina and point to something that looked edible and to something that looked like a bottle of beer, so I didn't go hungry very much.

Then, one of the only really bright spots of this trip happened. Out of nowhere, I met two gringos in an ugly International 4 wheel drive panel truck, painted god-awful green, and aptly named "The Green Monster"—an army surplus job, about 1942 vintage, with Michigan license plates. Two guys, about my age, were standing beside it. I wheeled up and stopped. These two gringos were just out of the U.S. Navy and they decided to take a tour of Mexico and Central America. C. P. Paris and Joe, his buddy, (I never could remember his last name) were in no hurry to get to anywhere, but I managed to get them to agree to our traveling together in case of trouble. From there on we had a great time stopping at all the little villages sampling the food and drink in all the cantinas we ran across. Joe spoke a little Spanish which helped.

We finally made it to Mexico City. The guys hung around for a while, but finally it was time for them to move on south down toward Panama.

I met Paris in Reno years later in 1961—we had stayed in touch—where he was living and working at Harrah's Club. We visited many times over the next forty years. Joe went back to Michigan after that Mexico trip and I never saw him again, but heard about him from Paris.

Paris came to visit me in Grand Junction, CO, in 2002. We spent a few days having a lot of fun moseying around the Colorado back country. He said we'd do this again soon, pulled out of my driveway, waved, and drove out of my life forever. He just dropped into a black hole. I quit trying to locate him after three or four years. During that last visit he said he was having some health problems. I have since learned he quit having them in 2009.

Constantine P. Paris, a Navy white hat, and John Sparks, a Seagoing Marine, being friends. Who would have thought it? Hasta 'luego, mi amigo. Vaya con Dios.

When I arrived in Mexico City, I bought a map, found my way to the college site and checked in with the front desk. They sent me out to the gymnasium where there were about thirteen or fourteen guys filling out forms. The guy with a whistle around his neck, that had to be the coach, waved me over, shook my hand while telling me he was Marvin Gray and to fill out these forms and get acquainted with the other gringos, and so it began.

My friend from Sam Houston State, two friends of his, and I decided we wanted to live off campus. We asked the front office if they had any information on places and within a few hours we had an apartment in a building on the Avenida de Hippodromo, the site of the old Spanish racetrack. It was close to the school and the athletic field where we would soon be practicing. We started getting into shape with stretching exercises, push-ups, calisthenics, and then somebody yelled "Wind sprints." There were about twenty of us on the field. We lined up, got ready, then somebody yelled "GO" and off we went. One guy made it the full hundred yards before he collapsed. The rest of us were scattered from thirty to eighty yards, rolling on the grass, gasping for breath. I was on about the 60 yard line in real pain. It was not possible to get any air in your lungs, much less get what was needed to run flat out. We all pretty much realized at about the same time that we were no longer in Texas where the altitude above sea level was between 1 foot and 300 feet. Instead, as one guy looked it up on the fact sheet we had been given, we were 7,350 feet high. That's 7 *thousand*, 350 feet up! No wonder nobody could breathe. We were only getting about 60 per cent of the oxygen we were used to. Suffice it to say, our little "tune-up before actual practice started" became more like a slave labor camp under Coach Gray. But at the end of the first week of actual practice, no one had died yet, and our outlook was much brighter.

The school part was great. Classes were in English and Spanish. All we gringos had to take Spanish. The Mexican students spoke English quite well and kept us afloat with help on our Spanish. I was taking classes in Journalism, Art, Conversational Spanish—with good looking senoritas—and how to make Cuba Libres with rum and whatever mix we could find. I made decent grades and our football team, the "Aztecas," was rolling over the Mexican college teams like a pro team matched against a junior high team. It was brutal at times. We ran up scores of 60 to 80 points to 0 for the opposition team. We played every player we had in uniform, all forty-one of them, every game. Among the seventeen Texans, we had both Anglo and Hispanic. One was a Little All-American Team member, two were All Blue-Bonnet Conference linemen and several had been first-stringers at some of the smaller Texas schools.

We played all the games at the Estadio Olympico, the stadium built for the Olympics before World War II, which would seat around 92,000. It was in the southwest part of the city, right next to the big Bull Fight ring. The crowds ran about forty-five to fifty-five thousand, all yelling "Yankee, go home!" in Spanish. The stadium had wire fences about 8 feet high, with ribbon wire all along the top, to keep the crowd off the field. We came into the stadium through a tunnel that connected it with the Bull Ring. This kept us inside the fence at all times. We arrived in uniform on the bus in the Bull Ring, played the game, made our escape back to our bus, back to our home field gym to clean up and get our street clothes back on. The Policia kept a pretty tight rein on the crowd. No bottled drinks or canned drinks were sold or allowed, but it was a good idea to stay away from the fence, especially after we had a sizeable score built up.

We won seven games straight. Then the Championship game came up with the University de Mexico, the last game of the season. Coach Gray got us prepared the best he could, even putting in some of the new "T" formation plays to go with our single wing attack. We had good speed, good size on the line and played very well together. What we didn't have were many reserves, about ten fair sized Mexican boys who played hard and gave it all they had, but they had no experience. The rest of the squad was pretty much just cannon fodder, filling up holes for a few plays while the regulars got a breather. All together, we had about forty-one squad members, two coaches and a water boy.

The day of the game, for the first time, we came directly into the stadium on our bus and stepped out at the end zone on one end of the field. The Mexican Army had been called in to provide security and keep order. The newspapers the next day put the size of the crowd between ninety and ninety-five thousand. That didn't bother us much as the fence and the soldiers should take care of us. What did bother us was the sight of the University of Mexico team. We knew they had a large size roster, but Coach Gray hadn't been very explicit when he told us that. We thought eighty or ninety would be the size of their squad. What we saw running and warming up on half the field were one-hundred and fifty big guys in football uniforms—*really* nice uniforms—*really* big guys!

One of our guards from Texas, Shorty Snodgrass, a great little 200 pound blocking guard, dropped the equipment bag he was carrying, turned around and looked at all of us standing behind him and said: "Jesus Christ, now I know what Jim Bowie and Davy Crockett musta thought when they looked out from the Alamo!" Nobody laughed. We knew he hadn't meant it to be funny. When he said it, it was pretty much what was in all our minds.

Well, it didn't turn out like the Alamo. We all lived over it. That was about the only difference. We scored two touchdowns in the first quarter because we were fresh; we opened our bag of tricks and turned it inside out to get them. Then they put the "A" team in. They put in a fresh squad every four plays, all of them big and most of them fast. They slammed two of our best backs and three of our regular defensive line by halftime. It was clean play, but brute force every play takes it out of you. I usually played all the offensive plays and a lot of the defensive end plays, if we were up against a fast backfield team. By the half I was lucky to just get out for offense. Our poor little subs were bewildered. They tried hard, but it was three downs and kick the rest of the game. To make it even worse, the crowd was so loud when we had the ball, you couldn't hear the guy next to you, much less Jack Wilburn, the quarterback. For the University, it was as quiet as it ever gets in Mexico City, just a low rumble until the ball is snapped, then pandemonium until the next play starts. It was a really long afternoon.

After the game, the Policia smuggled us out of the tunnel to the Bull Ring. Our bus had been parked there after dropping us off before the game. The officials knew from previous soccer games how difficult it was to handle these large crowds. The final score was 70 something to 14. All we got out of it was a little humility.

I went with the Art class to see the murals that Diego Rivera was painting at the University of Mexico in West Mexico City. They were incredible, hundreds of feet in length, 12 to 15 feet high on the interior hallways and more on the exterior. In context, they were heavily weighted toward the formation of modern Mexico as a socialist form of governmental enterprise, overcoming the colonial influences of the Spanish and later the French governing eras. Rivera had dozens of the University art students working on these as part of the Arts Program. Graduate students controlled the work as assigned by Diego.

The twenty-three student group I was in finished the tour in front of the Arts building, with a brief five minute oration by Diego. No questions were allowed. We simply listened as the future of art and Mexico was laid out by Sr. Rivera. "The social revolution would keep rejecting the excesses of Capitalism and its pawn to the north of Mexico, etc., etc."

His oratory could have used a little work, but there was nothing at all wrong with the way he could lay a line on plaster or canvas. Some art transcends social thinking. Some art, no matter what, will always be *ART*, no matter who eventually seizes control of "the great unwashed masses." Art as propaganda, i.e., Russia's monolithic murals and statuary, is one thing. Art as beauty beyond politics is something else. Rivera, I believe, will be remembered as a true artist, without reservations.

The time came for us gringos to renew our tourist visas. School was over until the spring semester started. It was a requirement for us to return to the border to renew the visas. Coach Gray had informed the team members that we would remain on scholarship the remainder of the school year, but, as always, there was a catch. He had been informed by the school administration that the Athletic Scholarship program would most likely be terminated at the end of the semester and would not be in place for the next football season. Coach Gray put forth his best arguments, but the outlook was grim.

Us football gringos had a team meeting and some of us decided we would go on back home, not renewing visas, and skip the next semester. Four of us, the three buddies I was rooming with and I, decided to go this route. We gave Coach Gray our decision and started packing. He said he didn't blame us and that we could play on his teams anytime, anywhere. He had married a beautiful Mexican girl from a very wealthy family several years before. His future was in Mexico, one way or the other. He was really a great guy and coach. He had been All Conference in Texas when he played there. He treated us all alike, gringo or Mexicano. This is what athletics was meant to be. It's unfortunate that television and modern sports ethics have changed this to a "Show me the money!" mentality.

We loaded our gear into my car and headed north. I took a different road west of the Pan Am highway and it was a much better road. It even had some paving on it. We went around Queretaro and through San Luis Potosi, Saltillo, Monterrey, and finally, Nuevo Laredo. We gave up all our papers, changed our money into greenbacks, at a loss, of course, eased across the river bridge into Laredo, Texas, and headed for Houston. At the first decent café we came to, we stopped and had chicken-fried steaks all around. Now we knew for sure we were home. It had been a great five months, but it was over—time to get on with whatever was next.

Little did I know that there was one more football game in my future.

•

Chapter 3 — Maybe Airplanes Would Be More Fun

I dropped the guys in Houston and headed north to Ennis. Mom and my aunts, uncles, and cousins had a great time stuffing me full of Texas cooking and listening to my mostly honest recounting of my trip and wild experiences. The employment picture hadn't changed any to speak of. I knew I'd have to go to Dallas or Houston or somewhere else to find a half-way decent paying job. I called my buddies in Houston to see what they were doing. They said they were going to work on a tugboat the first of next week. It sounded like a pretty good job. They said the tug company needed one more deckhand. I said to count me in and started packing. Mom said she wasn't surprised when I told her I was leaving again and going back to Houston in two days. She said, "I think you get it from your father." She also said it would be better than having me as far away as Mexico City. At least I would be home part of the time. Yeah, sure, as it turned out, I got home once in four months.

Two days later I was walking up the short gangplank to board the tugboat "Anna C," operated by the J. D. Cayton Tug Co. of Houston, out of Bloodworth Shipyards in the Houston ship channel area. My two buddies were already aboard. The third one had decided to go back to North Texas to his home for a while. With my coming aboard, the crew of eight was now complete. In two hours we were under way to Matagorda Bay, which was southwest on the coast between Galveston and Corpus Christi, to pick up some barges loaded with oyster shells, dug up by the dredges there, to haul them back to Freeport to Dow Chemical Company. We three new deckhands, just called "hands," were being instructed on how to handle the hawser lines and steel cables used in making up the tow lines. The mate who instructed us had control of the deckhands and their work. The engineer took care of the engines, pumps and all general maintenance. The cook took care of feeding us and other odds and ends. The Captain ran the boat, steered and navigated it, gave first aid, when necessary, and was backed up by the mate.

When I signed on, it was made clear to me and the other two new guys that the rules were simple and inflexible. The Captain's word was absolute. The mate was responsible only to the Captain and gave the crew their orders. The engineer was to be accommodated anyway necessary by everybody. The cook didn't take short-orders, except maybe from the skipper, and we *would* eat what was put on the table with no complaints. The senior hand was in charge of the junior hands and would instruct us in the shipboard knowledge we had to have. This included lots of safety items and general labor skills, such as "knitting" heavy rope "fenders" out of hawser line, using a "fid," a foot long tapered, polished, wooden pin, to do it. These fenders kept the hull from being banged up badly while we were alongside barges making up tows, etc. Working with wire cables, called wire rope, was difficult and could be damned dangerous if not done correctly. Splicing "eyes" into them was a bitch, even with two men working on the cables that were about the size of your wrist. Knowing how to tie (tether) the barges together and join them to the tug, especially for the on-the-nose tows, required knowledge, skill and brute force in that order.

When making up the tow, everybody worked straight through until we were ready to tow or were under way.

Duty time other than this, for the hands, was 6 hours on and 6 hours off. There were always two hands keeping watch on all the rigging of the tow, the waterlines of the barges, fire watch, helping the engineer if required, following orders of the mate or skipper, and doing hourly checks of certain things per a duty check list.

The cook, engineer, mate, and Captain (skipper) had flexible hours as conditions warranted. They might work a lot more or a lot less than the hands. Usually, the senior hand, the mate, and maybe the engineer were checked out for wheelhouse duty, steering, radio position reports, traffic advisory call, etc. This took much of the work off the skipper if we were in rough weather, in fog, or night in tight quarters, allowing him to concentrate on steering and navigation without distraction. This was really an "art" which took years to become proficient at.

If you had just ten barges (60 feet in length, 20 feet wide, carrying 30 tons of cargo each) tethered two abreast, five deep, on the nose tow, you would have a block approximately 320 feet by 45 feet, drawing 6 feet of water and weighing about 350 tons (700,000 lbs.). And this you might be pushing through 6 foot waves. Our tug, the Anna C., was built in 1949, in Wilder, KY, by the Nashville Bridge Co. She was 110 feet in length, 27.5 feet wide, twin screws, with two 900 HP diesel engines and had a draft of approximately 9 feet. You mostly steered a boat like this, during tow operations, by using differential power, along with the twin rudders. You brought one engine into reverse and left the other one in forward, then adding power or reducing power on them as needed to make the tow (on the nose) pivot toward the direction you needed to turn toward. Straightening up was the reverse of the first procedure, and then bringing the engines together in forward gear. Wind, waves, and possibly tidal currents had to be taken into account for each of these maneuvers.

This was why only the most experienced crew members were allowed to do these tasks. One mistake could put the whole tow underwater or drive it onto the banks of the canal or shore. Breaking or stretching the tether cables and pivoting the barges in the middle could result in collisions with other barges or vessels traveling in the opposite direction. A bad day at the office doesn't begin to describe these problems. Believe me, the front office will not be amused when you call this in on the company radio.

A standard work deployment on a contract is usually three weeks on duty, then a week off for the crew, and possibly the boat also. Working twenty-one days straight takes some getting used to, but having seven straight days off usually makes up for it. If a special charter or contract comes in that requires stretching the crew time out to possibly double the usual schedule, because of some mitigating factors, the crew is usually compensated for this and their time off is adjusted also. This type of work is not for everyone, but many crew members make a long and successful career of it.

Having served aboard a carrier, I felt right at home compared to the other new hands. I always called our tug the "boat," and one day the other hands asked why I didn't call it a ship. I told them that the way we were taught in the Marine Sea School to describe a naval craft is simple. You can put a boat on a ship, but you can't put a ship on a boat. Size *DOES* count.

We had been taking shell barges into Galveston and Freeport for a week when Captain "Andy Anderson," a good Norwegian, informed us that we were picking up some cargo barges in Galveston for a drop in New Orleans via the Intercoastal Waterway. This meant a thorough inspection of all the gear aboard and re-supplying in Galveston before we entered the ICW. Everything was checked. Our cook, who was a Cajun from Louisiana, took the skiff and brought back the galley supplies while we made up the tow. At first light we pulled away from the anchorage in Galveston and headed northeast and entered the ICW, passed through the canal on Pelican Island and headed into the main ICW channel after we crossed East Bay. I guess I expected a long, straight, wide, smooth water highway sort of thing. I quickly learned that this would be the most demanding work we hands had seen in the month and a half we had been on board. The ICW followed the natural creek and bayou channels with lots of turns and low banks. It had been dredged to a safe depth for small tugs and was maintained by the states it passed through and the U.S. Army Corps of Engineers.

Our work load changed. We ran from first light until last light, all hands on deck and then stopped for the night. There was no way we could navigate some of the tighter turns in the dark, no matter how powerful our search lights were, especially if there were currents or tides. It was three days of really hard work, but eventually we pulled out of the ICW and into the mighty Mississippi River. We parked our barges down by the Canal Street Ferry crossing at the south end of New Orleans. We had liberty in the French Quarter that night; the mate went with us to hold down the celebrating since we were starting back the next day about noon with a load of "shells" (empty barges). It was a fun night and a hell of a lot bigger, brighter, noisier, and more expensive than the Houston waterfront.

The trip back was pretty much like the trip out, except that the shells, riding high in the water, were like a bunch of corks bobbing around in the water. It took a lot of work keeping the rigging taut and making sure the chafing was kept to a minimum. One thing I remember that was a first for me was when we ran over a fairly big alligator and hit it with one of the propellers. We shut down so we could inspect for propeller blade damage. While we did this the cook lowered the skiff, went out to the 'gator floating belly up in the water by the bank, and after making sure it was dead, cut the tail off and brought it back to the boat. That night we had Alligator steaks. They were round and whitish, tasting somewhat like pork, but with a bit of "wild" with it. It wasn't bad, but although this was a great meal to a Cajun, to a kid from North Texas it wasn't even within range of a good Chicken Fried Steak with white gravy. I spent five months on the Anna C., saved some money, and went back to Ennis when they wanted the crew to sign on for eight months to a year or more to take a contract in New England and the Canadian Atlantic Provinces. I told them I had other fish to fry, wished them the best of luck, and bought a round for the crew at the nearest bar.

I still had airplanes on my mind.

After this last trip on the tug and a quick drink with the crew, I packed my gear and headed north. It was good to be headed home, although I had no definite plans. I only knew somehow that I was wasting my time in Houston. I was for sure not going to make my future revolve around the waterfront there, so home was the best idea for now.

Mom had been so patient and understanding with me I felt that I had to spend some time being normal for her. I wanted something I couldn't put into words for some reason. But after my close call as a Marine, I knew time was a valuable asset to be wasting without a goal. I didn't seem to be able to see the future except in terms of short periods of time, hours and days instead of years, no bright tomorrows and steady accomplishments toward my life's purpose. I began to wonder if there was too much of my father's personality in my makeup. With all his gifts of talent for music, personality and ability to make friends, he was fundamentally flawed in a way that made his life bring unhappiness to his parents, family, and people who trusted him in various ways. I was one of those people.

I never went to a school function with my father; no football banquets, no attendance to the senior play I was in, no clapping at my graduation, or any other life function that a young boy growing up will always remember. In all, I spent, counting the four brief summer visits with him and the four months in San Clemente, slightly less than a year in his company. If this was an indicator of *my* future, it didn't show much promise. My mother never quit loving Dad, even though she finally had to admit that there was no way to cope with his life style and retain her own mental wellbeing. The divorce, in 1947, had just been delayed by the war. Dad took up where he left off without missing a beat. Mother was a one-man woman. The day that she stood by his coffin in 1970, along with his two other wives, she was as distraught as if he had loved, cared and provided for her and me in every manner of his wedding vows in 1931. I only felt relief that this part of my life and hers had come to a conclusion.

My Mother would never allow me to denigrate Dad in any way as I grew up. She simply said that no matter what, he was my father, and deep in his being, he loved me as only a father can love a son. One of the last conversations I had with Mom while she was fairly coherent, residing in The I.O.O.F. Nursing Home in Ennis, was about the wonderful life she had had. She relived her past in the Tabernacle Baptist Church, the wonderful Pastors she had worked for, the multitude of friends she had and still has, the wonderful son who had made her so proud with his accomplishments in aviation, and the one true love of her life, a love she could never let go of, no matter how bad the circumstances. The last Pastor she worked for was Reverend Richard Moody. He and June, his wife, treated Mom like one of their family. They have even treated me like one of their family; letting me stay with them in their home on my occasional visits to Ennis. Although I have no feelings about religion one way or the other, I have to say that God has two dandy representatives in the Moody's. Their two daughters also exemplify the blessings that come to those with a strong faith in what they believe. These small town Texas folks are true examples of the American ethic and way of life.

When Mom passed away in 1991, she had been unable to comprehend the present for many months, but I knew that no fading ability to be part of the present could keep her from living in a past that she had found great happiness and great sorrow in. To have been so blessed with an acceptance of the reality of life and to live life as well as she did is a gift I think I shall never have.

I had only been home once in the last five months and nothing much had changed. In those days life in a place like Ennis wasn't comparable to floating down the river of time in a rowboat. It was more like wading across a vast, shallow pond in mud up to your knees. Now, this is not to say that a little ennui is not good for you occasionally, but you can become too comfortable in your life if it continues too long. I decided to make up some lost time with Mom and let everything else go for the time being. The day I got home, I took Mom out to lunch at Thompson's Café, and supper at Hoover's Café. I drove her around for a week to see all her old friends she wanted us to visit with. We visited with my aunts and their families. We went to Wednesday night prayer meeting. I continued to take her to lunch and dinner every day. She insisted on making breakfast at the apartment. Finally, I thought up the master stroke. After dinner Friday night I took her to the Plaza Theater to see a Cary Grant movie, as he was a special favorite of hers, and, in short, I tried to act like a son for a change.

I had a couple of dates with Nancy, my last high school sweetheart. She was a really sweet girl—the one who was with me the day I nicked Robert Mitchum's bumper. She was now dating a guy who was in her class in high school, a pretty good kid as I remembered him. She married him and it has worked out well for them—he went to college, became a lawyer, they have a family, and have enjoyed a good life together.

I looked around town for something to do, but there was still no work to speak of. I ran into a guy who had graduated a year before I did. He said he was setting "jugs" for a seismograph crew working up northwest of Ennis and they were hiring. I went with him the next morning and talked to the party chief. He liked the fact that I had been in the military, knew something about science and had no strings attached. He said if I would work as a rodman for the surveyor and sling drill stems for one of the drill rigs, if needed, he'd start me today. I knew as much about one of these jobs as I did the other, but I thought I could pick it up quickly, so I said, "Where do I sign?"

That sign-up sheet turned out to be a one-way ticket out of Texas for good. In May 1953, I learned the ropes to be a rodman, and then with the driller's help, how to work with him on the Mayhew drill, then the Failing drill—which had some differences that you had better know about. I found out how to take the stems (10 foot long steel drill shafts) off, put them on, stack them the right way, and still have as many fingers and toes at the end of the shift as I did at the start.

Everybody in Texas knows about "doodle buggin," but for folks who've never spent much time around an oil patch or the petroleum industry, here's a brief explanation. In order to locate the most promising strata of rock formations underground to locate potential drilling sites, a survey called a seismograph map is generated, sort of an x-ray of the ground beneath the surface, but done with sound waves instead of x-rays. To do this, a series of straight lines are surveyed along the surface of the area of interest to the geologists. Along these lines at evenly spaced intervals, holes approximately 5 inches to 6 inches wide are drilled to specified depths. These holes are then loaded at the bottom with a small charge of explosives, with a detonator and wiring to set them off. The holes are backfilled and tamped down to keep the energy of the explosion focused downward as much as possible. When the explosives are ignited simultaneously, the shock wave travels downward and sideways in all directions and is reflected back to the surface with different times and strength depending on the composition of the different layers of strata.

Along the straight lines surveyed on the surface, very sensitive microphone receivers, called "jugs" by the work crew, record the information of the reflected wave, including such information as frequency, elapsed time, and several other data points. This is all recorded on a set of computer tapes and when analyzed in the laboratory, gives the information to allow the strata at the different depths to be analyzed and maps to be generated. On the basis of this information, potential drilling sites may be located or the area may be dropped from consideration for drilling.

This was the way it was done in the 1950's, and, of course, like everything else, has been totally updated now to bring in better methods to analyze the information that has been generated to much better quality standards, allowing much better drilling results. My description of the work I did is the 1950's model. Let me make another oversight explanation as to the makeup of the work force crew. The party chief was exactly that, the boss. He runs everything with his orders, works with the "land man" to make sure the permits are in place and is the front man to deal with the front office, landowners and other officials. The land man obtains the permits to drill, etc. and works with local government officials as necessary. The surveyor does the surveying, makes the very accurate maps of all surface location points, BLM corner or survey monuments, etc., the drill hole locations and surface features of note. The rodman assists the surveyor, holds the position rod that is calibrated in feet and inches so that the surveyor can see it thru his transit scope and record the necessary information and map the lines and holes very accurately. He also does other related duties as required.

The driller is the boss of drilling ops, sometimes with multiple rigs to speed up the completion of a contract. The other drill operators are also called drillers, but everyone knows which one is *The* driller. Deck hands or helpers swing pipe and assist the driller in all ancillary work related to the actual drill truck and equipment. The "powder monkey" keeps control of all explosives and fuses, also the detonating lines and actuators; loads the holes and backfills them. The powder man's assistant helps in all these operations and others if required.

The "jug" crew lays out the jug connector cable, and sets the jugs at the exact surveyed position as per the map lines indications—very precise work, this. There might also be several general labor hands who help with all the brute force work, assist wherever needed, hustle supplies from the nearest community, and help with the driving when locating to a different survey site, possibly a state or two away.

And all this is named after the "Doodlebug," a little insect found all over the Southwest United States and Mexico. This little guy makes a trap for other little insects by digging out a hole in the sand or soil, shaped like a funnel. The sand or dirt is loosened on a 45 degree angle slope, so that anything that falls into the "cone" will slide down to the bottom and will be unable to stop its descent. When the trap is completed, the little "doodlebug" settles itself at the bottom of the cone and waits for its "dinner guest."

We were working south of Dallas on some ranchland belonging to some of the local ranchers on the Ellis-Dallas county line. We worked from Palmer across to Bristol. There were lots of fences to be crossed with cattle in the fields walking up to us to see if we were bringing them hay or salt blocks. I got used to the way the surveyor wanted things done with no trouble. But the driller was another matter entirely. He didn't talk much and what he did say was only said once. Every minute I wasn't with the surveyor I was at one of the two drill rigs, watching and making a list of things I didn't understand. Then when I had the chance, I'd ask the driller's helpers to fill me in, which they were able to do very well. One of the hands didn't show up one morning and I was put on the Mayhew drill as the helper. That ten hour day seemed a lot longer by the time the sun went down. I got my butt chewed about once an hour on average, but I survived and the party chief gave me a pat on the back when I made out my time card.

He said "That was better than I expected you to do first time out. Yessir, I think we can make a real helper out of you in two, maybe three years." Everybody in the office trailer laughed and cackled. I found out this was what he said to every new, inexperienced helper their first day. That was the way it was done. Everybody took their job seriously, but had some fun doing it. The days were long; you worked steadily unless something broke down. For the most part we worked five day weeks, six days if we were close to the contract end date.

I settled in, we kept moving along, getting further west and then north. We heard rumors every day. We were going south next, no, it was east. There was no new work. No, we were going to be so busy we'd be shorthanded. Then in late May, the party chief called everyone in about an hour before our usual shut-down time. We knew something was up. Half of us believed it was going to be a layoff, half, me included, just hoped we had a job for a while longer. Our party chief, he was in his middle thirties, said "Here it is. We're done on this contract in about two weeks. Then I'm going to take this unit to Colorado, lock, stock, and barrel. We will need every man who wants to go, but we're trying to work out swaps with other crews to switch some personnel so that men with families can stay here. We may be gone a year or so, depends on what the results are early on. We may have to hire some local extra help there, but the front office wants as many experienced crewmen as possible to go. Think it over and let me know either way in 48 hours."

Out of the seventeen members, other than the party chief, eleven of us said we would go. We wrapped up our last shot lines, took the trucks into the company garage for tune-ups and checks and headquarters assigned us two more trucks for hauling supplies. I had been spending as much time with Mom as I could, but her work schedule, along with all the activities at the church, kept her pretty well occupied. She truly loved the church and her place in it. I was very proud of her, her way of life, and her accomplishments. If she hadn't had this type of fulfillment to help fill the void the absence of my father and then I produced in her daily existence, I think I would have found it too difficult to leave her and try to find my own career out in the world. She urged me to do this. She was so proud of me. Later, as I started building my career in aviation, she contributed financial means from her limited income and resources. That was several years after this period of time I'm recounting. I felt guilty about leaving her this time for I had left and returned several times and I somehow felt this would be different.

I sat down with Mom after we came home from having supper and broke the news that I was once more going away. I told her I was giving her my car. I couldn't take it with me since I had to drive one of the trucks. I told her that I had spoken to the auto dealer who was in her church congregation and he had readily agreed to take both cars on trade-in for one Mom liked. She said "Well, if that's what you want, alright, but what will you do for a car when you come back?" I said "Simple, Mom. I'll just borrow yours."

The next time I did come home I flew down from Cheyenne in an airplane. She was glad to let me use her car some during the three days I was there. This was more than two years after I had left and turned northward.

The morning we left, the first week in June 1953, we formed a convoy with the party chief leading. We had nine vehicles and the best speed we hoped to average was 40 mph. Our trucks could get up to 50 mph without shaking themselves to pieces, but that was it. We went south of Dallas and Fort Worth, then to Amarillo, Dalhart, Clayton NM, Raton NM, Trinidad, CO, Pueblo, Colorado Springs and finally to Castle Rock, about 50 miles south of Denver. All of us flatlanders had nearly run off the highway numerous times while gawking at Pike's Peak and the Rampart Range of the Rockies before we got there. We had been on the road four days and three nights in cheap motels, one beer limit at night with our meal, four truck breakdowns—all minor, towed one stranded car to the next town with a man, his wife, mother-in-law, two kids and one infant and no clean diapers. All of us driving the trucks were nearly deaf for a couple of days.

Castle Rock was a fine looking town, the county seat of Douglas County. It was between four and five thousand people. It had a bunch of motels, bars, and one of the most attractive courthouses I've ever seen in my travels. Sadly, when I returned to Castle Rock in 1990, the courthouse was gone. It was burned down by a young woman who was trying to get her boyfriend out of the jail there. In its place was a totally unremarkable set of concrete boxes hooked together to keep the people and legal papers of the county out of the snow, but all the beauty had gone up in smoke, fire, and ashes.

We went right to work northeast of town about ten miles, then east and southeast of the town about fifteen miles. After a July 4th celebration fiasco—the whole celebration had to be cancelled due to about 15 inches of hail over the entire town and surrounding areas—we moved to the northwest quadrant and finished up in early September. We thought it might be back to Texas after these last lines were shot, but a few days before the last shoot things changed. A good sized contract had been bid on by the company and it was awarded to them. It just happened to be about 400 miles north of us in the town of Baker in Eastern Montana.

The party chief let two of the crew who had families in Texas, and whose families badly needed them, take one truck that wouldn't be needed on the new job and head home with it. None of us had any idea where Baker was. When we found it on the map, we knew it wasn't going to be easy to get to. And we were right. Remember, there were no super highways in those days, especially in this part of the west. We wandered across Colorado, Eastern Wyoming, Western South Dakota, over into Montana, and finally up to Baker, a little town of about 1,000 souls, with two motels, two bars, one pool hall, one movie theater, three cafes, and about one-hundred thirsty cowboys coming into town on weekends. We got along very well with these cowboys, as long as we left the local girls alone, didn't take much of their money playing pool and kept out mouths shut about Texas.

The country was fairly easy to work in, being mostly low rolling hills, grassland, a number of small creeks and ponds, and occasional fences that ran in straight lines north to south or east to west, as far as your eyes could see. The weather was good also, being the middle of September, real autumn, warm days and cool nights. The hills to the far west and northwest with tree cover were turning fall red and gold. A little frost one morning gave us a hint to check on warmer coats and coveralls. One morning we were at the jobsite, laying out the shot line just after daybreak getting set for the day. All of a sudden, we heard a soft, keening noise to the northwest of us which none of us could recognize and had never heard before. It got steadily louder and then dust was rising up on the northwest horizon. I wondered if they had earthquakes up here in this country.

And suddenly there was a wave of movement coming over the low hills, moving and flowing almost like flood waters, and in the first long rays of the rising sun in the east, we could see that this was a flow of running animals. Not cattle or horses, they were too small. Not sheep, not deer and then we heard one of the local men we had hired in Baker yell "It's the Pronghorns! The Antelopes! They're moving back to the Dakota flatlands for the winter."

And they came like a river out of its banks, thousands of them, male and female, smaller calves, spreading out and closing up constantly, headed to the southeast, to the Dakotas. They came by for half an hour or more, thinned out, and then were gone, only swirls of dust settling down to show that they had even been here. We found it amazing that this could happen right in front of us.

A short while later, a truck with two ranchers came by and stopped. From them we learned that the Bureau of Land Management (BLM) of the Federal Government was setting up traps to catch a lot of these "Pronghorn" Antelope in the Dakotas. They would move them to Idaho, Wyoming, Colorado, New Mexico, Nevada, Washington, Oregon, and possibly other states as well. This was to break up this last big herd, the last of herds that could number from twenty-five to thirty-five thousand animals, running across the prairie grasslands.

The Indian Nations had depended upon the American Bison, "Buffalo," and the Northern American Antelope, "Pronghorn," to provide food and hides for their lifestyles. The Buffalo herds had been gone for seventy years, and in the next five to ten years, this last herd of Pronghorns would be broken up and scattered through the country in small units held to forty to fifty head by hunting or other means. No longer would they be damaging crops in the Dakotas or Nebraska. No longer would they knock down the rancher's fences, eat his cattle's grass or herbage. No longer would they flow by like a river with so much life, so much beauty, and so much grace.

As I have driven through the west these last fifty years, I have always kept a lookout for the Pronghorns. When I do see them, there are usually no more than eight or ten in an isolated group, slowly walking toward ... what? At least I once had the chance to see them as nature intended.

The Antelope moving also portended something else. They knew something that we also knew, but hadn't given much thought to. They knew winter was just over the northwestern horizon. We knew it would slowly change from fall to winter, but that was Texas thinking. We didn't think the first part of October was going to be almost spring-like one day and 48 hours later we would be nearly snowbound. We had wondered about seeing all the folks in town working like beavers, putting things away, hauling coal and fuel oil into lots of places, cutting and stacking firewood. We thought they were just getting everything done before hunting season.

We went to town after work one late Tuesday afternoon about the middle of October. There had been a strong south wind during the day and a fairly warm temperature. About ten o'clock that night, as we were turning in, the wind was swinging to the west. I woke up at 5:00 AM, and heard the wind howling pretty loudly from the northwest. When I pulled the curtain aside and looked out the window there was nothing to see. My roommate was also getting up; this was our normal timing in order to be out to work about 12 miles east by 7:00 AM. He looked out also and said "The light in the parking lot has gone out." I said "No, I think the window is packed with snow." And sure enough, it was.

We got dressed and headed to the café by the motel where the crew met for breakfast every morning. The snow was coming down steadily, the wind drifting it into small drifts around corners and vehicles, about 4 inches deep. On the open ground it was 2 inches deep, but mighty chilly with a wind of about 20 mph. After breakfast, we headed out to the work area in the two Dodge Power Wagons, with 4 wheel drive, and had no trouble getting there. It was more difficult than it had been to get things done, especially for the surveyor and me, but we got it done by 5:00 PM and headed for town.

The next morning it was still snowing, the depth about 12 inches now, wind had died down a lot, and the temperature had dropped a lot. Instead of the 20 degrees when we went to bed, it was now 5 degrees. We went out, we worked, but it was so miserable we knocked off early, came in and ate. The party chief said "No drinking! We're breaking out the full winter gear and we'll go out at eight o'clock tomorrow." And so we did.

It was still snowing, depth about 16-18 inches, drifts 3-4 feet, and temperature –1 degree. We got the holes that had been drilled up to two days ago loaded and shot, but to set locations and drill new holes with precision was not possible. We gathered around the office trailer in early afternoon, built fires in two 55 gallon oil barrels, and everybody started gathering up the gear. We dug out, rolled up the pickup cables and jugs, broke down the drills and loaded the stems and, after three hours, had all of the equipment back up to the office and storage trailers. We still had several hours of work remaining to get things packed and stored, and it was cold! The wind went through the coats and padded coveralls like you were standing there in your skivies.

The fire in the barrels was way down and all the firewood we had was gone. The current temperature was −5 degrees, and there was no wood out on this prairie. Our powder man came back from the powder trailer with a wooden box in his arms. Everybody hooted and said, "That box ain't gonna warm us up very much." He said "Yeah, but this will." And with that, he pulled two sticks of 40 per cent dynamite out, whacked them in half with a hand axe and threw a half stick into each barrel. Just as all we hands were jumping up to run for cover, he said, as he was leaning over a barrel warming his hands, "Get over here and get thawed out, we got work to do."

Well, we went and stuck out our hands and that was a *warm* fire. He told us there was no danger in opening and burning TNT sticks as long as they were fresh, but leave old ones alone. If the stick is leaky, discolored, maybe with whitish crystals where it had been leaking, get the hell away from it after laying it *very gently* on the ground. Those nitro-glycerin crystals only need a small shock, like dropping them on the ground, to set them off. But, if it's clean, dry, not discolored, out of a new box, it will burn like a railroad flare, only with a great deal more heat.

So we burned half a box of dynamite, finished up, and went to town. This went on for a day or two, with the temperature staying between 0 and 5 below. We finally got everything packed up and back to Baker. The forecasts had been showing no improvement expected. For sure, winter had come to Montana.

Finally, with about a week left in October, the party chief told us that the company had informed him that we needed about four to five weeks to finish this job. They decided to mothball the equipment in Baker for the winter, if he agreed to this plan. With a temperature of minus 10 degrees, wind chill of minus 20 degrees and no improvement in sight by the weather bureau, he agreed this was the best option.

So the next day, we got all the equipment squared away for a three month shutdown, stored the trucks with a place that could keep them under cover, turned in all our company issue cold weather gear, and began to make plans to get out of town. That night the party chief threw us a party. We had a good time and even bought a round of drinks for the cowboys that happened to be in town. I think they had kinda gotten used to us and even hated to see us go. At least we had brought some excitement to Baker before that long Montana winter had set in.

The next morning we went to the bank with the party chief. He made a deal with them to cash our company checks or cut us cashier's checks. After we were through there, we all went to lunch for our last get together. The kid I had been rooming with was from Casper, WY, and had his car with him. I made a deal with him to pay half the expenses back to Casper. I just wanted to get a start on heading south. He told me I could probably find some work there if I wanted to stick around awhile and that a great many pretty girls hung out in the cowboy bars. That didn't sound all bad, especially with over $500 in my pocket, after I sent Mom a few hundred on what I owed her.

We shook hands all around, piled our junk in the car, waved as we drove out of Baker, Montana, and probably out of all of their lives forever. To this day I have never seen a single one of those men again. They were not my friends. They were my comrades, just as in the Marine Corps, the tug boat, the Mexico City College football team, and other instances in my life. We shared an interval of time, a common experience, our only bond being co-joined in this endeavor to a shared result. When that was accomplished, the interval was over, closed, and a new interval was begun. Adversaries belong to those intervals, also. We define our relationships with these titles. A comrade shows a uniting of purpose between you. An adversary shows a position opposing your own. These conditions may be short or long term in duration. They may or may not provoke violence or difficult situations to deal with in your life.

A friend, however, is part of every interval of your life, whether physically present or not. In most cases a true friend is part of a bond that defies time and circumstances. An enemy, on the other hand, has the same attachment only in reverse. They can be perceived to be a continuing threat to your physical or mental wellbeing, as you perceive the relationship between you, whether this is in actuality true or not.

My buddy (comrade) and I drove to Miles City, on to Bighorn, turned south and stopped at Crow Agency to visit the Custer memorial in the Little Bighorn Battlefield National Monument. It was a bitterly cold day and we were the only ones there. We then went south to Sheridan, Buffalo, and finally, to Casper. In Casper, my buddy had a married sister who let him stay in her basement if he pitched in on the utilities. She let me stay with the same condition, until I could find a place of my own. I now needed some transportation and a job of some kind. I had come this far from Texas and I wanted to spend some time in the west before returning to Ennis and perhaps getting locked in for life.

We looked all over Casper for a few days, but with the onset of winter, jobs had vanished with the warm weather. Winter had curtailed a lot of the things we had had in mind to try for. We heard about some work, applied for it, got it, and believe me, it was work and then some. We were hired by Harry Scott, the owner of the Natrona Lumber Co. in Casper. He had a string of seven or eight boxcars parked on the tracks outside the rear gate of the lumber yard and he needed them unloaded. Each of them was filled with bundles of sheetrock, except one which was filled with Portland cement in 80# bags. It took fifteen days to unload them, move the stuff inside and store it. I swore a solemn oath that I would never touch a piece of sheetrock or a bag of Portland cement again in this lifetime. My oath lasted two days. Mr. Scott kept me on as a delivery driver and roustabout in the lumber yard. My buddy went to a tire shop and garage as a helper. He wanted to get into that line of work anyway. I found a room close to town, bought a 1949 Ford coupe in rough shape, but a good price and started waiting out the winter. I started hanging out at the cowboy bars, getting drunk a lot and blowing too much of my money. I had a feeling this would get me in a rut pretty quick. It seemed like a long winter, working out in the cold.

Spring finally came. I had made several deliveries to the airport. I looked around the fixed base operation, the CAA Weather Bureau and Flight Service Station, and talked to a few pilots. This was exciting stuff, and got me to thinking again about possibly taking flight training on my G.I. bill. I managed to meet the owner and manager of Casper Air Service, the fixed base operation. I had talked to a few pilots on the field and every one of them said Dutch Werner was the man to ask if I wanted straight answers to anything about the flying business. Dutch was always busy, but when I told him I was interested in becoming a pilot he took time to sit down and have a cup of coffee with me and explained the facts of life—no, not those, the ones about the flying business—in no uncertain terms.

The amount of money necessary to get even a private license was daunting, but to continue on to get the commercial rating increased this by about 300 per cent—add the multi-engine rating, another 100 per cent, and finally, the instrument flight rating, the one that every would-be professional pilot had to have to advance in this field was another 100 percent. I had known that it would be costly to get started, but I think I had convinced myself that once I did get started, it would all fall into place somehow. Dutch Werner took about 90 per cent of the air out of my balloon. He pulled no punches. He told me he had seen dozens of young men start this course and maybe two or three out of ten would wind up with a commercial ticket in two or three years. He also said he saw nothing wrong with this system. It was the first fitness test of this profession; an early weeding out of those unwilling to dedicate every resource and effort toward entering a career that measured success or failure in terms of other people's lives and wellbeing, as well as their own.

He made a distinction between the private pilot/owner, flying his personal aircraft, usually in good weather and daytime mostly, taking very few chances, and flying from 100 to 300 hours annually. Some of these pilots do progress to higher ratings over time, but continue to stay non-professional.

Now, on the other hand, the pro pilot never stopped training and learning. There was no graduation set for them, only the next trip.

Dutch really impressed me with his straight forward, no nonsense approach to a life within the framework of aviation. All of his three boys had worked to get their tickets; no free rides just because Dad owned the flight service. Fred, Mike and Wayne all contributed greatly to aviation in Wyoming. Wayne went to Denver, sold airplanes for Combs Aircraft and later moved on to Idaho with his own sales operation. Fred and Mike stuck it out in Casper at the airport and on their cattle ranch south of there.

Dutch passed away in 2006, at the age of eighty-four. I always thought of him as the man who pointed me down the right road when I stood at the crossroads, without any hint of what lay ahead of me. Thank you, Dutch, from me and a lot of other guys you probably had a major effect on, for the better.

After Dutch told me there was no work at the Casper airport that he knew of that would help me get into training and since I was going to need more money than the $56 a month the G.I. Bill would give me, I followed his advice to look around some of the other places like Cheyenne or Denver. I called Cheyenne first, talked to Wyoming Skyways, and they said they would try to help me find some light employment around the airport and would use me in their shop and line service when they could. I decided that sounded like a good place to start. I packed my bag, thanked my buddies, and went to the airport to say goodbye to Dutch and his family. Casper had been a nice stop, but it was an oil town. If I stayed, about the only good paying jobs were in the oil patch.

That was a life I had no interest in. So, Cheyenne, here I come.

I don't know what I expected from the state capital of Wyoming, but whatever it was, I didn't find it. The old part of town was interesting and the airport was modern. The Wyoming National Air Guard was flying bright, shiny, North American P-51D "Mustangs" one of our premier fighters of WW II. (*Photo #3*) This was the first time I had had an opportunity to be around them, and what a piece of machinery to walk by. You could almost hear the Merlin engine softly purring, waiting for some really fortunate Guard pilot to take it out for some exercise. Sometimes on weekends, the Guard planes would come back from the practice area flying in the "finger four" formations, the combat spread that was used in the European Theater in protecting the heavy bombers, the B-17's and B-24's, on their daylight raids into Germany.

If you extend one of your hands, either one, in front of you, fold the thumb inward to the palm, out of sight, and spread the fingers as far apart as you can, this is the "finger four." The element leader will be at the tip of the longest finger, and his "wingman" will be at the tip of the index finger. The wingman's job is to protect the tail of the element leader as he is making an attack run on an enemy aircraft. The other pair operates the same way when they split off to protect the "lead" group or to attack other enemy aircraft.

When the Guard planes make their pass over the field, four, five or six combat spreads one after the other, pulling up and away, and breaking into "line of flight" formation for landing one after another, everybody in all the hangars rushed out onto the ramps in front of the hangars to watch. The first four touch down one after another, close together, roll out to the end of the runway and turn off as the next flight of four are touching down, rolling out, until all the planes are shutting down at the Guard hangar ramp. This was as close to the fighter fields of England, watching the birds coming home, as it could ever be for us young guys. Most of us young would be pilots had thoughts of regret, that we had been too young for this in the war, wondering if we could have done it, would have been good enough to make the grade, but knowing that we would never know.

All the Guard pilots knew that the end was near for this type of flying. The Mustangs would be put out to pasture very soon. The jets were coming. The Guard pilots were flying as much as they were allowed to. They probably already knew what I was to learn over the coming years. You can't store up flying.

The memories we all retain, whether wonderful or terrible, slowly erode over the years to a soft haze of decreasing importance. New memories mask earlier ones; smear the sharpness of facts into a soft patina of generalities. This is a natural mechanism of our nature, to help us retain the vital and discard the trivial, in order to protect our sanity.

I have tens of thousands of memories of flying airplanes. Some trips, because of circumstances that defined that particular trip as non-standard, are much sharper and produce more detail than others. We all have this ability to a lesser or greater degree. But, I cannot bring about a feeling of actually *flying* a trip. The smell of the hangar, the feeling of the fabric or leather of the pilot's seat, the vibration of the first engine starting, the feeling of slight increase of gravity as we rotate and lift off, the acceleration forces produced by turns or other maneuvers, the almost constant background noise level, air slipstream hiss, radio and cockpit chatter, the feeling of slight resistance, then release, when you flip a control switch and the constant programmed sweep of instruments for all functioning components. These things are no longer part of my life. I know for certain now, that the Guard pilots were all too correct in their fears. You can't store up flying.

All these memories provide me with gratitude for my career, and occasionally even moments of mirth or warmth. But they can no more evoke that feeling of being "one" with the aircraft, being integrated into a cooperative partnership that produces great satisfaction, than thinking about a favorite movie or book. I don't like today's movies very much, or maybe not at all would be more accurate. I like movies that "say something" to me, movies like *Fried Green Tomatoes* or *Driving Miss Daisy*. I liked *In The Heat of the Night, Places In The Heart, To Sir, With Love*, and *Shane*. But my favorite of all is *To Kill a Mockingbird*, and I'll tell you why.

I grew up in those times, in a place that was a lot like that town. The reason I'm bringing this up is because of one western movie that I saw about 1973, which is also on my favorites list. The name is *Monte Walsh* from a book by Jack Schaefer who also wrote *Shane*.

Lee Marvin plays the title role of Monte Walsh, and Jack Palance plays Chet, his riding partner. The Old West was dying, all the cattle ranches in Wyoming are broke after the cattle died in a terrible winter, the English are buying up all the ranches still working, and there's no work for cowboys. In one scene, Monte and his buddy Chet are sitting in rocking chairs on a porch talking. Jack Palance tells Monte that he's quitting cowboying and moving into town to marry "the hardware widow." Monte says he'd rather die than give up cowboying and move to town. Then Jack Palance had a line of dialogue that went through my heart like an icepick. He quietly said, "Nobody gets to be a cowboy forever."

When it ended I left the movie in a cold sweat. It had never crossed my mind that a statement like that could apply to me too. "Nobody gets to be a pilot forever." I was forty years old and time had been stretching out in front of me until it disappeared on the far horizon. I thought of the Guard pilots in Cheyenne twenty years ago. "Nobody gets to fly a P-51 forever." Well, the P-51 lived on after the Cheyenne Guard was changed over into a transport squadron. The '51's were sold surplus and many are still flying today, but not by those Guard pilots.

AIR-PLANE: n. (AM=BR. AEROPLANE) A heavier-than-air flying machine, powered by motors or jets and *LOTS* of money.

I had my first airplane ride in September 1933, at the Navarro County Fair in Corsicana, TX. It was in a Ford Tri-Motor "TIN GOOSE" and cost my Grandfather 50¢ for the 15 minute flight. It cost him another $1 for his ride; children in laps were half price. He said I sure must have been at home in an airplane, because I slept like a baby in his lap the whole time.

I've already written about my first two rides in San Antonio and my 5 hours of instruction in Dallas. In late 1953, I found myself in Casper, WY, looking for a job. I tried the airport, but nothing doing there. I did meet "Dutch" Werner, who owned Casper Air Service, and told him I had the G.I. Bill and wanted to learn to fly with it. He advised me to go to Cheyenne where they had two flight schools. I could probably find some work because it would cost more than the G.I. Bill would pay to learn and live at the same time. Over the years, Dutch, his wife, and three sons became good friends of mine as I flew in and out of Casper quite often after I got my career "off the ground."

I went to Cheyenne. I worked it out to fly on the G.I. Bill student program, work in the hangar shop and on the line servicing airplanes, parking them, and doing whatever else needed to be done. At night I slept in a hangar next door that housed The Cheyenne Ambulance Service and drove the Buick ambulance on night calls. In my spare time, I went around the neighborhood and found odd jobs, sawing wood, painting and scooping snow. With all of this I could just make the payments at Wyoming Skyways for the flight school. Later, as I flew more, I had to borrow money from my mother in Texas to keep going.

In the shop, I helped tear down engines, wash, clean, and prepare them for the mechanics to inspect, overhaul, re-assemble and replace them in the airframes. I also helped with fabric work on re-covering planes. There were more fabric covered airplanes at that time than metal ones at small airports. I learned a lot about sheet metal work on the more modern aircraft. I learned to help the mechanics bend and form sheets of aluminum to fit the repair work, drill the rivet holes through the stringers, put in removable "klicos" to hold everything together in the proper position as we riveted it all together. It was more than just labor. All the old time mechanics I worked and trained with were as much artisans as hammer and wrench guys.

In the early '50's, many of the flying schools ran the course as two parts, flying the airplane and fixing the airplane. I've known pilots over the years who have no idea where the cables or wires in the cockpit run to. Many times knowing something about the makeup of the aircraft made the difference in whether I got the airplane back home or was stranded somewhere.

I started flying in Cheyenne with an instructor in a 2 place Cessna 140, and also in an Aeronca 7AC Champ. After about 5 or 6 hours of instruction, Keith, the instructor, said one afternoon after the lesson "Well, I guess this is about as good as you're ever gonna get, so let me outa this thing and you go see if you can get it around the patch and back to the hangar."

This was what I had been waiting to hear. I jumped into the Champ, got it started, taxied to the end of the runway, did the little checklist in my head, CIGTR, (Controls-Instruments-Gas-Trim-Run-up) checked for other traffic, the pattern was clear, out onto the runway, power up, made the takeoff and flew around the airport twice feeling that I had everything well under control and now, the landing. I flew the pattern, carburetor heat on, check mixture rich, glide speed 60 indicated, lined up on the centerline of the runway, aim for touchdown 500 feet down the runway, check the wind, correct for wind to stay lined up, now down, down, 100 feet, 50 feet, 20 feet, back on the stick, back, back .... All of a sudden the plane shuddered and quit flying and started falling. I tried to pull the nose up, stick back into my lap. We fell about 6 feet, hit the tail wheel first with a god-awful bang, bounced four or five times, then swerved around in a circle and stopped. My instructor and a few people on the line ran out to help. My instructor said, "Well, we now have a new standard for *bad* solo landings!" One of the mechanics came up and said, "At least you got a souvenir out of it" and handed me the tail wheel assembly which had broken off at the attach plate.

I spent the rest of the afternoon repairing the damage. It was minor, thank goodness. Then I jumped in, took off and flew around the field and wheeled the Champ on two or three times and finally gritting my teeth, made a reasonably good 3 point landing and taxied back into a bunch of pilots and mechanics clapping and laughing. Keith, my instructor, came up and smiled as I got out of the cockpit and said "Now you know the difference between a landing and a crash landing." Then they dragged me down to the local pub where I had to buy a round for the guys—fortunately draft—and they explained that this was the customary solo celebration at this airport. It left me stony broke, but it was worth it. The solo flight is a rite-of-passage for any pilot. I now had it officially signed off in my logbook. "Solo flight successfully completed this date" and signed off by my instructor.

Since that afternoon I have probably made 15,000 landings, more or less, and other than a duster I put into a cornfield in Georgia when the engine quit on the pull-up (*Photo* #8), all have been successful, so I claim about 15,000 landings, and 1 arrival.

My training continued and one day I walked out with a CAA examiner to take my private pilot check ride. He asked me twenty oral questions which I answered about 80 per cent correctly—69 per cent was failing, into the Cessna 140, and an hour and twenty minutes later he signed off my temporary airman certificate as a "private pilot." I've always found it difficult to explain to others what a feeling of wonder that is. Perhaps doctors or engineers have the same feeling when they get their diplomas, I don't know. They are usually finished training and ready to go to work in their professions—not so in the flying business.

The private rating is a ticket that gets you in the door. Of course, you can fly all your life on a private license. There is a reasonable amount of enjoyment in doing this for sport, or light travel. But for some of us, that isn't enough. I looked at the P-51's, A-26's, B-17's, DC-3's, DC-6's, the first jets, the first turbo-props—this was where I wanted to be, among those pilots.

I knew this was a long term commitment, probably the best part of a lifetime, and a serious financial obligation to consider, especially for a guy with no assets to speak of. I won't bore you with the Horatio Alger scenario. I worked as much as I could, plowed all I could spare into flying hours, necessary study materials and took on any job my boss came up with.

One thing I do have great memories of from this time was the Frontier Days Celebration, the whole last week of July 1954. I'd heard about Frontier Days ever since I got to town, but I have to say these local cowboys had impressed me as some of the better liars I had been around, after all, I am from Texas. It was galling to have to admit that they had undershot the truth by quite a bit. I had been to the Pioneer Hotel Bar several times to try to mix in with the United Airlines Stewardess School students, but no soap. They had some real watchdogs with them, gals who looked like they had been in the Army M.P. Corps before joining United. None of us young pilots made any headway that I know of, but I didn't have the money to hang around a nice watering hole like that one, and I was more at home in the Antlers, or Longhorn cowboy bars.

The best memory I have of the celebration was the parade downtown opening day. I was on the sidewalk right at the curb and here came the Overland Stage Coach with six great looking matched horses and a driver that looked a lot like Gabby Hayes. Beside him on the seat was Harry S. Truman, wearing city slicker clothes, a single button suit with a bow tie and a straw boater hat, waving his arm and whooping. I thought those little round, gold rimmed glasses were going to fall off for sure. Ike Eisenhower had put him out to pasture the last election, but he looked like he was having the time of his life.

At the rodeo I got to meet Casey Tibbs, Jim Shoulders and about twenty-five more of the bronco riders, calf and steer ropers, bulldoggers and what all. The parties at night downtown with tubs of beer and dancing in the streets were one helluva lot better than the State Fair in Dallas. It was hard to get any work done at the hangar waiting for 3:00 PM, and then it was off across the highway to start the party. But unto all things there is a season and one morning it was so quiet, no cattle noises, no dust and no truck horns blaring. Frontier Days in Wyoming was over, and so was summer.

One day, I got to fly on one of the twin-engine planes we had at the hangar, a Beechcraft AT-11 navigator trainer from WW II. Ralph Johnson, who owned the Skyways Air Service, put me in the copilot seat and spent nearly an hour going over the controls, switches, instruments, and flight manual. To say I was overwhelmed is a vast understatement. We flew to Denver with Ralph flying and instructing me all the way. We landed at Vest Sky Ranch and I sat in the airplane 3 hours going over the cockpit while Ralph did some business. It was daunting at my experience level. On the way back to Cheyenne, Ralph had me take the controls—I was in the copilot seat—and make some gentle turns left and right, climb and descend, make some power adjustments with the throttles to control speeds during these maneuvers, and trim the airplane. I was in hog heaven!

He landed in Cheyenne so smoothly I couldn't feel the main tires touch on. The tail wheel made a little bump when it touched. After we turned onto the taxiway, he had me taxi in with his help to get an idea of how much lead you need to make the turns, also power on the left or right engine to help start and stop the turns, back pressure on the wheel to keep the tail wheel firmly on the ground to help with steering. The tail wheel lock had been taken off after rollout on the runway. All this time he was in contact with ground control, turning off equipment, setting trim controls, opening cowl flaps and running down the after landing checklist items.

When we parked he turned in the left seat, looked at me and said very quietly "John, you're moving from small airplanes into large airplanes. I'm going to tell you the basic difference between them, and you should never forget it. Small airplanes have big problems. Large airplanes have *FANTASTIC* problems!" I laughed, thinking that was a great joke.

I have since found out that he wasn't kidding.

I went ahead and got my commercial license, then my multi-engine in a Piper PA-23 Apache. I had about 200 hours. I was hot stuff. I had made a couple of trips in the Apache, one of them at night. A few nights later, I ferried an owner's Stinson Station Wagon with a 165 HP Franklin engine to Casper for him to have it to use the next morning. The weather was not very good, but good enough, I thought. There were a lot of low clouds with some light rain, but the Casper weather forecast said it would hold up well enough there.

I was about halfway there when I flew into solid instrument conditions, the red rotating beacon flashing back into the cockpit, nearly blinding me and nothing out the windows but rain, with water streaming over the windshields. I knew I was flying into higher terrain and had only been about 1,000 feet above the ground when all the lights went out as the clouds swallowed me up. The next 5 minutes should have been my last on earth. The Stinson had an artificial horizon, a turn-and-bank indicator, altimeter, rate-of-climb, and a magnetic compass. This was enough for a trained and experienced instrument rated pilot to work with, but not for me, inexperienced in instrument procedures. The instruments were all going in different directions, the airspeed high and then low as I tried to level the Stinson. I almost rolled it upside down a couple of times. I had no idea of my direction of flight. The compass was swinging wildly and I knew I wasn't far from Casper Mountain which was several thousand feet higher than I was. I was almost frozen with fear and afraid to move the controls in any direction. I kept remembering the old joke: An aircraft accident is when the pilot runs out of airspeed, altitude, and ideas at the same time.

It seemed that this had been going on for an hour, but time is subjective when fear overcomes you. It was about 5 or 6 minutes, maybe less, when a miracle happened. The airplane shook itself, like a dog shaking its fur dry, and we burst out on top of a solid overcast with a quarter moon shining through a higher thin overcast. My heart was beating so loudly that I could hardly hear the Franklin engine purring along now. About 20 miles ahead I could see the lights of Casper, with the airport beacon flashing white, then green, and suddenly I was back in the land of the living. I was drenched with sweat; my left hand was hurting from squeezing the control wheel so hard. I had been terrified.

I landed at Casper knowing that the Goddess of Aviation had given me a spot quiz, and I had squeezed by with a D-. If I had gotten an F, everybody in Wyoming would have read about it in the morning papers.

More than 23,700 hours of flying have passed for me since that night flight to Casper. Have I ever been scared, apprehensive, or alarmed since that night, you might ask? Of course, I have. That's not unusual in flying. But terrified? No. Training is the key element in aircraft emergency procedures, and the first thing that has to be trained is the pilot. Emotions cannot be excluded in cockpit operations, but they can be limited to ordinary responses to unusual, unexpected, or dangerous conditions. I firmly believe that flying is one of those very few career fields that demand that your performance improve as the situation deteriorates.

The Goddess of Aviation does hand out problems to air crews or pilots very frequently. Most are simple spot quizzes. Very rarely will this quiz demand 100 per cent to pass and that 99 per cent or below will be failing. That problem has only *one* correct solution. But, sooner or later, an air crew or pilot receives a "Zero Sum" problem.

There is *NO* solution. Everybody hears about it. It has always been this way. It will always be this way.

Even the very best training comes in second behind good luck.

Ralph Johnson had two Douglas B-18 army bombers in Cheyenne, along with a lot of other war surplus aircraft of WW II vintage. They were based on the DC-2 and DC-3 Douglas airliner design that became famous as the Army Air Corps C-47 troop, freight, and paratrooper haulers. He had removed the 800 HP Wright engines from them and replaced them with the engine and propeller power packages from a Boeing B-17, the Wright 1820-56A with 33D/150 propellers which gave it 1,150 HP a side.

Ralph contracted these aircraft to the Dept. of Agriculture to use as spray planes. (*Photo #4*) In the upcoming season they were going to be spraying for the control of the Mexicanus, the migratory grasshoppers that were taking over the central and western states. I helped our mechanic, Jay Yotty, in the preparations for the season on these planes. One of Ralph's pilots for these aircraft, Art Loomis, was a WW II transport pilot who had flown the "Hump" as the Southern Himalayas were called by the plane crews. He and I became friends while we worked and he asked Ralph to give me a try as a copilot on one of the planes. Ralph talked to me about the job, it would be for four or five months, and he decided to give me a try. It worked out, fortunately for me.

I had about 350 hours now. The job wasn't going to pay much, but with the expenses being paid and flying on a DC-3 class aircraft made it a real stroke of luck for me. I would get about 200 to 250 hours of large, multi-engine time logged. I would also get to fly with two of the best pilots in the Western U.S. and get paid for it. Ralph Johnson was pretty much a legend. Let me tell you a little bit about him.

Ralph was born in Indiana in 1906, about three years after the Wright Bros. made history. In 1930, he graduated from Purdue University with a degree in mechanical engineering. He joined the Army Air Corps and, after receiving his wings, served as the personal pilot for the 8th Air Corps Commanding General. He became the chief test pilot at the United Airlines Cheyenne maintenance base. He developed the stabilized approach which is still used today. He developed cockpit crew techniques, visual approach slope lights, propeller de-icing equipment and the scrolling checklist. He held five patents.

In the 1930's, he helped test fly and evaluate the DC-3, and he evaluated the little-known DC-5. He was a test pilot for United Airlines at the age of thirty. During WW II, he was based at the Cheyenne Airport where he was responsible for engineering and testing of hundreds of B-17's, B-24's and PBY naval aircraft going through the modification center. After modifications for many types of special uses were made, Ralph and his test pilot crews flew these aircraft to the ragged edge, to develop manuals to train the service pilots that were going to fly them in combat.

Ralph left United in 1948, and started a general aviation business that offered high altitude aerial surveys, modified military aircraft to fight forest fires, insect pests, fire ants, and grasshoppers. He had an aircraft sales agency, a fixed base operation for repairs, annual inspections and crash repair. His flight school, in Cheyenne, WY, was the one I got my training at. I think everybody in aviation in the Western U.S. knew Ralph.

Ralph flew his big airplanes until he was eighty-two, when he finally sold his business. He was married to his wife Ruth, a great lady, for seventy-two years. She died in September 2009, and Ralph followed her in January 2010. He was one-hundred three years of age. I last visited with him in his office at Master Equipment Co. at the Cheyenne airport in the early 1990's. I was on a Learjet trip while I was flying for International Jet Aviation in Denver. We visited for 25 minutes or so and I told him I'd take him to lunch next time I came up. I still owe him that one.

We always used to say that Ralph could fly better in his sleep than any of us could wide awake. One dark early morning in Safford, AZ, Ralph and I were taking the first trip of the morning out to spray on the San Carlos Apache Indian Reservation which was about 30 miles northwest of Safford. We had to cross the Gila Mountains by climbing about 4,000 feet and then drop down into the valley about 2,000 feet to the farmlands where they had grasshoppers by the billions. We had 1,100 gallons of diesel fuel mixed with a poison called Aldrin. One gallon covered one acre, and we put the load out in 8 minutes of spray on a swath width of 300 feet and had a kill rate of 92-96 per cent. We would fly about 25 feet off the ground at about 120 mph indicated. We wanted to get started just at daybreak before the dew dried up and the heat started lifting the spray.

This morning we had 1,100 gallons of spray in the spray tank and a light wind from the left as we lined up on the northwest runway and started the takeoff. At takeoff speed I called out Rotate; Ralph did and then called gear up. I unlocked the gear handle on the cockpit floor and raised it, watching the gear lights go from green to yellow to red, showing gear up—"Gear shows up, hydraulic pressure up." I called out. When I sat up and looked out the windshield, I didn't see any runway lights. There should have been about six or eight visible on each side. Instead, nada. I said "Ralph," and he said "I know. No lights. I've got oil running across my windshield."

I looked closely at mine with a flashlight. Oil was coming across it from Ralph's side. When I looked out his side window with the flashlight, I could see a jet of engine oil about the size of my index finger spraying out of the prop governor and right into the propeller which was flinging it across Ralph's windshield pane and the airstream was pushing it across mine to the point that I didn't really have any forward visibility. Zero. I looked out my side window and it was nearly clear. I told Ralph I could see enough to get us lined up on the runway if we could get the plane around the pattern. I knew we had to get on the ground before we pumped the 40 gallons of oil out of the left engine oil tank and blew up the engine.

"Do you want me to dump the load?" I asked, knowing we had less than 5 minutes before we ran out of oil. "Hell no!" he said. He was already in a left turn on instruments for the pattern. "That's $600 worth of spray. I'm turning on the downwind now, you talk me down." And that's what we did. I told him when to start the turn, stop turn, descend to pattern altitude, right 5 degrees, keep descent at 300 feet a minute, the flaps are approach and the gear is down, right of centerline, left 3 degrees, 100 feet high, flaps down, right just a little, 20 feet high, flare straight on this heading. SCREECHHhhhhhh! The brakes slowed us down. I shut down the left engine. We stopped; our pickup with the mechanics was there in a flash, putting a new drain plug in the prop governor, pumping the oil tank full, wiping the worst of the oil off the windshields, cowling and wing.

Ralph fired up, we got off in good order and were 38 minutes late starting our first run. Ho hum, just another day at the office. We finished this contract on the reservation and went to Alamogordo, NM, to spray for spruce bud worms in the Lincoln National Forest northeast of there. This was completely different for us. We had to climb to the top of the ridges and then come downhill all the way to the bottom, contouring the ridges and valleys all the way down, then climb back up to the top and do it again. There were a few valleys we could go lengthwise rather than crosswise, and I mean a few. We had one B-18A on the job, the Biegert Bros. from Washington State had a B-17D working and some company had a PBY-5A "Dumbo" and I got to ride in these sprayers. It was a real thrill to fly in the B-17, but it was a lot more demanding on the crew than our bird was. The Dumbo was slow, but it put out a great spray pattern. I would have never gotten used to those overhead engine controls that they had, but the crew had it down to a fine art, just like being in a baby carriage. I got nearly 5 hours in the two birds as an observer. Nobody rode with us. We didn't have any room for them. It was pretty tight just for the two man crew in our cockpit.

We sprayed Cloudcroft, NM, early one morning and I don't think we made any friends there. We were right on the tree tops at 6:00 AM, but at least we didn't see anyone shooting at us. We got through in one week there; the weather was just right, the winds were almost calm and we were through two days ahead of schedule. The B-17 headed north, the PBY headed west, and we headed east to the Texas panhandle.

We flew with both our B-18s out of Perryton, TX, in the Hansford County area where we sprayed about 130 sections for The Bivens Cold Water Creek Cattle Company. Now that was easy work. The runs were so long we didn't have to turn until the spray tank was empty, 8 minutes to flow out 1,100 gallons, and then turn to go back and get another load. When this area was finished we worked in Sherman County and around Fritch just west of Borger. Then it was back to Cheyenne and finally, to finish off the season, we did a job for Mel Chrysler to help him out. It was in Dillon, MT, a beautiful place to spend a couple of weeks. When this job was finished, it was back to Cheyenne. Now for some R&R we all thought, but in a couple of week's time, Jay Yotty and I were sent to Hill Air Force Base in Ogden, UT, to get a Fairchild C-82 "Flying Boxcar" ready to fly out of there to Cheyenne. Ralph had bought it surplus with the idea of making a sprayer out of it.

We drove a Ford pickup, filled with tools and parts, over to Ogden. I was just the mechanic's helper and we got a mechanic from the Air Service on the municipal airport to help with some work at the end before Ralph, Art Loomis and Jim Stevenson got there. We had only a short time to get it running and flyable and off the air base or we would have to truck it out. Nobody wanted that. After a week of long, long days and short nights, when the flight crew showed up we had it in reasonable, fairly flyable, we hoped, condition. Jim went through the inspection, and although he wasn't particularly happy with it, he grudgingly said with any luck, we could fly it as far as Cheyenne. After run ups and taxi tests, we chained down the pickup in the cargo bay, picked up our ferry permit, got our parachutes on, required to depart a military airbase, and taxied into position for takeoff. Ralph was flying, Art was copilot, Jim was in the flight engineer position behind the center quadrant, and Jay and I were behind them in the two bulkhead seats wondering if we'd forgotten anything critical. Hill tower made certain we were aware that the instant they could see daylight between the tires and the ground, the airplane could not return to Hill, but in case of a problem would have to go to the Ogden Municipal Airport or continue on to Salt Lake.

Ralph had kept the weight down so the airplane would perform better on the climb, so when we were cleared it lifted off about half way down the long runway. We tucked the gear up and turned west to circle over the Great Salt Lake to gain altitude. We were climbing at a solid 800 feet a minute and when we passed through 10,000 feet we turned east and continued climbing, joining V-6 airway. Finally we reached close to 11,000 feet as we crossed the Wasatch Mountain Range and leveled off, and we were looking ahead to Ft. Bridger. We had no VOR navs so were using ADF off of Rock Springs as primary nav. We were just under 10,000 feet when we passed Ft. Bridger drifting down to 9,500, and suddenly #2 engine starts sputtering, spitting and surging, although the fuel pressure was still up. Jay said "It might be pickling fluid, try changing tanks." Jim switched to the outboard and in a few seconds the power starts to come back in and gets a lot steadier.

Everybody is giving a big sigh of relief, when about 5 minutes later #1 quits dead without even a sputter and this "boxcar" immediately assumes the "lead sled" disguise; the rate of climb is showing 400 feet a minute down before anybody can reach for anything. By the time we get the tank switched to the outboard and the engine "saws" its way back to nearly normal power, we're down to 8,600 feet and about 35 miles out of Rock Springs. Art asks "We going into Rock Springs?" and Ralph says "Not

yet. Let's see if we can get the power stabilized first."
Well, we all know there's not enough fuel in the outboards
to get us home. We only had 100 gallons in each one just
to keep them wet. If we don't get fuel from the mains we
could be in deep doo-doo.

For the next 20 minutes, Ralph, Art, and Jim are like
a ballet dance team, back to mains, change to aux when
engine starts dying, back to mains when power restored,
from #1 to #2, then back again. We're down to 7,700
feet passing Rock Springs and both engines start running
more smoothly, no barking and spitting, the fuel flow
meters show normal flow to each engine. The cylinder
head temps are nice and warm and although the crew
members are still breathing a little shallowly, things seem
pretty normal with the power plants.

We've just passed Elk Mountain on the north side,
about 1,700 feet above the ground, when we see Laramie
airport with Cheyenne a smudge in the distance. The
power is steady, we ease it back, start a slow let down
into Cheyenne, touch down on the airport 2 hours and
18 minutes after lifting off at Ogden. It was believed that
some pickling fluid had gotten trapped in the rear of the
main tanks and when we leveled off at cruise altitude
it was released to dilute the fuel. Eventually we pulled
enough of it through the fuel system to get almost pure
avgas to the system. There was about 15 gallons of
pickling fluid drained out of the main tanks during the
post flight inspection.

Ralph took us to the airport café and bought all of us
the best thing they had on the menu. Today it was pot
roast, biscuits, mixed salad, and apple or peach pie, iced
tea or coffee. I was told later The C-82 was parked by the
hangar for some months and then flew away one day. It
was one of two that Ralph made into sprayers. Both were
sold to New Frontier Airlift Corp. in 1961.

My four and a half months on the B-18's gave me four
years of experience. Ralph S. Johnson weighed about
150#, stood about 5'7" tall. He was one of the biggest
men I ever met in the flying business. If you should get

to Cheyenne sometime, stop at the airport terminal, walk inside and see his memorial. He was one-hundred three years old when he passed away a year or so ago. They don't make many like him anymore.

I wish I were one of them.

Chapter 4 — Go East, Young Man, Go East

I worked for a while in Cheyenne after the spray season was over. I then went to Greeley and worked between "Coach" Dick Nolan and Ed at Low Level Dusters ferrying airplanes, cleaning them up and getting them ready for sale. It got so slow that I had to sell my old clunker car and walk to the airport. I could see it was going to be a long winter if I got caught in Greeley so I went down to Sky Ranch airport—just east of Stapleton, but Don Vest had no work available just then. I met Don, Eddie Dyer and Don's right hand man, Eddie Mehlin, who was really a key person at Sky Ranch airport and in many respects for Vest Aircraft Co, while I working for Ralph Johnson. Don made a call to Combs Aviation and Clinton Aviation and gave me a recommendation. Clinton didn't need anyone, but Combs needed a couple of guys with some experience for line personnel. I went over, applied and got a job. Having experience paid off for me right away. Instead of 75¢ an hour, I was hired at 85¢ an hour. I finally moved down to Denver.

Don Vest, like Ralph Johnson, was known all over the intermountain west. He had aircraft dealerships, shops, a good flight school and was known for his honesty and integrity. He had a wonderful, pretty and very smart wife. His son, Don, Jr., was a pilot who lost his life in an aircraft accident. Don's wife was thrown from a horse at the Vest Ranch in Castle Valley east of Moab, UT, about 1960, and died as a result. Don took a demo ride in a modified Beechcraft Bonanza with two engines on it in the fall of 1962, and died when it crashed. Eddie Mehlin stayed in the aircraft business and I last saw him at the sales operation he worked with at Centennial Airport in Denver about 1993. He filed his final flight plan in April 2009, with over 40,000 hours in his log books in over 300 different models of aircraft. Believe it or not, this is true.

I somehow wangled another old clunker out of a used car dealer near the airport while working on his lot on my time off and made $2.50 a week payments until the $35 note was paid off. Combs had a flying club for employees only and I got to fly the 1948 125 HP Piper Tri-pacer for $6 an hour. I couldn't fly much, but a couple of hours a week kept me from getting too rusty. I did start making contacts though. Many of the other ramp rats, as we called ourselves, were really neat guys. I stayed friends with many of them until we lost contact over the years. The one I have stayed in contact with the longest lives about 100 miles south of me now. His name is Don "Pinky" Sellars. When I met him on the line at Combs, he was making money from Uncle Sam by pretending to be a Sergeant in the Air Force at Lowry Air Base. Apparently, he got away with it pretty well. They kept paying him and giving him more stripes.

Don also did quite well after he got out of the Air Force. He went to work in the Aircraft Sales Department for Combs, working his way up over the years from Bonanzas, to Queen Airs, King Airs, Learjets and their trade-ins. He sold a lot of Lear's for Combs. Then he flew one for "Tiger" Mike Davis, a real character in the oil business around Denver. Later he flew a Lockheed Jetstar for a German company in Germany, during the time I was flying for an Italian movie star in Rome.

Don returned to Denver and flew for Bill Daniels, who more or less invented cable TV here in the west. Daniels Cable TV's Lear 35 was really well known. Don finished up his career about the same time I did mine. He is still a fine friend of mine. I've always thought it was a toss-up over which one of us liked flying the best. I'll be glad to settle for a tie in this one case.

Another lifelong friend I met as soon as I went to work at Combs was a lanky pilot/mechanic named Ernie Green. Ernie was a WW II veteran and served with the Army Air Corps as a crew chief and airplane mechanic on a B-24 Liberator named "Troublemaker". He was in the African and Italian campaigns and won The Soldiers Medal for putting out a fire on a bomber when every aircraft was desperately needed. Ernie was a true westerner. He was born and raised on a ranch near Cheyenne, Wyoming. He loved hunting, fishing, horses, a gorgeous blond airline stewardess named Shirley, whom he met and married while working for Alaskan Airlines after the war, and who gave him a passel of good looking kids, and … and … , darn, there was something else—oh yeah. Airplanes. That was it. Airplanes.

Ernie spent almost all of the last part of his whole career flying out of Stapleton in Denver. He worked for several large companies, flew everything from Cessna 180's to Lockeed Super Venturas. Everybody knew Ernie, but not everybody liked him which was okay with him, and, as a matter of course, he didn't like everybody either. You had to prove to be the kind of person and pilot that had the same dedication to country, family and occupation that he had or something close to it. He was a good pilot and proved it with 13,000 hours in his logbooks before he hung it up in 1982. He never put a scratch on a passenger or an aircraft, except maybe a duster or two when he first started his career. The two or three times I flew with him, he was as smooth as a freshly oiled pump shotgun.

I used his name as a reference on many an employment application and I always got a good mark from him. I wish I could write about all the great guys and gals I met in those early days, but there are just too many of them. Of course, there were the usual two or three bad actors we all knew and avoided as much as we could. Flying is a business with practically "Zero" tolerance for anything except honesty, responsibility, dedication to improving performance, and acknowledgement of your actions no matter what they are. Ernie was just a little more sensitive to this code than most, but maybe it had something to do with "The Code of the West."

Ernie filed his final flight plan in April 1995. Like most of the pilots I know, he really enjoyed the work of Ernie Gann. We all think Captain Gann was given the gift to speak for us, both as pilots and human beings. He had the ability to bring out something of the wonder of our way of life that most of us can't adequately express. So, Ernie Green, from me, all the gang at Stapleton and your many other buddies, let me say, in the words of Ernie Gann, ".... fair winds, old friend ... fair winds."

A Lot of interesting things happen at a large airport fixed base operation and Combs Aircraft was certainly no exception. Like the morning we were unstacking (moving airplanes outside) the big hangar and one of the linemen inadvertently let the 90 foot long hangar door down on top of Rocky Mountain Helicopter's brand new Bell 47, the first chopper in Denver, and reduced the height of it from 12 feet to 6 feet. Hershey Young, his wife and his brother were not amused, since they had been waiting for months for this Bell to be delivered so they could start building their business.

One afternoon, a young salesman from the Combs Used Aircraft Sales Department was sent over to Sky Ranch Airport to bring back a Beech Bonanza that was to be evaluated for a trade on a newer plane. I was working the front line with two other ramp rats. There were several pilots doing things around their aircraft. All of a sudden every one of us looked up to see where this banging, grinding, noise was coming from. The only thing to be seen on the ramp in our vicinity was this Beech Bonanza taxiing up and in a few seconds it whipped into the front line to park.

One of our linemen chocked the wheels as soon as it stopped. The engine was shut off and very quickly the cabin door popped open and our young Combs salesman stepped out on the wing, onto the step and to the ground. He walked around the right wing and came up to all of us standing in front of the plane and said "Call the shop to come pull this in and take a look at it. This thing would hardly fly coming over, I had to hold the nose up all the way to keep from losing altitude and I couldn't get it over a 110 indicated and there was a lot of vibration, too."

All of us were just standing there looking at the back of the plane. One of the linemen started laughing. It caught on like a wildfire. In a few seconds everyone in our area was walking to the back of that aircraft, while the poor pilot is just standing there watching us go. One of the other pilots that had been cleaning his airplane and had strolled over to see what this strange noise was, walked past the Bonanza tail, reached down to the ground and picked something up. He was laughing as he turned around and lifted up a pretty stout iron chain about 10 feet long with a 3 foot iron stake attached on one end of it. The other end was hooked onto the tail tiedown.

He looked at the young pilot and said "Sonny, I bet you'll find it does a lot better on your next flight if you untie it from the tail tie-down before you take off." The poor salesman was really mortified. He kind of slunk off and it was three months before everyone quit ragging him about checking the tail tiedown before he started up. All of us pilots with some experience couldn't believe this could happen. You couldn't taxi out with all that noise and banging going on. Apparently we were wrong. There was no damage to the aircraft.

One time Norm Cramer, the owner of the Alamosa, CO, Airport flight operation flew his new STOL (short take off/landing) Helio Courier demonstrator into Stapleton to show it to a potential customer. They looked it over and Norm made a remark, which several of us heard, that he could land this airplane in 250 feet. The potential customer said he found that very hard to believe. Norm said "Get in the airplane and I'll prove it to you."

Well, they took off north and got clearance from the tower to wheel around left and land on runway 12. As all of us at Combs watched from the front ramp at the hangar, Norm turned in on final, full flaps down, hanging on the prop, as they say, came over the fence barely moving and just as he crossed the end of 12 runway at about 20 feet high, it stalled, fell flat down on the belly, splayed out the landing gear and balled the propeller up to about half its normal length. It slid to a stop. We were out to it in a minute or two on a tug with a fire extinguisher which we fortunately didn't have to use.

Norm and the potential customer were climbing out of the plane as we got there. The customer said "Well, Norm, I have to agree with you. That's about 250 feet I guess, but I had planned to buy something I could get back home in too." As you might guess, the sale went out the window and Norm changed it to 500 feet for landings after the airplane was rebuilt and back in flying status. Just for kicks we measured from the end of the runway to where it came to rest. It was 273 feet. Close, but no cigar.

Another cold morning and still pitch black at about 4:30 AM when one of my linemen—I had made crew chief and another 15¢ an hour so I had to handle all the chaff that came up—ran up and said "There's somebody fooling around the airplanes on the front line." I grabbed a flashlight, went out to the front parking line where we had about 14 or 15 airplanes parked in two rows, and saw a tall man slowly walking between the rows with his hands in his coat pockets and a hat pulled down low on his forehead. I put the light on him and said "Sir, this is a restricted area. No one is allowed to be in this area without permission. I'll have to ask you to return to the airline terminal."

He turned and said "Oh, uh, I'm very sorry. I just thought I'd kill some time waiting for my flight. Sorry." He turned and started toward the terminal. I called out to him "Just a minute, sir. Are you by any chance Jimmy Stewart?" He turned and grinned and said "Well, I guess that I have to admit that I am." I turned the flashlight away from his face, and said "Mr. Stewart, we would be glad to have you come down and wait for the flight in our flight lounge. We have hot coffee and tea."

He smiled and said, "Well, that would be just fine." So Jimmy Stewart, who had come in on a red-eye from L.A. to catch an early Frontier trip to Durango to make a movie with Audie Murphy called *Night Passage* sat with all us ramp rats for an hour in the flight lounge talking about airplanes instead of movies. One of our boys, who was ex-Air Force, made the mistake of calling him General Stewart, since he was a Brigadier General in the Air Force Reserve. Jimmy put his hand up and said emphatically "Nope, it's just Mr. Stewart to you guys. I'm just another throttle jockey like anybody else." When it was time for his flight, I gave him a ride down to his gate in our golf cart right to the airplane steps of the Convair 440. You could do that in those days. He thanked me again, tipped his hat to the stewardess and went up the stairs.

When the picture came out everybody at Combs went to see it. It was a good western. Jimmy Stewart looked and sounded exactly like Jimmy Stewart. Not a single one of us thought to ask him for an autograph that cold, dark, morning.

Sad, very sad things can also happen. I have this date written in the margin of my logbook. November 1, 1955. That evening I was working late to cover for one of my friends who had a hot date. It was a chilly day which was turning into a cold early evening. I walked down the main ramp to a Continental gate to see if this buddy of mine would go to a party in Aurora with me when he got off work at eight o'clock. He had to work until nine o'clock, but then we could go. We set it up and I headed back to Combs walking under the wings and in front of all the airliners. You could also do that in those days if you were wearing a ramp I.D. badge. I walked under the wing of a United DC-6 that was just getting ready for pushback and engine start. It was just about 6:15 PM, full dark with a cold wind picking up.

Later, we were putting our hangar storage aircraft inside the big hangar with three of us out on the ramp, when we heard a faraway rumble. A small bright light flashed in the sky to the north of us about 40 or 50 miles away. Alarm sirens started to wail almost immediately. I looked at my watch. It was 7:08 PM. Police sirens were screaming down Smith Road north toward the highway that goes toward Longmont and Cheyenne. The word came down from the tower. A United DC-6 had blown up north of Longmont and crashed.

This was the DC-6 I had walked under a little more than half an hour ago. It was the United DC-6 that John Gilbert Graham had put his mother on with her suitcase containing a homemade bomb which exploded and caused the death of all persons on board. John Gilbert Graham had purchased a flight insurance policy on his mother's life. I believe it was $25,000. Graham never got to enjoy the money. It was definitively proven beyond any doubt that he was guilty and within five years he was executed. We can't carry out sentences this quickly anymore. Today it might get done in twenty years, if at all. This bombing was the first proven act of terror or criminal gain by bombing an American civil airliner.

I met Captain Jack Talkington of TWA Airlines who was flying a DeHavilland "Mosquito", the famous British bomber that was incredibly fast—it could outrun many of the German fighters—and was built almost completely of plywood. He was basing it out of Stapleton to do some high altitude photography of the front range of the Rockies on a contract that TWA had with the U.S. Forest Service. He was an American who had flown the Mosquito and Spitfire fighters for England in the Eagle Squadron during the Battle of Britain. We became acquainted while I fueled and serviced his aircraft. When he found out I was training to be a pilot and had already flown on some converted American bombers, he offered to take me on a maintenance flight the next morning if I had the time. He said I would find that there were some small differences between what I had flown and what the Mosquito was like. I readily agreed, got another lineman to cover for me, and the next morning we went out for a 45 minute check of the high altitude equipment, mainly the superchargers on the Rolls-Royce engines, at 31,000 feet of altitude.

There really is no way to describe that flight, even to another pilot. The airplane was like something from another dimension the way it performed. I think this flight for a pilot was as close to aircraft heaven as I will ever be allowed to be.

President Dwight Eisenhower and Mrs. Eisenhower came into Combs four times while I was there. The President liked coming into Stapleton better than Lowry Air Force Base south of us. There was very little fuss made. Some security met the Lockheed Constellation (Air Force One) and the presidential party, usually about ten people in all and they were driven to Mrs. Eisenhower's mother's home about 15 minutes away. The President always took time to shake everyone's hand and say hello, coming and going. Usually, us ramp rats were the first and the last ones to be by the ramp after we had wheeled it up, so we were first to get a handshake and a good morning or good afternoon. Then he would go into the flight lounge and do the same thing to everybody in there. He was our favorite V.I.P. at Combs, hands down.

We had many many celebrities come into Combs. That is the way it is in the airplane business. Many were easygoing, many were preoccupied, a few were gruff, and a very small percentage of them were a giant pain in the gozanga. We tried to treat everyone equally, but some were much higher octane than others. One day, a sleek Lockheed L-18 Lodestar twin engine silver beauty rolled up to our front line. We flagged it in, parked and chocked it. The door opened and the copilot stepped out and asked if we could fuel the airplane right away and put some fresh coffee aboard. I sent one of the guys into the flight lounge to get the coffee and the pilot stepped out. It was Charles Lindbergh—*The* Charles Lindbergh.

Our line manager, along with Harry Combs and Wayne Brown, our top execs, came out because the tower had called and told them who was on the airplane. None of the line personnel got a chance to visit with him. We were smart enough to let Mr. Combs and Wayne Brown, the company president and a handful of other top executives do all the glad-handing. We just serviced the aircraft, fueled it, put on some hot coffee and got out of the way. The copilot said they were on the way to Los Angeles to do some promo work for American Airlines about new routes. Mr. Lindbergh was a spokesperson for the airline and did a fair amount of these types of trips all over the country. I only remember that he nodded a lot during the conversations and was really thin looking. He did wave as he stepped back into the Lockheed. The copilot closed the door and in 5 minutes they were lifting off headed west.

We had so many great customers, you got used to it after a certain number of them had come through. Elliott Roosevelt came in a lot on his way out to his ranch at Meeker, CO. His son Bill lived and worked in Denver so we saw a lot of him. He loved airplanes and had managed to get his pilot license, after a lot of instruction. He acted just like all the younger guys who hung around, even though when his grandmother Eleanor died she left him several million dollars. The Roosevelt name didn't hurt any either. He used to go out to parties in Aurora with us and we all had a good time. Most of the time, I think he forgot that he was rich and came from a very well known, powerful, political family line.

People like Adolph Coors, Jr., Bud Maytag and many of the better known Denver families had airplanes based with us so we were on a first name basis with them. But it was always understood that our only real job was to keep the airplanes in the best manner we knew how. Everything else was a distant also ran.

I could go on for two more pages about the celebs and non-celebs that stopped in at Combs, but some of them we really liked to see taxiing in. I'm going to finish with this one whose company name I've changed. There was a Texas oil company by the name of *Good Old Boys Oil* that came in frequently, about every other month, from Houston or Dallas. They had a beautiful, shiny, Douglas DC-3. Their pilots were nice Texas guys who would help with the luggage and sit and talk about flying with us for hours if we weren't busy. The airplane had a great interior. There were four big leather chairs grouped around a coffee table, a ten foot couch, a bar about the same length, and a couple of sets of regular seats at the back bulkhead. It was always the same four passengers, Mr. Good and Mr. Old, his partner, and two really nice looking women we figured were their wives.

Mr. Good and his partner were both in their early sixties, I would guess, and so were the two ladies. It was said that the two men had dropped out of school in the 5th or 6th grade to go to work in the east Texas oil patch in order to help their families after their fathers had passed away or moved on. They worked the rigs as deck hands, did tower and pipe work, worked a 12 hour tower, as a day's work was called. Over the years they got pretty savvy about the oil business. Mr. Good found a small piece of land that had never been filed on and he and his buddy got some money together and leased it from the owner.

Everybody in the oil patch said they were crazy as hell if they thought there was any oil there and it began to look like they might be right. After two years, working off and on, drilling with a beat up cable tool rig they borrowed from a buddy, they were about to call it quits. But some of their friends came over and helped out, dropped in some money, enough to keep them going for another three months. The well came in with two weeks to spare.

Over the years they took some more calculated risks, insane chances other oil people called them, and darn if they didn't pay off too. Now Good Old Boys Oil was a small but productive company held only by Mr. Good, his partner, and the dozen or so friends who had helped them. About the only fancy thing they had was the DC-3 and most of their travel was to fishing spots, hunting areas, and Las Vegas every so often. They had a place up north in Colorado. They played around in the oil patches in the 4 Corners area, and were well known and liked in the Denver oil community. They were easy going and we always looked forward to seeing them again.

The time I remember best is when the Denver Post decided to do a short article on the company for a Sunday section on the mining, oil, and gas business in the Rockies. They sent a reporter and photographer out to Combs to do the interview in our flight lounge before the plane left with the Good Old Boys party. They took some pictures and the reporter started to interview Mr. Good about his early life, about struggling to help support his mother and four or five brothers and sisters, how he had made a go of it, and now paid his employees well, and sent money to charities, hospitals, and schools.

I will never forget the question and answer that broke up the small audience into laughter and ended the interview. The reporter, having noted that Mr. Good had to drop out of school in an early grade, asked a few more questions, got the answers, and finally said, "Mr. Good, what do you think about higher education?"

Mr. Good rubbed the side of his face for a minute as he thought, then looked at the reporter and said with a wry smile "Well, I think higher education is a really wonderful thing. I don't have none of it myself, but I don't have no trouble at all hiring people that do".

We all laughed, even the reporters. Mr. Good got up, tipped all of us linemen on the way out. They all got on the big, shiny DC-3 and they left. The article was well done. We never did find out if the ladies were their wives.

Sometimes, the meek do inherit, against all odds.

Besides working at Combs, I flew charter for Rocky Mountain Aviation which was owned by Don Neil. Don had a beautiful Cessna 195 with a Jacobs 275 horse engine *(Photo #9)* and a Beechcraft 35A Bonanza. These aircraft would handle mountain flying if you were very careful and knew the country pretty well. I made many a trip to Aspen in the 195, taking skiers there and bringing folks in leg casts back to Denver.

We also provided pilot services to people who had twin engine planes, but didn't need a full time pilot. Don flew pilot with me as copilot. We flew as far as Cleveland, Pennsylvania, Detroit and other fun places back east. I really learned the finer points of multi-engine operation from Don which I credit as a major reason that I'm still here to write this. What with this work and being a line crew chief at Combs, the occasional delivery of an airplane someplace, I managed to make a living, have a few dates and keep my junker auto running.

Don traded trips with Eddie Drapela's charter service quite often. Eddie was one of the most notable characters around Denver aviation circles and we had plenty of them. He started flying charter out of Grand Junction, CO, in 1932, in an Eagle Rock biplane with two open cockpits. Eddie knew every tree, every rock, and every valley on both sides of the continental divide. He was of medium height and build, had wavy gray hair, a mustache and always talked about himself in the third person.

He would say "Drapela took off into the snow storm. Was Drapela afraid? No. The weather got worse. Ice began to build up on the airplane. Was Drapela afraid? No. Suddenly, Drapela couldn't see the ground. Was Drapela afraid? You damn right he was!"

There wasn't a better mountain pilot in the west than Eddie Drapela. I flew many a trip for him and in several cases the people had flown with Eddie lots of times. They would ask "Why isn't Eddie flying us?" and I would say, "Oh, he has a hot date tonight, but not to worry. I'm his illegitimate son and I fly just like he does, only better." Eddie always got a kick out of this kind of thing. He said one time "If you keep saying that to my customers, I guess I'll have to adopt you so I'll have somebody to take care of me in my old age." We had a lot of fun and I did a good job for him. He gave me several really good recommendations over the years for pilot positions. He was one of a kind.

Another notable, who came into Combs several times a week and would sit around in the little snack bar room, drink coffee and chat with all the pilots and mechanics, was "Captain" E.B. Jeppesen. The "Captain" title was in honor of his being one of the first airline captains with United Airlines. We all called him this just to tick him off. He just wanted to be one of the guys. Several times he was mistaken for one of our line personnel by pilots who didn't know who he was. But nearly every pilot who flew cross country on airways and flew instruments to make approaches to airports knew his name. Jepp charts and Jepp approach plates were usually the first things you made sure you had in your flight bag. It's too long a story to tell here, but all of us in aviation who made our livelihood by getting down safely owe a tremendous debt of gratitude to the man who single handedly started the notation of charts to find airport runways safely, even in really lousy weather conditions. His offices were at Stapleton Airport in those days, but now the company has grown so large, producing nav charts and approach plates for most of the modern world, that they have their printing plants and offices scattered over many countries.

Thank you, "Captain" Jepp. If I ever missed an approach, it was because of my flying, not your approach plates.

One of the best known pilots based at Combs was Charley Dilahunty who had been in the Air Corps in WW II and was now flying a terrific looking silver DC-3 for Shell Oil Company. Charley was cussed and reviled by a lot of the other pilots at Combs, but that didn't bother him a bit. It wasn't his flying that had the other pilots hacked off, but his deportment on the golf courses around Denver. He absolutely refused to let the other throttle jockeys win a nickel when they played with him. He finally got to giving so many strokes away, and was still winning, that there was a rebellion among the sheep he was shearing.

They insisted that he drop down to only six clubs in his bag. A few hundred dollars later, it was down to two, and Charley was breaking even with a nine iron and a putter, but at least the hackers had somewhat of a chance.

One day in the Combs coffee shop, Charley grabbed me by the arm and said "I want you to go to lunch with some of us guys. I have to take our Shell Oil Chief Pilot from Holland out and I thought you guys would like to meet him. Besides, I'm paying." Well, that made it a done deal, so we all met at one of the better steak houses close to the airport at noon. We were seated in one of the side rooms, eight of us, and were introduced to Shell Oil's Director of Flight Operations for Europe and U.S. operations. His name was Doug Bader.

Many of you will not be old enough to remember WW II, the Battle of Britain between the German Air Forces and the English Royal Air Forces, but most people have seen movies or series on TV about it. The name Doug Bader was synonymous with the fighting and winning of the air conflict by Britain and came to symbolize the courage and fortitude of the RAF fighter pilots. Bader lost both his lower legs in the early 1930's in a fighter crash. He was fitted with two artificial legs after the RAF retired him, but by dint of much work and pain he overcame this disability and returned to service in the RAF in the late 1930's, just as Hitler was overwhelming the continent with his military might. Doug shot down something like 22 German aircraft as a squadron commander of a Hurricane fighter group. He was then shot down over France and spent the last three years of the war as a POW. We six pilots were blown away. Dilahunty had never mentioned we were going to meet a superstar. It was a great experience for all of us. Mr. Bader was as congenial as pilots get; laughing, telling a few raunchy stories. And he refused to transfer Dilahunty to Holland so some of the airport duffers could win now and then. He invited us all to come see him in Amsterdam if we got over to the continent. What a once-in-a-lifetime-lunch.

Harry Combs owned Combs Aircraft which sold Beechcraft planes and serviced all types of airplanes as a fixed base operator. He also owned Mountain States Aircraft, which was the sales agency for Piper Aircraft in the intermountain west. Harry and his partner, Lew Hadyn, had a small airport in north Denver during WW II and trained civilian pilots to prepare them for entry into the Army Air Corps. After the war was concluded, they moved the operation to Stapleton Airport to set up a fixed base operation for the sales and servicing of the new aircraft that would soon be coming into the post-war market. Harry has an interesting story, but just about everyone I came to know in those days had an interesting story to tell. It sort of came with the flying business. Later on Harry became the President of Gates Lear Jet Corp., after he sold Combs Aircraft Co. to Charley Gates of the Gates Rubber Co. Combs-Gates was later sold to American Airlines and is now known as AMR Combs with numerous fixed base aircraft servicing operations in the U.S.

I got a big break in December of 1955, when I got to fly with one of the local pilots on a Beechcraft C-50 Twin-Bonanza for three trips. (*Photos #5 & #6*) This was a bigger twin engine plane than the Piper Apache and a lot more sophisticated than anything I had been flying in smaller aircraft. Frank DeCastro was an extremely knowledgeable pilot and gave me very good instruction in this machine. To my surprise, in January of 1956, he asked me if I would like to interview with this airplane's owner to fly it for him, since he, Frank, was moving on to a better position. I said "You gotta be kidding!" but he wasn't and after a quick interview with E. E. Peterson, the man who owned the airplane, I had a job, on approval for a couple of weeks. I walked out of the interview after being told the pay would be $100 a week and travel expenses. I'll never forget thinking to myself, "How can you spend $100 in one week?" I soon found out the answer; very easily and quickly.

For the next three months I flew this airplane all over the west and the midwest. We made a lot of trips to Utah, to Green River, the Hanksville area, Salt Lake, Moab, and Las Vegas, among many other destinations. I didn't have an instrument rating yet, so I did a lot of "sneaking" in and out of airports and around the weather. I got as far away as Washington DC, Fort Worth, Dallas, (*Photo #7*) and Des Moines, IA. It was the end of March and the end of the line. I walked out of Combs Aircraft, our base, to get the airplane ready for a trip and found it had padlocks on the tie-down chains. Mr. Peterson, who was a Uranium Mine Stock Promoter, had leased this aircraft and was behind on the lease payments. Needless to say, I was back at Rocky Mountain Aviation flying charter the next day.

I got a two week stint flying a Piper Apache for a Denver businessman named Odie Colquit in early May. We toured mines in Arizona and New Mexico, drumming up sales for the "Porta-drill," his invention to drill holes in limited space mine tunnels. When this was over, a pilot friend called me in Denver and recruited me to fly a duster dusting cotton and tobacco for an operator in southeastern Georgia. What little dusting and spraying I had done in Greeley had shown me I could do it. I had nothing better on the fire at the moment so I signed on. On May 29, 1956, in Dublin, GA, I checked out in a Cub duster with a 100 HP Lycoming engine, packed all the necessary spare parts and my bag in the airplane and headed south to Baxley, GA. On the way down I noticed that most of the countryside was tall pine trees, with fields and pastures cut out of them. I saw some smoke coming up out of the thick pine forest. I curved a little out of the way to see if it was a forest fire starting. When I flew over it at about 100 feet high, I saw a bunch of men and equipment. They waved and motioned to me and I waggled the wings and went on and finally landed in Baxley. I got out of the airplane and the first thing I saw was a bullet hole in the fabric of the right wing. The mechanic/helper from the duster company drove up and started laughing when he saw me staring at this hole.

"Didn't they tell you to shy away from any smoke if' you see it?" he said. "The moonshiners will shoot at anything that flies over 'em. The revenuers fly Cubs so they thought you were a fed sniffing out their still. I wouldn't do that again if I was you." He got my attention. I never did that again.

In Georgia, the feed and seed stores usually sell the dust and the dusting as a package. They mark the field to be dusted on a big county map. They give the farmer a numbered 3 foot square of cloth with 4 stakes to put out horizontally in the tobacco field so the pilot is sure to get the right one. I was warned by the feed store owner that sometimes an adjacent farmer will move a flag to his field to get the dust on his crop and then will swear on the Bible that the farmer who had bought the job has snuck over and put the flag in his field just to get him in trouble with the law, so we had to check our marked map carefully.

The fields were about 20 to 40 acres on average. A 100 acre field of tobacco was a big one, since we were putting out about 25# to an acre. I could only carry 650# in my dust hopper which meant that I had to land on a country road or pasture and pick up more dust for any field bigger than 25 acres. I was flying so low that I had tobacco blossoms from the top of the plants on my wheels and landing gear strut braces nearly every day. You had to coat the top of the leaf with the dust as it was going down, then it coated the bottom as it swirled and bounced back up. It was close tolerance flying requiring an exact airspeed, height, pull-up, turn around and positioning, so that the swathes overlapped by about 2 to 3 feet. The really big time decision, though, was whether to go over or under if you had a power line or telephone line crossing the field. You had to keep in mind that the crop was 3 feet tall when you started, and at the end of the season, it was 12 feet at least, so it got pretty tight under some of those wires.

I always checked to see if there were wires in the fields as I circled it before starting the first pass, but one time I got snookered on a field and knocked 2 counties out of power for a day. The poles for the wires were in the trees on two sides of the field and couldn't be seen. The wires were running at a 45 degree angle across about a third of the crop so you couldn't see them. Since wires are pretty much invisible until they're about 50 feet in front of your windshield, that's when I saw them. It was too late to pull up over them, there was not enough space to go under them, so all I could do was to put the prop, which has sharpened leading edges for this exact purpose, right on the wires and cut them. They cracked the plastic windshield, whipped over the wings and slashed a 5 foot cut through the fabric on top of the left wing. The aircraft was a little noisy with the fabric flopping around, but it flew alright so I finished the field, flew back to the Baxley Airport and called it a day. We repaired the damage that afternoon, and I was back in the sky at 5:30 AM the next morning. My boss, however, was not amused when I reported in to him, but he understood. He had cut a few wires in his career, but he hated to have to haggle with the power or phone company about the repair bill.

The only other thing of interest in this summer of dusting was when I pulled the nose up at the end of a pass looking at 50 foot pine trees dead ahead of me and at about 40 feet the engine quit. I didn't say sputtered, coughed, missed, I said quit. Dead. I still had about 25 per cent of my dust aboard, so fortunately, I was pretty light which helped a lot. I held the nose high, kicked in full right rudder, and as we wheeled over on the right wing, dumped the nose. I flattened out to stretch my glide, went under the power lines on the edge of the gravel road bordering the field, across the little country road and I hooked the landing gear struts on a fence post at the edge of a corn field that had been harvested and had only a few stalks in it. I hit the ground, bounced up in an arc and came down on the nose to a stop, with the tail standing straight up. The plane finally fell back on its belly, with no gasoline leaking out onto the hot engine. I always kept my shoulder harness and seat belt tight. They kept me from hitting anything in the cockpit. Other than a few bruises, I came out of it smelling like a rose. You can't count an episode like this a landing. We call it an "arrival." This is the one arrival in my logbooks. (*Photo #8*)

We ended the season after the tobacco crop was finished by de-foliating cotton fields with lampblack. This gets the leaves to absorb heat from the sun, wither and fall off the plants so they can be machine picked. I can say in all honesty this was one of the worst experiences I've had in flying. I was two weeks getting all that black soot out of the skin on my face and neck.

The season was over the first week of September 1956. I bought an old DeSoto sedan and headed for Denver 1,800 miles away. A young guy named Gene Clements, who had helped around the duster hangars at Dublin, asked if he could come with me. He was a Georgia native, but he wanted to see the west and Denver sounded great to him. I told him if he'd do half the driving he could come along. We drove day and night, averaged about 40 mph, and rolled into Denver two days later. Georgia was full of nice people. I enjoyed the experience, but about the only thing I really, really missed when it was over were those fried catfish and hushpuppy dinners on the Altamaha River outside Baxley and Hazelhurst. They rate right up there with chicken-fried steak and white cream gravy—sorry, Texas.

I helped Gene get on with Combs in the line service department. He stayed in Denver for quite a while, but time takes people away. I went to Utah; he went to California and the last I heard of him he was selling Bibles on the west coast.

I went back to Don Neil at Rocky Mountain Aviation and was really happy to be flying charters in the Bonanza and Cessna 195 (*Photo #9*) in the Rockies again. Eddie Drapela told me that several people I had flown for him on charters had asked him about me (his supposed illegitimate son) the next time they had a trip with him. He told them I was on vacation in Georgia knocking down tobacco plants. He said they thought the way that I had flown them that I would be very good at that. The charter business was slow, so I put in some more time with Combs in the line service department.

One day a beautiful Douglas A-26 medium bomber from WW II came taxiing in for parking in front of Combs hangar. It had been made over into a corporate transport for an oil company in California, carried two pilots, with seats in the cabin for eight passengers. This is a fairly big plane with 1,800 HP engines. I was going to stop it out in front without turning it around and move it to wherever it needed to be with a tug and tow bar. I motioned them in to about 100 feet from the door of the line service passenger lounge and signaled them to stop. Instead, the pilot revved up the right engine, held the left main gear brake and spun it around with a lot of engine power. The prop blast was so great that it picked up a little Piper Tri-Pacer, a 4 passenger single engine fabric covered private aircraft, and spun it upside down in the air and then dropped it on top of an almost brand new Beechcraft D-18 twin engine. This occurred in front of the flight lounge door. I hit the deck, trying to stay away from the right prop, as the plane turned and saw the whole thing while lying on my back.

Well, the next hour was interesting. We could have sold tickets there were so many people out to see this mess. The pilot claimed I had signaled him to spin it around and the copilot backed him up. The airport police were there writing it up for insurance purposes. I was questioned and said flat out the two pilots were "fabricating" that story and that I had crossed my arms in an X, the signal for a full stop. By good fortune, several pilots and mechanics witnessed the entire thing and all of them said, positively, I had signaled for a complete stop, but the pilot gunned it, spun around and almost ran over me. The upshot of it was that I was cleared, the California oil company got a hell of a repair bill, and the pilot was given a ticket for improper ramp operation. He also had a date with the local FAA office for a heart to heart talk about operating big airplanes in the vicinity of small airplanes.

The next day one of Clinton Aviation's linemen was towing a Cessna 180 to tie it down in their parking ramp area. He swung around by a tall chain link fence close to their hangar and ripped the entire right wing off when it hit the fence. Now, that's difficult to do, unless you're running the tug wide open at about 25 mph. We all wondered what would be next as these things always come in three's. It did happen, but not at Stapleton. Two weeks later the Air Force, at Lowery AFB south of Stapleton, mis-fueled a Convair B-36 giant bomber by putting jet fuel in the tanks for the gasoline engines. The aircraft crashed some ten minutes after take-off about 8 miles northeast of Stapleton on the Rocky Mountain Arsenal property. Several of the airmen didn't get out. We had a bitter taste in our mouths over number three. But unfortunately, it comes with the business.

It was November and the days were short and cold. The flying business was in the pits. Nobody was hiring, the charter business was down to about half of what it had been. Some of the Greeley duster pilots were going down to the Imperial Valley in southern California to work on winter produce crops, but I had done my time in ag aviation. It was good experience, but a steady diet of it wouldn't get me to where I wanted to be. When you're young you're eager—always looking for that shortcut, a way to cut a few corners—to get on the straight away quicker. Several of the well-established corporate pilots at Combs took time to give me good advice by telling me that this business is one you earn your way into, not talk your way into. And, they said, if you get a reputation for using poor techniques, poor judgment, poor standards and, worst of all, won't take responsibility for your performance, everyone will tell the truth about it if they're asked. No pilot is going to step into a top job without having his past currycombed right down to the skin. Like all professions, there is an area where the half-assed performer can scratch out a living and maybe get by, but it's the end of the line, not the beginning.

I took this advice to heart as much as I could. There was a quality about these men in general that I liked and wanted to emulate. Not to say that some of them didn't have hard edges and sharp tongues. Others possessed an air of calmness toward life that was so low key they didn't seem to be effective, until you sat in a cockpit with them. After that, you saw how far you had yet to go to be included in this unique grouping. Still, the smoothness, the confidence, the ability to integrate with the passengers and give them that sense of trust that they *want* to have, *need* to have, that can only be a result of how you feel about them. It is a part of our profession that has great meaning. A "Sit down, shut up, and don't bother the flight crew" attitude does not give the passengers a sense of security. You need to counter their natural trepidation about possibly putting themselves in danger. Your attitude will set the comfort zone for them on the trip.

I once briefly knew an airline pilot who, while figuring the weight and balance for take-off, would ask the copilot, with the cockpit door open before engine start, "How many pounds of flesh we got on board?" This could be heard halfway down the aisle of the DC-3. This cavalier attitude toward the "cargo" was probably meant to be humorous. Still, it put the importance of the passenger's welfare into a diminished position in the minds of any of the fare paying passengers who heard this. They had the right to expect the highest level of striving for safety and comfort by the crew. This pilot probably was a good technician, but this job required a higher standard than that alone. It required a great deal of willingness to make the unskilled passenger feel that he or she was a welcome member on this team of travelers.

One of the finest of corporate pilots I had the privilege of getting to know very well over a lot of years was Jack Waddell, who was Chief Pilot for Potash Company of America. They had their offices in Carlsbad, NM, and Jack had a DC-3 there at the Carlsbad Airport. His copilot/

mechanic was Guy Lowder. They made a great team. Jack was a transport pilot in the Air Corps in WW II, and later flew for Frontier Airlines out of Denver. When he changed jobs and became the company pilot for PCA, they bought a brand new Beechcraft D-18S Twin-Beech, which was the Queen of the Skies in those days. As the company grew through the'50's, they moved up to the DC-3 and eventually to a 4 engine turbo-prop, the Vickers "Viscount" which was being flown by Capitol Airlines out of Washington DC. This gave PCA a thoroughly modern aircraft—at that time—to travel to their plants across the U.S. and Canada. The heavy maintenance was done for them by Continental Airlines at their base in Denver. Continental was operating Viscounts at that time and had a fine service facility at Stapleton Airport in their hangar.

One day I flew into Denver from Moab, UT, where I was based at that time. Jack was in Combs having coffee with "the usual suspects," the pilots who were based there. I had a cup of coffee with him and he asked me to go to lunch after he checked on the Viscount's progress at Continental's hangar. He needed to find out if the inspection was coming along as scheduled. We went over to the hangar to his airplane and he conferred with the lead mechanic. Jack needed to leave the next morning to get home to get the big guys in the top echelon of the company and leave for New York City. They said it would be ready for the test flight by late afternoon. About then Jack looked up, grabbed my arm, pulled me down the aisle to the hangar wall and stopped in front of a man and woman. They were nicely—but casually—dressed and certainly not working in this shop.

Jack pushed me up in front and said "Bob, I want you to meet one of my buddies who flies for Charley Steen over in Moab. This is John Sparks. John, meet Bob Six, the president of Continental and his wife, better known as Ethel Merman." I said hello, shook hands, then said "Miss Merman, I've seen you in several movies and always enjoyed them, but I wish I could have seen "*South*

Pacific" on Broadway." She said "Kid, that was a heck of a long time ago and I'm just glad to be in the airline business now. That show business is a tough way to make a living." Mr. Six laughed and said "Who you kidding, Hon, you know you love every minute of it."

She threw her arm around his neck and said "Well, I guess it wasn't that bad, but as soon as I do this next TV show, I'm hanging it up for good." Bob Six smiled at Jack and me and said "That's what she said before the last four TV shows." I saw Ethel on TV sometime after this meeting, and she nearly blew the tube out of the set. What a voice!

It turned out that the Viscount was ready for the test flight at 6:30 PM just after dark. It had started to lightly snow, with high ceilings, so there was no problem in doing the flight. The problem was Guy Lowder, the copilot, couldn't be found so Jack dragged me into the airplane and he and I flew a 45 minute ride in light snow. Jack knew the airplane so well that all I had to do was read the checklist, pull the gear and flaps, talk on the radio, put the gear and flaps down and watch him handle this 64,500 pound, 4 engine Airliner like it was a kiddy car in his front driveway. The head mechanic rode the jump seat and made all the notes for the write off in the log books. I basically just went along for the ride. This was what I wanted to do in my career, only with something a little smaller and a few less engines to have to keep up with.

I stayed in contact with Jack for a lot more years— nearly thirty of them. We were both flying out of Denver the last years of our careers. Then we retired. Jack fell off a ladder in his garage about ten years ago and took off on his last flight plan. I have a feeling that when I do show up at the pilot's coffee shop up (or down) there, Waddell will be sitting there with all my other old friends. I can just see him telling them, "See, I told you Sparks wasn't late, he was just lost in the holding pattern again."

Chapter 5 — Dearly Beloved, We Are Gathered …

I met my future wife, Ella "Ellie" Hubbard, in Denver. Don Neil introduced us; I as one of his pilots, and her, as in the accounting department of the oil company that had a financial interest in Rocky Mountain Aviation. We were also crewing a plane for the owner of that company, Irving Pasternak. I took her for a brief flight over Denver in the Cessna 195 (*Photo #9*) late one December afternoon with the snow softly falling as the night came down with it. The Christmas lights were shining all over the downtown district. It truly looked like a scene from one of the Yule Season movies. Six days later on December 14, 1956, I had a trip to Reno, took Ellie along, and at 10:00 PM that evening we were married. As I write this we will soon be celebrating fifty-six years together. She has insisted that one paragraph about her is more than enough. This young bride of mine followed me to Moab, UT—17 years there; back to Denver—3 years; Connecticut—6 years; Florida—6 years; Rome, Italy—2 years; Denver again—6 years; Grand Junction, CO—11 years; and finally, our last move (we hope), Smith Center, KS, her home town—7 plus years so far. I was so broke as a young pilot in Denver that she had to buy the wedding rings. I've always thought that was the best investment she ever made.

Back to the narrative—I had gotten a fair reputation as a dependable and capable charter pilot in the mountain west. I had flown quite a bit in the Rockies and hadn't hurt anyone yet—scared them, yes—hurt them, no. I flew a Beechcraft Twin Bonanza for several months for a uranium promoter, until the leasing company repossessed it. I made many trips into Utah, Arizona, New Mexico, Wyoming, Montana and Nevada. I came to really enjoy flying in the desert southwest.

I went back to Combs and Rocky Mountain Aviation after a summer season of crop dusting in Georgia, got married, and one day was approached on the ramp at Combs by Dick Kaiser. He was the Chief Pilot for Utex Exploration Co., the big uranium mining company in Moab, UT, owned by Charles A. Steen, the first of the big strike uranium millionaires. His flight department needed a good mountain and desert qualified pilot. They hadn't been able to find one and, being desperate, they took me instead.

Actually, I *was* very lucky. Dick Kaiser knew several pilots in Denver based at Stapleton. He was in Denver on a trip and asked four of his pilot buddies if they knew of any good mountain pilots looking for a job. I have to say that luck has always played a big part in my life. All four of them suggested that he contact me at Combs. He walked up to me on the ramp, we talked awhile and I had a job. They were going to pay me $500 a month and rent me a company house for $50 a month. It was like winning the lottery!

We moved to Moab on April 1, 1957. I went over first to get everything set up. Ellie had to train her replacement and made the move a month later. I had been in Moab two or three times while flying the Twin Bonanza for E. E. Peterson, the uranium promoter. On the first trip I had to sleep in the airplane at the airport. My boss got to sleep in a sleeping bag on the floor of the motel room that his friend had. The uranium boom was on in full force. There wasn't a room, a house, a trailer, or a tent to be found to rent and people slept wherever they could. Private homes were renting space on their living room floors with bathroom privileges for $5 a night. I thought it was great. It was like being trapped in one of the old cowboy "B" movies. About 1959, at the height of the boom, Moab was composed of 35 per cent houses and 65 per cent trailers. That's why the nice two bedroom house in the Utex housing community called "Steenville" for $50 a month was like finding money in the street. I was one of three pilots working for Charlie Steen and his companies, Utex Exploration Co., Moab Drilling Co. and URECO (Uranium Reduction Co.), the mill that handled the ore. Mr. Steen was the first uranium prospector to make a *big* strike in the U.S. He was living in a dugout in Cisco, UT, with his wife and four sons. He had an old WW II Jeep and no money. He had been prospecting for nearly a year on a very short shoestring. He had been a geologist for an American oil company and was working in South America. He came up with a novel idea about where to prospect for uranium on the Colorado Plateau and the 4 corners area. He quit his job, borrowed some money from his mother, a couple of businessmen grubstaked him, and he headed out to Utah. For one to two years he worked his plan. He was down to almost nothing when he picked up a black rock south of Moab. He had two or three dollars in his pocket. The black rock was pitchblende, a very rich uranium ore. Six months later he was handed a check for $5,000,000, advance funds from New York financiers, to exploit the ore body. The *Mi Vida* mine, Spanish for *My Life*, changed the history of the Colorado Plateau. It also changed my life forever.

My assignment was to fly the Piper PA-23 "Apache" 4 seat light twin (*Photo #10*); the Cessna 310 light twin with 5 seats (*Photo #11*); and the Cessna 180 single engine 4 place, when we needed to get into desert strips or small, rough runway airports. And also to fly copilot on the large, 10 seat, twin engine Lockheed L-18 Lodestar (*Photo #12*), when needed. Later, we added the Beechcraft D-18S (*Photo #16*) which I also flew.

I also got to help clean these aircraft, fuel them, and assist our mechanic if he needed an extra set of hands to get black and greasy. *Wow*! No wonder they were paying me so much.

Moab was a little boomtown and it had boomtown rules. If you wanted to find anyone in this community in the morning, you went to three cafes and they would likely be in one of them. First you went to Fern's Café and next to the Westerner Grill. If you hadn't found them it was a good bet that they were at Milt's Stop & Eat waiting for a stool at the counter. Milt's had only a counter with eight stools. You didn't dawdle at this counter. You ate, paid up, and got out. If you started talking after you finished eating, you might get a tap on the shoulder from one of the four or five guys waiting by the marble machine for the next vacancy. He might say "You thinking about homesteading that stool, buddy?" or maybe "If you're thinking of staking a claim, friend, Lisbon Valley is that-away" pointing to the south.

Afternoons, you looked in at the "66 Club," the pool hall, waved to our sheriff, John Stocks, noted how many penny stock promoters were waving handfuls of stock around in the air, looking for a trade or sale—"1,000 shares in *The Never Say Die* claim for $10 cash money, no checks." After the 66 Club, it was the Wagon Wheel Bar or Woody's Mill Creek Tavern.

Suppertime: back to Fern's, the Arches Cafe or the Uranium Club. If you hadn't found them by then there was nothing for it but to head south to the edge of town to "Bad Jack Day's" Alibi Bar. No luck? Head back to town, stop at the courthouse and check the jail. If they weren't there they had probably gone to Price or Grand Junction to pick up some supplies, or raise some hell.

It was a great time to be young, to have a job flying airplanes for a real rags-to-riches millionaire, and to be living in a giant movie set. (*Photo #13*) The seventeen years I lived in Moab would make another entire book—don't panic, this is the only one I'm going to write, I swear, but that town, those times, the main characters, the heroes, the villains, the good, the bad, and the ugly—well, you just had to be there. (*Photo #14*)

We flew a lot. It was really the only way to get around in country this vast, especially if you were in the mining business. We flew all the southwestern states, Mexico, Central America, Canada, and Alaska, with lots of trips to Salt Lake City, Albuquerque, Denver, Grand Junction, Phoenix, Farmington, Amarillo, Dallas, San Antonio, Houston, Casper, Cheyenne, Billings, Boise, Reno, Las Vegas, and dozens of little towns, especially in the western plateau country. We really earned our money flying the Rockies and Wasatch in the winter; ice on the airplane, on the ground and in flight, snow, poor or no weather reports, no instrument approach at the Moab Airport, no lights for night operations. And yet, somehow we made most of the scheduled trips. We flew many emergency trips also. Mr. Steen would do anything possible to help in emergencies. I went on five or six flights to pick up injured miners, hunters, or accident victims—landing on highways or roads and then flying them to medical facilities in Grand Junction, Price, and Salt Lake or to the closest available help. Our big Lockheed Lodestar flew into Monticello, UT, and picked up six or seven burn victims, when a café or motel blew up, and flew them to Grand Junction or Salt Lake City. One of these emergency trips, on the night of December 13, 1958, was the best piece of flying I think I ever did in Moab.

I was at home in the early evening of December13th. It was cold with low clouds over the valley and at the south end where the airport was located. Occasional light drizzle was on and off as it got full dark at about 6:00 PM. The phone rang just after 8:00 PM. It was my boss, Charlie Steen. He said "John, would it be possible to fly to Salt Lake and bring back some blood in the next couple of hours?" He explained that the situation, for one of our friends who was having a baby, had turned very critical. During the birth at the hospital she ruptured inside the birth canal and was bleeding profusely. As luck would have it, she was a very rare blood type of B negative. We had only one donor with that type in the community and who was at the hospital having blood drawn as we spoke. I told Charlie I would check the weather and know in 5 minutes if I thought it could be done and I would let the doctor at the hospital know either yes or no. He said "Do whatever you can, but don't take any rash chances."

The weather bureau in Grand Junction gave me a report which was barely good enough to even think about a trip like this. I called Dr. Paul Mayberry at the hospital and asked whether we could pick up blood in Grand Junction instead of Salt Lake. He said there were two pints there and they were on the way over to us by the Highway Patrol. They would be here in an hour and a half. That would hold Mary Allen, the patient, until about midnight, but she was too weak to even think about operating until they could cover the blood loss. That meant that if we couldn't get a case of blood by 1:00 AM, her chances for survival were virtually nil.

I told him I'll get the blood; you call Salt Lake and arrange to have it at Thompson Flying Service at 10:30 PM and let Thompson know I would need a quick fueling service on the aircraft. He said he would and told me the Sheriff was on his way to pick me up to take me to the airport and the Sheriff would then get whatever I needed set up for the landing when I got back.

I called the airport operator and asked him to get the Cessna 310 (*Photo #11*) out of our hangar, tow it down to the pumps, fill it with 100 Octane and check the oil. I told him we'd be there in 20 minutes. He said it would be ready. I also told him the Sheriff would have the plan for getting things set up for landing when I got back.

I had made a plan to handle a possible emergency night operation after I had been flying in Moab for about a year and had really gotten to know the valley. The LaSal Mountains were 12,000 feet high just 5 miles southeast of the runway, the canyon walls were 600-900 feet high, running north to south from town to the airport which was 9 miles south and there was a difference in elevation between the town and the airport. The elevation at the

[128]

airport was 4,950 feet and the elevation in the center of Moab was 3,950 feet. I had to climb 1,000 feet between town and the runway. The rimrock of the Colorado River just to the north of town was about 4,300 feet. We were really "down in the valley," but I had a plan. I had tried it out a few times in daylight when I was coming back home with no passengers to see how it might work. It was okay, but it required tight control and wasn't for the fainthearted.

I phoned our local radio station, KURA, 1450 kc and told Les Erbe, the manager, that we had an emergency. I needed his help and here's what I wanted him to do. He usually signed off and left the air at 10:00 PM (FCC regulations), but tonight I wanted him to turn off the audio and leave the carrier wave on radiating until I was back, carrier only and no modulation. He said "You must be thinking about ADF" and I said "you got it." He assured me it would be done just that way. I hung up, grabbed my coat and opened the front door just as Sheriff John Stocks pulled up with the lights flashing yelling "C'mon, c'mon!" I ran out, hopped in beside him and we roared off like a bat outa hell. I saw someone in the back seat, turned around to see J. W. Holland, a friend of mine and a cousin of Charlie Steen's wife, M. L. Steen. Dr. Mayberry had told me J. W. was the only one in town with the right blood type and had given all they could legally take at the hospital a few minutes ago.

I said "J. W., you did your part, buddy. Now I'll go round up some more." He said, "I'm coming with you." I said "Like hell you are. This is dangerous enough for one guy in that plane, much less two." J. W. and I are both Texans so we speak the same language. He said "Sparks, I've got some sandwiches and hot coffee in this sack and I'm coming along to make damn sure you don't nod off and besides, I'm bigger and meaner than you, so let's get this show on the road." J. W. had been on several flights with me. He was in the infantry in WW II, fought in the Battle of the Bulge, won some medals and I knew there wasn't a thing in this world he was afraid of, except maybe that raven haired Texas beauty, Tina, he was married to. I said "O.K, you dumb tool pusher, I guess they can put us both in the same grave if this doesn't go well and it won't have to be a very big hole." He just laughed.

We were at the airport in 10 minutes. I gave everybody the plan for the return, we got in the Cessna 310 (*Photo #11*) and within 5 minutes we were rolling on takeoff. I told the airport operator how to put the cars on the approach end of the runway with the lights shining down it so I wouldn't be blinded on short final, especially if I had a really wet windshield. I would call on unicom radio frequency for a weather check at the airport when I was about 10 minutes out. If it was heavy rain or the ceiling was below 200 feet, I would have to go back to Price and have the highway patrol drive the blood down as fast as possible.

We took off north and climbed straight to the radio tower downtown. We were in the clouds after the first 400 feet on solid instruments. I turned to the northwest and checked that the KURA radio signal was loud and clear. I climbed to 13,000 feet on instruments with oxygen on, straight to Provo, turned north on the approach to Salt Lake, made the ILS approach, landed and rolled into Thompson's Flying Service. We fueled, hit the rest room, strapped the case of blood in the back seat and told the State Police to let the Moab Airport know that our ETA was12:35 AM.

We took off at 11:25 PM. Man was it dark in those clouds climbing out. We flew direct to Provo, then at 14,000 feet direct to Price. We let down to 9,000 feet after Price on a heading toward Moab in heavy clouds all the way. There was some light ice, but the defrosters were keeping the windshields in pretty good shape. I had the low frequency radio tuned to 1450 kc, but was getting nothing yet. Grand Junction weather was reported at 400 broken, 900 broken, 1,100 overcast, 3 miles visibility in light rain, so we could always get in there, if necessary. Finally the ADF radio needle started kicking around to directly off our nose, pointing just about where it should be pointing.

About those three letters, ADF—they stand for Automatic Direction Finder—one of pilots very best friends. This instrument points at a radio source when you tune it in and identify it, and shows on a round compass dial (with north being the nose of the airplane) where that source is in relation to the airplane. If you turn the airplane so that the needle points straight ahead, it will take you directly to that source and when you pass over it the needle will swing around 180 degrees and point straight behind you showing that the source is now behind you.

I called Moab Airport on unicom radio frequency and they reported that the clouds were pretty solid against the canyon walls, but about 300 feet high over the runway with a light mist and the wind almost calm. I had them call the dispatcher at the sheriff's office to get a report about the weather over town as that was the key to getting down. The dispatcher had them tell me that it hadn't changed any. She could still see the light on top of the radio antenna. I knew the radio tower was in the center of downtown. I needed about 400 feet of ceiling to do this safely. I could go as low as 4,300 feet mean sea level on my altimeter, but that was it. If I went down to that altitude and didn't break out, I would have to climb back up and go somewhere else.

Oh, did I mention that I had to circle tightly around the transmitter tower site because once I got below 4,500 feet, I would be below the cliff walls east and west of me. They are about 4 miles apart and if I'm in the clouds, I can't see them.

Now for the rest of the plan: when I break out, I will orient myself and roll out heading south, find and follow the old highway which leads me right to the end of the runway. I'll be climbing all the way from town, as I'll be 700 feet below the airport elevation when I'm 300 feet high over downtown.

So, here we go; power back, trim nose up, flaps down ½, airspeed 115 mph indicated—100 mph is as low an airspeed as you *ever* want to see in a 310, pass over the KURA antenna, 40 degree bank angle as soon as the ADF needle swing indicates station passage, left turn so I can see the glow of lights out my left window when I break out, keep the ADF needle 90 degrees to the left, call unicom and tell them to stand by with the vehicle lights for the runway. I'm passing 4,800 feet, 4,700 feet, 4,600 feet and 4,500 feet. Suddenly, there are breaks in the clouds, house lights and some car traffic. I have good ½ mile visibility at 4,400 feet, then about a mile at 4,300 feet. I turn south on the old highway, put the landing gear down, landing lights down and on and call the airport for vehicle lights on. I power up to keep climbing, maintaining about 150 feet above the ground, 115 mph indicated. Suddenly, through the mist about 2 miles ahead, red tail lights are flashing and headlights shining away down the runway. Now fuel boost pumps on, check landing gear down with 3 green lights on, prop controls up to full low pitch, mixture rich, put landing flaps down full, ease power off crossing the cars on the end of runway, flare, touchdown, roll out, pull off the runway onto the main parking ramp, shut the engines down. The Sheriff's car is right there; we transfer the precious box to it. They are gone in a flash, lights whipping the night with red and blue flashes. I look at my watch. It's 12:37 AM. J. W. says, "Can I open my eyes now?"

He gave me a hand getting out of the plane. I stretched, yawned, and said "Well, you were right, J. W., just another day at the office."

The blood and the doctors did the trick. They extended Mary Allen's life by some fifty odd years, and the baby, their only son, was just fine also. The Allen's thanked me over and over for a week or more. I could never bring myself to tell them that I would have gone for the blood that night no matter who it had been for. It was what you do for your neighbors.

Charlie had a 75 foot yacht at LaPaz, Mexico, at the tip of the Baja peninsula. On some of the trips we went down on we carried supplies and boat parts. We had to pay mordeda (bribe money) to get them past Aduana (customs) in Santa Rosalia on the way in. I only got arrested for smuggling twice, but I knew the Jefe' at Aduana and I got off with a $25 U.S. fine each time. Usually we would take Charlie's guests down for five or six days. Often they were Utah State Senators and Representatives. The pilots on the big airplane and I were detailed to keep them out of trouble at night. Yeah, sure. We knew the bouncers in the cantinas and the "Casa de Puta's." (surely, you know what that means in Spanish) So spreading a few bucks around usually kept things under control.

The yacht was 75 feet in length, and every day that the weather was good, it would go out into the deep water between Baja and the mainland to fish for marlin and sailfish. The Mexican Captain knew where to fish and the big fish that were taken in on that day got strung up on the dock and pictures were taken with the happy fishermen. The catch was carted off to the orphanages and homes for the elderly to become the evening meal. If you came up with a trophy fish and wanted it on the wall in your home in Utah, it could be shipped into the U.S. cleaned, packed in ice, and delivered to one of the U.S. border towns for about $100 U.S. Remember, this was 1958,'59 & '60. $100 then would be like $1,500 today or even more. Not many were sent back. If Charlie said to the pilots "Come along and go out with us." It meant only one thing. The engines needed some work or some things needed to be fixed, painted, varnished, or polished. Did we ever get to fish? Are you kidding?

I worked for Charles A. Steen for nearly five years. I liked him and I got along with him, his wife (a Texas honey) and his four sons, who I had to take to Salt Lake to the dentist, get their school clothes, sometimes for check-up physicals and other similar chores. Charlie kept a suite in the Hotel Utah and two days there with the boys was more like a week with those little devils.

I never stole from Charlie. Several in the company did, however—*big time*! My wife and I remained good friends with Charlie and M.L. throughout all of his tax troubles, the company melt-down, the loss of most of his fortune and friends—in that order—and during the bitterness about the remainder of the estate and how it would be divided among his sons and then the final slide into ill health, old age and mortality for both of them a few years ago in Colorado. His youngest son Mark and I have kept in touch over the years. Mark was the faithful son; he took care of his folks to the best of his ability and resources. I think I was about the only ex-employee who did keep in touch very much.

A lot of Moab people didn't like Charlie, mainly because he didn't give them any of his money or enough of his money. He left a legacy of schools on donated ground, churches on donated ground, money and support for many civic improvements when he had good finances. He was a man of many moods. He thought *so fast* that at times his words couldn't keep up with his thoughts, which made it difficult to understand him to some extent, especially when he was talking about new ideas or projects.

He only fired me once and then only for 5 minutes. His wife, M. L., explained to him why we were three hours late getting into Raton, NM to meet him. She and J. W. Holland, her cousin, were my passengers in the Piper Apache (*Photo #10*) flying from Moab to meet Charlie at Raton for a family funeral. It was a cold February day with lots of heavy snow showers over the route from Moab through the Colorado foothills, into New Mexico and over into the Raton area. The weather report sounded as though I could make my way along the Alamosa Valley, down to north of Taos, turn east across the valley, through the Sangre de Cristo Range Pass, and drop down into Raton. No sweat. Wrong. *Plenty sweat*.

I had turned east across the valley toward the pass under very heavy clouds with snow all around the perimeter, except straight ahead. I could still see bright sky on the other side of the pass, until I got within about 3 miles from the throat of the pass and realized that the "bright sky" I was seeing was really a terrific wall of solid snow. There was no visibility ahead at all. I made a quick 180 degree turn to head back and more bad news. The snow had moved in behind us and closed the back door. I was now in a flat valley about 6 miles long. It was a big horse ranch with some nice, flat pasture land alongside the gravel road running through it. I knew that trying to fly out either direction, with no visibility, was a lot like playing Russian roulette with only one of the six chambers empty. To try and climb out with no de-icing equipment in this type of weather was also very short odds for a happy ending. I elected to land and wait it out or get help if we couldn't get going in the next four or five hours before dark.

I told my passengers the plan. They said do what I thought was best. It was about 12:30 PM when we rolled to a stop in the middle of the valley alongside a gravel road that hadn't had any traffic on it for several days. We were in about 4 inches of loose snow. I shut down one engine and idled the other one so I could keep the heater running, as it was only about 10 degrees. I rotated them every half an hour, switching to the other engine to have it warm and ready when we needed it.

I tried to radio our position to an airliner I heard on the radio, but had no luck. I got out and walked about ¼ of a mile to a cabin beside the road. It was deserted, but the roof was still on it, if we had to use it for shelter. I had survival supplies in the baggage compartment. We never flew the kind of country we traveled in all the time without them aboard, summer or winter. So we could eat and stay warm and get help the next day, if necessary.

Nearly three hours went by. We still had about an hour and a half of daylight left. Suddenly, a ray of sun shot in and I could see the eastern pass coming out of the snow with large breaks forming overhead. Earlier I had walked about ½ mile east ahead of the airplane to make sure the snow was not too deep to get out. It would be okay if I packed it a little, so we fired up. I taxied east and back about three times, then firewalled the engines, bumped the flaps down when we hit 60 mph indicated and the little jewel leaped into the air. Twenty-five minutes later we touched down at Raton airport. The storm wasn't over yet, at least not for me.

The engines had barely stopped when the boss came running out to the airplane. As soon as I got M. L. and J. W. out on the ramp, he hugged her, shook J. W.'s hand, and fired me. This didn't surprise me much because Charlie wasn't noted for his patient understanding when his family was concerned. But, as I thought might happen, M. L. and J. W. grabbed him and said I had done a great job of taking care of them. M. L. then said that not only was he not going to fire me, but he was going to give me a raise and that she felt safer flying with me than any pilot he had ever had.

The way it worked out they had the funeral—although somewhat delayed—I was un-fired, got a raise and put on notice that if I ever worried the boss like that again, not even the devil himself would want what was left of me. This was straight from the boss. My belated New Year's resolution was to not get the boss riled up again, and I have to say I did take it to heart. It was nearly a year before I got in hot water again. But that didn't count as the boss never heard about it.

When I first came to work for Mr. Steen in Moab, the big buzz in town was about the movie company that was coming to film another western with filming to begin in a few months. This was a pattern that repeated over and over in the seventeen years I lived there. I worked with several of these productions, sometimes as an extra, sometimes flying the "dailies", as the exposed film for that day was referred to, over to Grand Junction to catch the United flight to California for processing at the studio. I would bring back the processed film that was waiting there and my wife and I would run it at the downtown movie theatre that evening for the production crew to evaluate to see if anything had to be re-shot at the director's orders. (Close friends of ours owned the theater and when they were out of town, we managed it for them) There were approximately fifteen or sixteen films, plus some automobile commercials, made in that seventeen years; some very small, low budget, others medium budget with fairly well known film actors, and four or five big-time ones with top of the line "names" that were "money in the bank" when they went up on the marquee after the film was released.

Mr. Steen loved to throw a party whenever an occasion called for it. There were plenty of July 4th, New Years, Utex Company birthday and Utah Statehood Celebrations held at the airport hangars or in the city park and the whole town was invited. The movie cast parties were always at his big "house on the hill" overlooking the Moab Valley. These parties were formal to an extent. There was an excellent buffet, the game room had a 30 foot bar with bartender, the gardens and the swimming pool afforded ample room to circulate. The dance floor in the game room could hold twenty-five couples with no real crowding. The top people working in his organization, including the pilots and their wives, were always invited. The most memorable one I can remember was for *Warlock* with Henry Fonda, Anthony Quinn, Richard Widmark, Dolores Michaels and Dorothy Malone, along with ten more character actors who are well known when seen on the screen.

This was my favorite party, because I got to dance with Dorothy Malone and Dolores Michaels. My wife, who was a brunette knockout in those days and still is, chatted with Henry Fonda at length at the bar and was tendered an invitation to go catfishing on the Colorado River the next day by Mr. Fonda. This was not to be, however, as the last Tequila Margarita of the evening had too much of an effect on Hank and they carted him off to the motel to sleep it off.

There were a number of other really good movie cast parties. *The Comancheros* with John Wayne, Stuart Whitman, Ina Balin, and Nehemiah Persoff was a winner.

Later in the picture shoot some of the guys and gals from wardrobe, makeup and stunts that we met on the set came over to our house and brought steaks and beer. After it cooled off from the heat of the day, we had a whale of a cookout. They brought with them Ina Balin and Nehemiah Persoff, "Nicky" as everybody called him. When it was time to wrap it up (makeup call was 6:00 AM), Ina and Nicky, along with everybody else, refused to leave until they had cleaned up the yard and washed and dried all the dishes. You couldn't find any better visitors for your community than these Hollywood folks. I have a picture of Ricardo Montalban and my wife. There is another one of John Wayne with his arms around my wife and her two friends. (*Photo #15*) Mr. Wayne was the nicest guy off the set you would want to meet. On the set he was all business.

One other Hollywood "semi-star" my wife and I had the chance to spend an evening with is one of our favorite memories of those days. When the movie *Gold of the Seven Saints* with Clint Walker was filming, Ellie and I went to an historic, beautiful old ranch house on the edge of Moab that had been turned into a quite unique restaurant that served some of the best food in the valley. It was crowded as usual, but we had a table within a few minutes. While we were looking at the menu, the owner, whom we knew very well, came over and asked if we would mind having one of the Hollywood people sit with us as there wasn't another table available. We said that would be fine and shortly he was back with a portly, bald headed gentleman who had a set of white teeth that nearly blinded us as he smiled and sat down. He was Robert Middleton, one of the best "also starring" actors in Hollywood. In the early 1960's, he was in twenty-five or thirty movies and quite a few TV productions. We spent over an hour at dinner, while he kept us delightfully entertained with stories of his two sons, his new Chrysler 300, the drive through the Indian Reservations to get to Moab, and about what goes on in the show business industry. He had a small part in the *7 Saints* film and would only be in Moab for three days. We saw him many times in movies and television during the next sixteen years. Sadly, he passed away in 1977.

There was one other well-known place to eat in Moab that everybody who came from Hollywood to work in Moab knew about. You had to go down Main Street to this alley entrance in the downtown area, walk half way down the alley to a red light bulb hanging on a rod over a red door and you were there. The "Red Door" was a restaurant owned by Ray and Ethel Scovil. It was the best place to see movie stars, state governors, multi-million dollar uranium mine owners, and a few scoundrels in all of this part of the west. Ray was also the local Justice of the Peace. With his bald head, goatee beard, black T-shirt, and white (sort of) apron around his rotund belly, he fit in perfectly in this dimly lit, two-tier café built around the kitchen where he cooked everything right in front of everyone. You had to knock on the Red Door to get in. If he liked you, after he had a look through the peephole, the door swung open. If he didn't like you, you could stand out in the alley all night.

Ethel was also a very interesting character. She was a clairvoyant and could read palms. If you were hiding a dark secret—beware—she didn't sugar coat her readings.

Ray's steaks were 2 pounds each, the salad, potatoes, hot sourdough rolls and desserts were the stuff of legends. The place was packed every night from 8:00 PM to about 2:00 AM. A 30 minute wait for a table was pretty normal. One night when about forty of the stars, production crew, director and producer were there eating and partying, our local State Highway Patrol Trooper brought in a speeder about 1:30 AM. "J. P." Scovil had him stand in front of the entire audience while he conducted the hearing. He pounded on the big wooden block meat preparation table with a meat tenderizing hammer and asked the defendant if he had been driving 80 miles an hour in a 60 mile zone. The poor guy looked like he was going to faint, but he did admit it was probably somewhere in that neighborhood.

Ray fined him $20 for speeding, $10 court costs and further sentenced him to have a roast beef sandwich, potatoes and coffee before he went on his way. The defendant told Ray he didn't have enough money to pay the fine and that he was headed down to Farmington where he had a job waiting. He'd left all his money with his wife and kids in Heber. Ray said that wouldn't do. He grabbed a cooking pan off the shelf and walked by every table saying, "Throw a dollar in the pot, I'm not doing no more cooking 'til we get this kid on his way." We all chipped in, the loot was counted out on the cooking table, and the last dollar was thrown in by Ray. It added up to about $49. The kid had his meal and coffee while Ray wrote out the receipt and gave it to the young guy with $19 on top of it. Ray told him to get the job and take care of that family and if he was ever caught speeding in Grand County again he would be eating "jail chuck" for thirty days. Ray was our special "Goodwill Ambassador" for Moab—but not always.

Jim Winbourn, our local State Game Warden, brought a guy in one time for attempting to poach a deer on the LaSal Mountains—out of season. He shot at what he thought was a deer in the dark while spotlighting, an illegal shining of a spotlight to reflect the eyes of the animal. Instead of a deer it was a mule which belonged to a prospector who was in a sleeping bag right beside said mule. Well, the poacher was traced down quickly. By late evening he was standing in front of the meat cutting table, oops, I mean the judge's bench, at The Red Door. Seeing that they had him dead to rights, he admitted his guilt. Ray sentenced him to a $150 fine for attempted poaching. Also, he was to replace the mule to the prospector and eat one pound of mule meat every night for two weeks. To make sure the last part of the sentence was carried out the guy had to come to the Red Door every night before Ray opened up and consume the meat of the murdered mule in his presence.

One of the very favorite movies of the community was *The Greatest Story Ever Told* with Max Von Sydow as

Christ. The Sermon on the Mount scene was the only big scale scene made in Moab. Because it was a large crowd scene all the town folks were invited to come out and be extras for a day, and over four-hundred did so. It took from 4:00 AM until 4:00 PM to get the shot completed.

The last one of the sixteen or so movies (I wish I had the space to go through all of them) that I will mention is the last western film that the greatest "Western" genre director, John Ford, would "put in the can." This was *Cheyenne Autumn* with Richard Widmark, Carroll Baker, Jimmy Stewart, Karl Malden, Edward G. Robinson, Ricardo Montalban, Patrick Wayne and many other fine supporting actors. They were in town in the early fall, when the leaves were turning in the LaSal mountains and along the Colorado River in Castle Valley. The George White Ranch, along the banks of the Colorado River with its fort of palisade log walls and buildings was a beautiful set. The colors are some of the best ever put on film in this part of the country. I hope you can see this movie sometime on the TCM or AMC movie channel on TV. The cast party at the Steen home was a classic, too.

In my logbook, there's an entry for 11-16-1960. It says Moab-Salt Lake, Lockheed L-18 Lodestar, N10JC, copilot: 1:00. Charlie Steen was selling URECO (Uranium Reduction Co.), to the Atlas Minerals Corporation which was headed by Floyd Odlum, a very well-known name in mining circles in the U.S., Canada, and elsewhere. He was almost as well-known as his wife, a cute little lady who had made a big name for herself in the aviation world. She was born near Mobile, Alabama, May 11, 1906, and christened Bessie Lee Pittman. She married a man named Cochran before WW II and later changed her first name to Jacqueline. During the war she had a vital part in transporting bombers and fighters to operational squadrons overseas using female pilots. She was the head of the WASP's, (Women Air force Service Pilots), who performed this work. She still holds more speed and altitude records during her career than any other pilot, male or female, living or dead. Miss Jacqueline Cochran is the foremost aviatrix of aviation history in this country, Amelia Earhart notwithstanding.

Jackie, as everybody called her, married Floyd Odlum, who was head of RKO Pictures in Hollywood, among other things, and was reputed to be one of the ten richest men in the United States. When he had to travel from California around the west, Jackie would quite often fly him in her vintage L-18 Lockheed Lodestar. (It was still outfitted in the cabin with the same seats and furnishings as when it rolled out of the Lockheed factory in Burbank, CA in 1939) The registration number was N10JC (for Jackie Cochran), a number as well known as the one on the Grumman Gulfstream bought by Walt Disney personally, which carried the registration number (or just N number in aviation circles), N234MM. It so happens that this Gulfstream is the one I flew for Walt Disney World in Orlando, FL, for two years. Wherever we flew, it was always "234 Mickey Mouse." Many aircraft have their owner's initials worked into the N number, but few were as well recognized as these two.

Floyd Odlum and Jackie were in Moab discussing the URECO deal up at Charlie's big home on the hill north of town. Charlie called and asked me to come up to his home. I dropped everything and rushed up there. I had never met Jackie, but had met Mr. Odlum when he flew into Moab on several occasions in the Atlas corporate plane out of Salt Lake.

I was really happy to meet such an accomplished and well known aviatrix. Charlie told me they had offered to give me a ride to Salt Lake to pick up the Apache, which had just finished a 100 hour inspection in one of the shops there. He asked if that would be all right with me. I could barely say yes fast enough and that I was ready to go right now or whenever they chose to. Jackie said the sooner the better, so we hopped in my car to go to the airport, as I had to have it to get home when I got back.

Twenty minutes later we were starting engines. I was in the copilot "right" seat and I asked Jackie if she wanted me to read the checklist. I had told her on the way to the airport that I had 50 or 60 hours in Lodestars as Mr. Steen owned one and I was familiar with the cockpit. She laughed and said that she didn't use a copilot, but I could handle the radios when we got into the Salt Lake area. She would do everything else because she had her own routine. I said, "Sounds good to me" and away we went. I mentioned in the early part of this chapter that the airport is 1,000 feet higher than town and that we should be that high when we go over town if we don't climb a foot after we lift off.

Well, as a matter of fact, we went over town at 200 feet altitude and 250 mph true air speed. Jackie lifted off the runway, leveled at 200 feet, and we flew between 200 feet and 600 feet all the way to Price. She climbed over the Wasatch Range, then after crossing Provo, turned north and descended into the Salt Lake Valley, stopping the descent at 1,000 feet. She then slowed to about 150 mph indicated to be somewhat legal in the pattern. She had me ask for a straight in landing on 34 right, which was approved, we slowed to gear speed about 3 miles out, got flaps down at about a mile on final, wheeled that babe on at about 120 indicated and made the third turnoff. There was not a wasted minute or motion. We chatted all the way about Chuck Yeager, about flying the F-86, and the F-100 (supersonic), which made her one of the fastest women in the world. The Russians had quite a few female fighter pilots with some flying supersonic equipment. I didn't touch anything but the radios the entire trip. Floyd sat in the last seat aft in the cabin and read the Wall Street Journal all the way. She made the trip 10 minutes faster than we had ever made it in Charlie's Lodestar.

She said goodbye, I shook hands with Floyd, they jumped into a waiting taxi, and that was when I thought about an autograph as they were driving out the gate.

The little Apache felt like it was stuck in second gear all the way back to Moab. I kept checking to make sure the gear and flaps were up. Unfortunately, they were.

Jacqueline Cochran filed her final flight plan on August 9, 1980, leaving from Indio, CA. She was never the public, newsy figure that Amelia Earhart was, partly because the public is fascinated by people who die inordinately young and under tragic circumstances. Also, there was not the "rags-to-riches" side to her story, seeing as how she had married one of the richest men in this country. Her achievements were so many, so diffuse, so empowering for women who had an interest in aviation that she has to be put, not in a class of her own, but into a strata of her own. I thank the Goddess of Aviation that I was selected to be one of the few who had a moment in time, in the air, with one of the legends.

Another log entry dated 4-26-1961, has a special significance for me. Under the Remarks column, an entry says, "Met Ernest Hemingway and A.E. Hotchner in Las Vegas." The trip that day was in our C-45G Beechcraft "Twin Beech", from Moab-Delta (UT)-Ely (NV)-Death Valley (CA)-Las Vegas (NV). I had four company engineers and we ended the day at the Sands Hotel in Las Vegas where we always stayed. They were going to a dinner show and I was going to eat in the bar café and go to bed. It had been a long day with probably another one coming up tomorrow. I checked in, put my stuff in the room, washed up a little, and headed down to the main lobby bar and café. The Maître D' recognized me and gave me a small table on the quiet side of the room.

As he seated me he said "You're not supposed to know who is eating at the table behind you, but I know you won't bother them. They would probably give you an autograph if you asked nicely, but don't try to sit down or anything." I turned and it was just dark enough that I could see it was two older men, dressed in very informal type clothes, but that was all. I said, "Who the heck is it?" He said "It's Ernest Hemingway, the writer, and some guy who travels with him."

I have always been a Hemingway fan and I had read somewhere that he now traveled with another author named A. E. Hotchner. I ordered something simple and when I finished eating and got up to leave I said to myself what could it hurt? I walked slowly up to their table, and Ernest Hemingway looked exactly like the photo I had seen of him a few months before with a heavy grey beard, tired, dull eyes and very thin hair.

Holding a small amount of wine in his glass, he looked up at me and I could see that the dull eyes were just that—dull, no life. The mouth was slack, the beard unkempt. I turned to the other man, who looked keen and alert, wearing a polo shirt, probably about the same age as Hemingway, wearing glasses and holding a highball glass, but was much more alive and attuned to what was happening around him.

"I'm sorry, I don't mean to intrude, but I wanted to see if this really was Ernest Hemingway. Are you Mr. Hotchner, by chance?" He smiled gently. "Yes, I'm A. E. Hotchner, and if I might ask, who are you and what do you want?"

"I'm just an airplane pilot here for the night and I guess I don't really want anything. I have been reading Mr. Hemingway's books since I was in high school. Part of what I thought I would want to do with my life came from ideas that I got from those books. But there was so much hidden, so much I couldn't figure out, that didn't fit in right. And I still feel that much of his work has been, and might continue to be, beyond my understanding. I thought if I saw him in person perhaps it would help me find more depth in his work. But seeing him this way, I don't think I will find it any easier to absorb the meanings of his works. All I can do is keep reading, I guess."

Mr. Hotchner turned to Mr. Hemingway, reached out and took the hand with the wine glass in it. "Ernest, here's a young man that wants to tell you that he likes your work." He looked back up to me and said, "He has some good days, but by this time of evening, he usually is worn out, and doesn't communicate well, if at all. The doctors are trying some new medications, but they seem to put him into more isolation at times than he had before using them. I'm sorry, but I think it's best if you just smile at him, and walk away. He won't remember much of this evening tomorrow. But thank you for wanting to interact with him. Ten years ago he would have stayed up half the night talking to you. Now, he mostly has just 12 hour days."

I turned slowly to face Mr. Hemingway. I leaned down slightly and said softly, "Thank you, thank you for what you've given us. Goodbye."

Mr. Hotchner stood up about halfway, steadied himself with one hand on the table, and put his other one on my arm. "Thank you for stopping by. Ernest hates being like this, he rants about it during the day sometimes, curses the doctors. Keep reading his work. I don't understand some of it myself, but the parts I do understand bring a satisfaction to my mind." He smiled a sweet, simple smile.

"And take this with you, you have brought your gift, and given it. By caring, you have proven that you have understood what he was trying to say, and understood it very well. Thank you. Goodbye."

I went to my room and wondered why it had to be so disappointing to have an idol that you have considered to be eternal, turn out to be a frail mortal after all. I wrote as much of the conversation down as I could remember. I put it into my odds and ends drawer when I got home, and it was still there when I was looking over the things I wanted to draw upon for this book. I still read Hemingway once in a while. I can still see him sitting there looking up at me. He never said a word that night.

On July 2, 1961, some sixty-seven days after I met Ernest Hemingway, he took his favorite shotgun out of the gun case that bright morning, loaded it, put the barrels into his mouth and pulled the trigger. He had lived a life that was bigger than life. He had formed words that put the world into an orbit around us. In *The Old Man and The Sea* we struggled against life with the old fisherman, winning, and then losing against the natural odds of nature. In *For Whom the Bell Tolls, Islands In The Stream, The Sun Also Rises* and a large amount of all the body of his work, he deals with man's battle against the continuing, overpowering forces within himself. This is augmented by the pressures of a world that is essentially brutal and heartless, caring little for the balm that love could bring to relieve this misery. It is not for me to attempt to tell you about his reasoning, for I do not have the capacity to understand it well. It is this struggle to reach peace that each of us must accomplish on our own. I think Ernest Hemingway once referred to it as "reaching maturity in spite of everything."

Other trips didn't have the pizzazz that these did perhaps, but they certainly could be interesting. The head of Mr. Steen's geology department was Andy McGill, an irascible old Canadian. He had been Charley's boss in South America. I flew him all over the west looking at mining properties of differing types. One such trip was a lulu and he never let me forget it.

Andy wanted to go to Beatty, NV, which was about halfway between Las Vegas and Tonopah, where he would meet some mining people to look at some property. I had never been to Beatty and I looked it up on the Nevada aviation map. It showed a little airport there and I said no problem. We flew out of Moab in the Twin Beech (*Photo #16*) just at sunrise the next morning. By 7:30 AM, I was topping the last ridge of hills, dropping into this little valley with a highway running through it and seeing the little town of about 800 people some 10 miles ahead. Very shortly I saw an airstrip beside the highway about 2 miles east of town. I circled it and landed. It was just a dirt strip with a small parking area in front of a big ranch house with barns and fences. We pulled up and shut down. I didn't see a phone booth or gas shack. I told Andy we would have to get the people in the house to call a taxi for us.

I secured and locked the airplane and we walked up ten or twelve stair steps on the big front porch. When I pushed the buzzer switch we could hear a gong go off in the house. In no time at all the door was thrown open and a very curvy gal about thirty years old said "Geez, you guys are sure early, but, c'mon in and we'll take care of you."

The reason I knew she was curvy was because she was wearing just enough gauze here and there to pad a crutch. I thought Andy's eyes were going to jump right out of his head. He turned, stared me right in the eye and said "*This is a brothel. You brought me to a house of ill repute!*" I'm trying to explain that I had no idea it was anything but a little hick airport. The curvy lady is leaning on the doorjamb listening. I turned to her and said "Please excuse us, we thought this was the Beatty Airport. Is there a taxi we could call to get to town?"

She laughed, waved her hand to come on in and said "I'll get the town marshal to come get you, and in the meantime you can have a cup of coffee." She yelled back towards the hallway and told someone to call the marshal to come get us. Fifteen minutes later we're on the way to town, where we stopped at (I think it was) the Hotel Nevada. It had a Casino and Café all rolled up into a two story lap sided building that was probably built as the first stagecoach stop in this valley.

When Andy's people showed up, they talked him into staying over that night near the property they were going to look at. I got his bag loaded in their vehicle; told him I'd be here at the Hotel when he showed up tomorrow and watched them take off for the Death Valley country. I got a room, ate, slept awhile, walked all over town for half an hour, lost $5 playing 21, took a nap and then settled in to watch the sunset. At eight o'clock I ate again and decided to take a walk. I arrived at the little airport about 8:45 PM, checked the airplane and thought a cold beer or two would get me ready for the walk back to town.

When I walked up to the porch, I saw two Sheriff Department vehicles parked in the lot. As I walked past them, I saw California on the plates, not Nevada. This time the door was open, so I just strolled in. It looked like a Hollywood western movie set, except for the shiny chromium and glass jukebox blaring away in one corner. There were about seven or eight guys at the bar and at a table talking to three curvy gals. At the bar were two guys with cowboy hats, pistol belts with pistols, handcuff pouches and beers in their left hands. They looked me over with one glance and turned back to talking to the female bartender who was wearing a lot more dress than the other girls. I recognized her as the lady who had met us this morning.

"Well, here's the flyboy now. I was just telling the law dogs about the big shiny airplane (we were in the twin Beech on this trip) parked out front. You all fixed up in town?"

"Everything worked out just right, the boss is over in California somewhere, and I'll get that big, shiny airplane out of your way tomorrow afternoon sometime. Meanwhile, I'd like a beer and if these guys are raiding the place, I'll be glad to get the hell outa here without the beer."

The Sheriffs smiled and waved me over to a stool. "Ah, you look harmless to me." The older one said. "Sit down and have that beer. Where you from?"

We chatted about the trip, about inspecting a possible mining property and some small talk. Finally, I said "Well, if it's not a raid, did you guys come all the way over here just to get a drink? I thought California was a wet state." The younger one, a deputy according to his badge, said "Naw, this is our monthly run." They then told me the story of how a previous Sheriff of Inyo County had made a deal with a jail full of really rowdy, hard to get along with prisoners. If they kept quiet, did their jail work, didn't give him any trouble and had some money, at the end of the month he would take them all over to Beatty to the cat house for a night of "relaxation." This worked out well, so well, that it was still going on several years later.

"Yeah," the Sheriff added "we got the only jail in California that guys are trying to break *into* and not *out of*." We chatted, told risqué stories, drank a few more beers, and at 10:30 the deputy stood up and yelled "Fifteen minutes, we load up. Finish whatever you're doing and get down here." By 11:00 the Patrol cars were loaded up and pulling out with the girls waving from the front porch. I turned down an offer to ride to town with them; it was a pretty night, soft warm breeze, no moon and a sky full of stars. I wasn't going to waste a night this pretty just to keep from walking two miles.

The next afternoon we flew back to Moab. Andy McGill told everyone and their dog about Johnny, the pilot, taking him to a "House of Ill Repute" in the middle of the desert. Half a dozen or so guys in the company said they would like to tag along on the next trip to Beatty, but there was no next trip planned. The next time it was Death Valley (*Photos #17 & #18*), 121 degrees and no shade. I knew it was too hot for me when I saw three California grey fringed desert lizards run across the road next to the airport. All three of them were carrying canteens.

Another experience I had on a Nevada trip with the Twin Beech was one of the darndest ones I ever had. It only happened this one time, but that was enough for my entire career. I had to pick up some passengers early one morning in Las Vegas for a trip to northern Nevada and Idaho. We were scheduled to leave Las Vegas at 6:00 AM. I departed Moab for the 1 hour trip at 4:15 AM, on a very chilly morning. I had the heat turned up as I climbed to 12,500 feet altitude, and was cruising along on a beautiful night flight as smooth as silk. I could see the glow of lights from Las Vegas when I was about 80 miles out and without any warning, a very loud explosion occurred in the cabin of the aircraft, nearly deafening me. What I thought was smoke filled the cabin and cockpit, burning my eyes, but not my nostrils as I had an oxygen mask on. I just knew the tail of the airplane had blown off. I didn't dare turn around and look, as I was afraid I would see stars where the tail section should have been. I was waiting for the bird to roll over on her back and start that last long descent.

It had been about 20 seconds, which seemed like 5 minutes, and I realized that so far nothing had changed. The engines sounded the same, the control yoke I was holding was steady, and rudder pedals weren't flopping around. I gingerly moved all the controls, slight turns, nose up, nose down. All was normal. There was still plenty of smoke in the cockpit and in the cabin when I turned on a flashlight and looked back, but it was thinning out rapidly. I descended slowly and carefully, flew into the pattern at McCarren Airport, put the landing gear down, the operation was normal, flaps on the approach, normal. All the smoke or vapor was gone, the airplane was as normal as it ever was. I was cleared for landing, touched down, rolled out, exited the runway, taxied into parking at Hughes Aviation, shut down and noticed my shirt was entirely soaked with sweat.

After I walked around the plane and visually inspected it, I had them fuel the airplane. There was not a single thing out of place and I'm now starting to think that maybe I've blown a gasket. The lineman got in the cabin to get the hot coffee container to fill it. He told me when he got out that he had kicked something on the floor. He and I got flashlights and started looking. We found the CO_2 fire extinguisher underneath one of the seats with the top blown completely off of it. It should have been on a holding bracket on the forward cabin bulkhead, but somehow the lock clips that held it in the bracket had opened and released the extinguisher, letting it roll around the floor. It finally came to rest blocking one of the main vents for hot air to warm the cabin. We found the marks where it had blown the entire top of the bottle off after the hot air had forced it to overpressure and the safety vent hadn't released the CO_2. I had two other extinguishers aboard, so I was legal to continue the flight, which I did.

This was one of the few times I truly thought about dying in an airplane, but it taught me a lesson I never forgot. Don't take anything for granted. I had flown that airplane the previous day and everything was normal. An extra 2 or 3 minutes for a cabin inspection would have located this problem, put it back into standard operating parameters, and I would have had a dry shirt to start the trip with. Thank goodness it was only my shirt that was wet.

I have had so many experiences, especially with weather, that I think I will write an entire chapter in the latter part of this book to relate some of them briefly with the hope that any pilots who read this can get a little more insight in the way to think about flying the mountain west, if they haven't done much or any of this. Sometimes, though, things happen that there isn't any way to prepare for and you just have to ride it out. One such occurrence as this happened on a trip between Moab and Salt Lake one nice late winter morning on March 2, 1958.

I departed the Moab airport at 8:00 AM for Salt Lake City with two passengers who resided in Salt Lake. They had returned the day before from a trip on the yacht in Mexico. I had flown them numerous times, so this was just another "milk run" getting them back home. We were in the little twin engine Piper Apache PA-23, a great airplane for short trips like this. (*Photo #10*) The passengers were Tony Hatsis and Jennings Phillips. Both were well known in Salt Lake. In the future Mr. Phillips would be elected mayor of that city.

About 20 minutes into the 1 hour trip, Tony tapped me on the shoulder and asked me what that thing on the left wing was. I swiveled around to see what he was talking about, and to my shock, I saw a bullet hole in the top of the wing skin, about one-third of the way out toward the wingtip. I knew it was very close to the inboard main fuel tank, a rubber bladder cell, but there was no spray coming out and everything was normal. I was just passing the city of Price, so I called into the Price airport on unicom radio and had the manager call the Sheriff's office and report that we had been hit by gunfire and would like to have the authorities standing by when we landed in Salt Lake, in approximately ½ hour.

I elected to continue on to Salt Lake because we were showing everything normal. It would have taken almost the same amount of time to descend and land at Price as it would to continue on to Salt Lake. We would have only saved about 10 minutes and by going on, Mr. Hatsis and Mr. Phillips would be home, instead of possibly being stuck in Price for a day or so. Upon arrival at the Salt Lake Airport, we were met at Thompson Flying Service by the Salt Lake County Sheriff's department, the FAA Chief of the Salt Lake office and the FBI.

It was indeed a bullet hole, from the bottom of the wing, missing the fuel tank by 4 inches and exiting out the top skin. After a careful inspection of the entire exterior of the aircraft, this proved to be the only damage and would require minimal repair work. Over the next three days, Mr. Steen, Mr. Hatsis and Mr. Phillips each contributed $1,000 to a reward fund for the arrest of the guilty party responsible for this incident. This was also a Federal offense, so it made all the papers in Utah and Colorado. I told the authorities that I didn't believe anyone could hit that airplane with a .22 caliber rifle once we got up to 2,000 feet above the ground. The FBI had determined that it was consistent with the size and shape of the hole that a .22 hollow point, long rifle projectile would make with an air speed of 150 mph. They would have had to lead the aircraft by about 200 feet, and the average person would shoot at it instead of leading it, especially that far. They agreed and we started the investigation at the Moab airport with the notice of the reward in all the papers. It was less than a day until a person reported seeing two young men hunting in a field just north of the airport, with the time consistent with our departure. The two young men, both about thirteen years old, claimed to have been home at that time, with the mother of one backing up their story.

Two other people who knew these boys also reported seeing them with their .22 rifles that morning walking out into the field that I flew over just after takeoff. John Stocks, the Grand County Sheriff, told Mr. Steen he had all the probable cause he needed for an arrest, but Charlie said he wasn't going to send any kids to prison if it could be worked out some other way. Sheriff Stocks had a talk with the mother of the one boy who was giving them their alibi. After explaining that the boys would get off with some community service and an apology to Mr. Steen and the passengers and pilot, if they kept their noses clean for three years, there would be nothing on their record. She recanted and said it was a different day she was thinking about and she would make sure her son and his buddy did everything required. Sheriff Stocks had a heart to heart chat with them and they tearfully admitted that they had done it, but said it was just on impulse and they hadn't been able to sleep nights since then as they were so ashamed and scared. They worked for a year in an informal community service program and over time became two of the better young men we had in our school system and our town. The three witnesses each got a $1,000 reward. I was grateful that they had been such lousy shots. Both emptied the clip in their rifle, a total of 18 rounds, and one strike.

It wasn't totally unknown that you should fly higher during hunting season, and several times aircraft have been hit, usually without serious damage. But in one case I am aware of, because it happened about 50 miles south of Moab, it was very serious damage. A single engine airplane that had been missing for nearly five years was found in heavily wooded hill country by some backpackers. The skeletal remains of the pilot were still in the cockpit area. The investigation revealed that a large caliber rifle had fired a round that went through the bottom skin of the cockpit area of the cabin, through the pilot's seat, through the pilot's body and exiting out the top of the skull. This aircraft disappeared during deer hunting season in Southern Utah. This homicide case remains open. More than 600 aircraft have been reported missing in the western states in the last sixty years.

That brings me to a completely different episode. I was still drinking during this time, gambling and losing, really getting into a financial sinkhole, even with my wife working. I would come home from a trip from some place where there was gambling, Las Vegas, Elko, Reno, Winnemucca, Battle Mountain and others, and within a week my bank in Moab would call and ask me to come down and cover the checks I had written there. I would go down and plead with Mr. Carlson, the head of the bank, to loan me the money to cover them. This he did for a while, but told me one day this was the last time, even though I was keeping up with the payments. I was at the point that I was going to crash financially if I kept this up, but I couldn't seem to stop myself when I got to drinking.

I had been in Moab about three years and had met a lot of smooth characters and a lot of rough ones also. I gambled in town a lot and got to know some of the prospectors, miners and "desert rats" fairly well. Everybody knew I was a pilot, went to Mexico frequently for Mr. Steen, and was kind of a character in my own right.

There was quite a lot of small mining around the area, in a circle about 100 miles across, in Utah and Colorado. A lot of gold was found over the years in small quantities in the rivers and streams. You could only legally sell it to the U.S. Government for $35 an ounce. A lot of the old prospectors wouldn't do that, but would try to smuggle it into Mexico where it brought $80 to $90 dollars an ounce. They would have 20 or 30 ounces saved up over a few years work and sometimes several of them would try to get it out in one shipment, maybe 100 to 150 ounces or more.

After a panguine game, a western card game, one night and I had lost all the money I had with me and signed a few markers, I was moaning and groaning about what terrible luck I had had the past year and it had nearly flattened me. A guy I knew from the gambling games came up to the bar and asked me if I would like to get most of it back. He said he and some friends wanted a package taken to Mexico and would be willing to give 10 per cent of the value of it to a pilot who would fly it in to a desert strip across the border and bring back the proceeds in American dollars the Mexicans would pay off with. He said the trip would be just a 100 kilometers into

Mexico and back. They had a Cessna 140 in southern Arizona I could fly and I would be paid in cash on the spot when I returned.

I asked what kind of total are we talking about here and that I wouldn't stick my neck out for a couple of hundred dollars. He said it should be about 400 ounces of gold at $80 an ounce and my end would come to $3,200. Now that sounded like a lot of money to a guy who's in serious debt, so I said to let me think about it. He said it had to be there in the next month to get that good a price. I had to decide within a week and let him know. When I woke up the next morning I remembered every word, even with the hangover and loser's remorse. I thought that with a half a year's pay for one night's work, I could catch up on all my debts and current obligations.

I would pay off the notes at the bank and get a fresh start just by helping these miners get a better price for what they've worked damn hard for. That's really not doing anything like committing a real crime. I thought about it all day and the next day. It would be easy flying, quick in, quick out, get my end, jump in the car and in 12 hours I'm home—just once, just this one time and never again.

I had made a friend in El Paso during my stops there going in and out of Mexico. I decided I needed some advice. He was the only one I could think of that might know what the odds were on making something like this work. I called him at Champs Aviation in El Paso and after a couple of minutes, I told him someone wanted me to drop a package off in Chihuahua one night, turn around and come back empty. What could he tell me about this kind of thing? He said that the way it usually goes down is that you bring the contraband in, land, they check it out to make sure it's as advertised, then they take you to the truck to get the money and when they hand the bag with the money over they include a bonus for you—a 3¢ bonus. That's what the .38 or.45 caliber round costs that they put through your ear or the back of your head. They take your watch, belt, anything else of value, roll you into a shallow grave, have one of their men fly the airplane down into the interior where it's prepped for sale further south, and they head back to the Jefes' place with the consignment.

He said that about six to eight airplanes a year disappear into Mexico along with the pilots, and if they ever show up again, that is, the airplanes, they've been painted, new ID numbers, and the pilots are rarely ever heard from again. I thanked him and told him I'd be in soon on my way to Mexico for the boss. I thought all along that it couldn't be as easy as it sounded and furthermore, I knew that I couldn't have done it in any case. No matter how much trouble I had made for myself and my wife, I was basically an honest person. I had been raised to believe that a person who broke the law willingly was worthless and should be on the chain gang or in prison. If this was a test, I didn't do very well. I should have rejected it out of hand and told the guy not only hell no, but that he was lucky I wasn't going to tell the Sheriff about it. Later on in my life some criminal action overtures were made to me again, but I did better with them. I told them to wait here while I get the Police. They left without saying goodbye.

I was arrested in Denver one time while flying for Mr. Steen. However, it was only for "Grand Theft-Auto." I had flown several passengers to Denver and since we would be there two days, I booked a room at the Skyways Motel just off of Smith Road, and rented a car at the Terminal at Stapleton. I checked in at the Skyways, washed up and since it was about 7:00 PM, I strolled down to the bar to have a cocktail or three or four before deciding on eating. I ran into a pilot I knew named Bill Haynes who was from Kansas. After a few drinks we decided that as I had transportation, we should go eat at the Aurora Lounge, about 8 miles away in Aurora. Lots of pilots, stewardesses and good looking gals hung out there. You could get a good meal, have a few drinks, maybe dance a few rounds with the gals, and in general have more fun than sitting in your room watching *Bonanza* or *All in the Family*.

We strolled out of the bar, hopped into my rental, backed out and zoomed off to Aurora. We spent about 3 hours eating, drinking, and wishing there were some good looking girls to talk to or dance with. Finally, knowing Bill was leaving fairly early the next morning, we paid up, got in the car and started down Colfax Avenue west bound, then north toward the airport and the motel. As we got close to the Airport, sirens and red lights went off right behind us and I pulled over to let them pass—only they didn't pass. I pulled over and stopped, put the window down just in time to have a Denver police officer come up with his pistol drawn. His partner on the other side of the car was doing the same thing. "Get outa the car with your hands up, keep'em up where I can see 'em." We both got out of the car and I started to protest, but shut up when he said "You're under arrest for grand theft auto. Put your hands behind your head."

I said "Wait a minute, this is a rental car from the airport, we're both pilots who have our airplanes parked at Combs and we are staying at the Skyways Motel." The second cop has checked the VIN and plate and he said "Yep, this is it, the one reported stolen two hours ago at the Skyways."

I said, "Wait, wait, I have the rental papers in the glove compartment." The first officer opens the door, gets in the driver's seat, opens the glove box, there's a lot of stuff in it, but no car rental papers. "Okay, we're done fooling around. Get the other guy, Al."

Suddenly, I get a flash. I looked at the cop, and said "Would you do one more thing before we go any further? Would you take out the keys and look at the tag on them." He leans in, pulls the keys out and puts his flashlight on them. There, on the key ring, the most beautiful piece of plastic I'd seen in years. It said "Dollar Rent-a Car, Denver, Colo."

The two officers looked at it and the one who talked to us first said, "You ain't kidding us? You really rented this car?" I said "Yes, I really rented this car or one like it. Look, why don't we go on to the motel and straighten this out. It's only a mile." And so we did, one officer riding with us in the car, followed by the patrol car. At the motel we pulled up in front. They went and got the man who reported the theft. He identified the car and the officer asked him for the keys. He handed them over, the officer sat in the car, inserted the key, and it started with the first twist of the man's key. He pulled out those keys, took my keys, put them in the ignition and it started with the first twist of the key.

I was looking down the row of cars by the side of the motel and down by the side entrance door to the bar we had come out of. I told the officer "Come with me a minute, I think I know what happened." We walked down by the side door and there, parked behind a car closer to the side door, was an identical car to the one in front of the motel; same style, same color, identical to the eye. We went and tried the keys. My keys unlocked it and started it. His keys wouldn't unlock the door or even turn in the ignition. The man had driven in and parked beside the side door, but on the other side of it from my car, which was then hidden by another car that parked after I did. When we walked out of the side door to go eat, the other car was sitting in plain view and I never gave a thought as to where I had parked in the first place. So we got in and drove off.

Ten minutes of paperwork later, we were no longer under arrest, the guy who reported his car stolen was on the way home, he had only stopped in for a drink. The cops didn't apologize, for after all, they had just done their job and cleared a crime report. They did say just before they drove away," We didn't think it was you guys all along. You two didn't look smart enough to steal cars!" They laughed, waved and drove away.

Bill Haynes, my pilot friend from Kansas, shook his head and said "Sparks, the next time we see each other, will you pretend you don't know me? I will if you will." We stayed friends for a lot of years. We had a lot of laughs about this. Bill would say "Go steal us a car so we can go to the movies." He developed cancer and died young at about sixty years of age. He was the Junior Kansas State Pool Champion in his youth. Everyone who played pool with him knew they had been beaten by the best.

A few years after this incident, the County Sheriff in Moab, Hector Bowman, approached me about becoming one of his deputies and working in my spare time. Heck was a great Sheriff, but he only had a fifth grade education and he was having trouble with all the paperwork that came with the badge. Someone told him that I had worked in brigs as a Marine and he wanted me to help out with investigations and paperwork, especially with the Federal Agencies. He asked Bob Curfman, the TGS manager at Moab and my boss (and a great one) if the company had any problems with this. The answer was no, as long as it was on my own time and didn't interfere with my company duties. I told Heck I would be glad to help out. I took the tests and qualified with weapons—I had an expert qualification in the Marines—was cleared by the State of Utah and sworn in. For the next four years, until I was transferred to Denver by TGS, I worked in the Sheriff's Office as my schedule permitted, and I hope that I gave some material benefit to the work that I did for it.

In a previous chapter, I made the statement after returning from playing football for Mexico City College that went, quote: "Little did I know that there was one more football game in my future." unquote. Well, it wasn't all that much of a game on my part, but the end justifies the means, I guess.

We had a movie crew in Moab making a western, and many of the crew had played football in high school or college. The Moab High School football team was putting on a drive to collect funds for new uniforms and equipment for the team. The old uniforms were in bad shape and since school would shortly be out for the summer, somebody whipped up a scheme to have a Varsity versus "Has Beens" football game with the proceeds going to the uniform fund. Sounds great, huh? All the old football players around town were recruited, myself included. We practiced a few plays, worked out a couple of hours to get into shape and the night of the game everyone in the county was at the stadium. When the Varsity ran out on the field, the "Has Beens" really got a shock. Not only were the coaches suited up, but three of the movie crew were among their ranks; not just any three, but three who had played some minor league pro football.

Well, it was the longest 48 minutes I can remember. The Varsity absolutely cut us to pieces and then chewed on us. I came down with double charley horses in the third quarter and was spared the last 12 minutes of this slaughter. The uniform committee made a ton of money, all the bars in town did a land-office business after the game and none of the "Has Beens" had to be hospitalized. It was a really successful event, all in all.

Photo Section

Photo #1: John on the right, Ben & Clifford, Ennis 1948

Photo #2: John in uniform 1951

Photo #3: Mustang P51D

Photo #4: Douglas B18 sprayer

Photo #5: Twin Bonanza, DEN

Photo #6: John & Twin Bonanza, Ennis, TX

Photo # 7: John, Mom, Carol Sue & Mary Jane

Photo #8: GA Duster Crash 1956

Photo #9: Cessna 195 B

Photo #10: Steen Piper PA23 Apache

Photo #11: Moab Drilling Cessna 310

Photo #12: Howard 250 Lodestar Moab

Photo #13: Ellie & John at Dinner Dance, Moab

Photo #14: John & Lincoln in Moab

Photo #15: John G., Peggy P., John Wayne & Ellie

Photo #16: D18S Twin Beech

Photo #17: Andy McGill in D-18, Nevada

Photo #18: John in Hammock, Twin Beech

Photo #19: Aero Commander at SLC

Photo #20: TGS open cockpit drawing

Photo #21: John & Aero Commander

Photo #22: John & Aero Commander in Den

Photo #23: TG Twin Bonanza

Photo #24: John & Jim Estep in 421 at Rock Springs, WY

Photo #25: Shan, John, Bob, 421 engine out

Photo #26: John & Lear Star Trip

Photo #27: G1 at Pamlico River, NC

Photo #28: G1 & Ellie in Denver

Photo #29: TG Hangar in White Plains

Photo #30: John in G1 cockpit

Photo #31: G1 Instrument panel

Photo #32: Jetstar & TG Pilots

Photo #33: TG Fleet

Photo #34: Typical 731 Jetstar

Photo #35: John in Jetstar cockpit

Photo #36: TG Cessna Citation 500

Photo #37: John Beury & John Sparks in Bahamas

Photo #Photo 38: AC 685 in Tampa, FL

Photo #39: Swearingen Merlin 2

Photo #40: John's Cessna 152

Photo #41: John & Dave Howe

Photo #42: Chief Justice Warren Burger & John

Photo #43: John, Dave & passengers

Photo #44: G 1 on way to Rome Italy

Photo #45: John & G1 Italian crew in Rome

Photo #46: Carlo Pedersoli AKA Bud Spencer

Photo #47: Cessna 208A

Photo #48: Swearingen Metroliner

Photo #49: Cessna 340A & Pikes Peak, Co

Photo #50: IJA Lear 25D N225DS

Photo #51: IJA Make A Wish Foundation Lear

Photo #52: Lear & IJA Pilots

Photo #53: John & Al Unser, Jr. at Mansfield, OH

Photo #54: John, Rich & Stearman

Photo #55: John, Ellie & Dogs

Photo #56: John & Ellie Xmas 1996

Chapter 6 — Got a
Job for a Pilot?

In the late fall of 1960, I began getting frequent trips to Reno, NV, sometimes with Mr. and Mrs. Steen. The Super Ventura was also flying there and to the west coast more frequently. This continued into March of 1961. Those were the sort of trips I had been flying for UTEX, the main company for almost four years now, so nothing in scheduling was much of a surprise. There were no standard weekly trips. The trips came up; we flew them, waited for the next pop-up. When the office called me one afternoon and told me to pick up a passenger in Reno at 10:00 AM the next morning and return with him to Moab, it was very standard. They told me his name was Mr. Mayhew and he might have some light cargo to bring along.

I met him, loaded four file boxes, two four foot long large map tubes and his medium size suitcase into the Apache. I couldn't get it all into the baggage compartment so I had to use most of the back seat. I apologized to him for having to sit up in front with me, but he said that was what he preferred. On the trip we chatted about the pleasant weather. At some point I asked him if he was in the mining business and he said that no, he was an architect doing some work for Mr. Steen. I was smart enough to not ask what it was. I did find out that he had studied under Frank Lloyd Wright in Arizona. I would guess he was now in his fifties so I assumed that that must have been some time ago.

We were met in Moab by Charlie's gardener who loaded him and the cargo into his vehicle and took him to the Steen home. Staying at the Steen home and not a motel was unusual and almost unheard of. Three days later the Super Ventura took Mr. Mayhew, Mr. & Mrs. Steen and Charlie's executive assistant back west somewhere. This was all very puzzling. Nothing quite like this had happened before. Usually, the trips were pretty transparent within the company structure, but this had the office and laboratory staff scratching their heads.

Three weeks later the shoe dropped. Charley called all employees into the office conference room for a meeting—laboratory, trucking, accounting, and aviation departments. He wasted no time, one of his characteristics, in telling us that most of the company was being sold and what he wanted to keep was being moved to a new office building in Reno that was being constructed on the Reno Airport. There were a few key employees who could go if they wanted to. The company that was buying the mine, equipment, and other facilities would probably interview the current staff for possible employment. The timing for the move would be late summer or early fall. I was asked about a week later by Carol Rippy, our chief pilot, if I had any interest in moving. I told him Nevada was not my idea of where I would like to live, so if nothing came up around this area, in Salt Lake or Grand Junction, I would probably head for Denver. I still had good connections there.

In the early days of making the western "B" movies, when they started to run out of money, they shortened the film by "cutting to the chase" to get it over with quickly. Hang on; I'm cutting to the chase. A company named Texasgulf Sulphur had started to develop a potash mine 12 miles from Moab. They were a Fortune 1,000 Company. They already had a flight department in place in other locations around the U.S. and Canada. I met their local Project Manager and asked if they were going to have an airplane based here for company travel. He said he wanted one, but there was not one readily available in their flight department. I told him there was a really nice Aero Commander twin engine aircraft (*Photo #19*) based in Moab that a mining company wanted to sell or lease. I thought I could get him a swinging deal on a lease and I'd fly it as the lease pilot. I took the management crew on a demo flight to Salt Lake. They loved it and put the request in to company headquarters in New York City. In two weeks we had a deal.

In September 1961, I started working as a lease pilot for Texasgulf. The Steen move had been made, but they left one of their airplanes in Moab and I also flew it for them a few times to help them out. Texasgulf had started the development of a shaft 28 feet in diameter and 3,250 feet in depth into the potash ore body. They had to do a lot of work with different companies in Denver, Salt Lake, Kansas City, Albuquerque and several other locations, so we were really busy for the first ten months. I flew into Canada numerous times to Calgary where they had a district office, Saskatoon where they had a large potash mine, to Regina, Winnipeg, and some smaller locations. The shaft was being dug by Harrison International, a construction company based in Houston, TX. They specialized in this type of work.

There was also major construction in progress for the surface facilities—the processing plant, warehouse, shops, and office building. It was a fine tuned effort with very knowledgeable staff at every level. Several trips by the Texasgulf aircraft that was based in Texas or New York City came into Moab bringing company engineering, chemistry and rail experts to consult and plan for all the many necessary contingencies to complete the surface programs. One major project was to plan and start site work on the 28 miles of railroad to connect with the Union Pacific main line for hauling the cars of potash to market upon completion of the facility.

Starting a complex set of operations like this had quite an impact on a little town of five-thousand people.

It went into the "boomtown" mode again to some extent, but nothing like the uranium boom. An infrastructure that didn't exist in the first boom had now become a standard part of the community and the result was a soft landing in most cases. You could find a house to rent or even buy. The trailer parks had expanded, cleaned up and added better facilities. We bought a new house for $16,750. It was a nice split level, no garage, but a carport, which was a standard thing in those days. The job was just what I wanted and I was told that it would likely become permanent with the company if the mine operation turned out as expected.

We flew a lot the first three months. Out of 92 days until the end of the year, we flew 64 days, with 105 legs (landings) in 152 hours. (*Photo #20*) The Aero Commander (*Photos #21 & #22*) was a wonderful aircraft to fly. The only drawback was that this was not a supercharged model which limited my ability to climb with ice or above weather. But no plan is perfect. At least I was working, was where I wanted to be, doing what I wanted to do, and making more money than I had made with my last job. I had hopes of doing such a good job that the Manager of Aviation in New York would put me on permanently rather quickly. But one of the first things I learned about a large corporate flight department was that the man who runs it rarely likes any plan that he doesn't originate himself.

The company people I flew were just great. The original project manager was just one of the guys once he got out of the office. From what I heard in the office it was a different matter. He was fair, but expected nothing less than your best effort and the truth no matter what. I worked for five project managers that were all pretty much that way, but one was a little more rigid than the rest. He was an ex-Marine officer, Korean veteran and came out after ten or twelve years to follow his engineering degree into the corporate world. Of course, with me being an ex-Marine "grunt" you would have thought we would get along famously. We got along okay once I convinced him that the Marine Corps ceased to exist at the entrance door

[193]

of the airplane. Eventually, we got comfortable together, as long as it wasn't overdone.

The trips were to a lot of the same places I had been going to with Mr. Steen, so it was like a stroll in the park most of the time. Many new destinations were added, especially to Texas where the company had the largest sulphur mine in North America and possibly the world. It was at Newgulf—about 50 miles southwest of Houston. It was a company town, everything in it being owned by the company, houses and all. We had a good company airport with large hangars, lights for night operation and our own fuel system for avgas. I went down several times in the Aero Commander to do survey work in the Gulf of Mexico for offshore bidding with the federal government. Our petroleum division engineers and geologists spent lots of hours looking at a lot of seawater. It was a bearcat trying to find all the corners of the bid areas on nothing but Omni radio bearings and ADF to help. But they seemed to think it was fine and as a result of the bidding, we eventually had forty some producing well platforms offshore.

I had some trips to North Carolina, New York City, Toronto and Montreal, but one in particular I was glad to make a second trip to. I had been to Annette Island, Alaska, on a Steen trip shortly before the change over to Texasgulf and this was an interesting experience. We had to land at the Ketchikan International airport, located on an island about 21 miles southwest of Ketchikan, then take a Coastal Ellis Airways charter in a Grumman Goose amphibian to an inlet on Prince of Wales island about 60 miles west. A 300 foot long merchant vessel, the mine headquarters, was anchored there about 50 feet from the shore. I stayed aboard the ship while the mining engineers went ashore to see the mine. I was standing by the railing looking at things ashore when I felt a hard bump on my leg and hip and something took hold of my hand. I looked down and saw a dog, a very large dog, standing about 4 feet high and weighing about 120 pounds, looking up at me with my hand in his mouth. One of the men walking by said "He wants to go fishing. There's the skiff. Everything you need is in it, go out into the middle of the channel and troll about 60 feet deep." The dog turned and took me to the skiff, let go of my hand, hopped in the skiff, sat down on his haunches, and tilted his head when he looked at me, as if saying "Well?"

The dog was named Kaita. He was half husky and half grey wolf. He could climb any ladder on the ship, even straight up. We fished about three hours with Kaita watching intently from one side of the skiff or the other and came back with a forty pound King Salmon which the cook turned into salmon steaks for us visitors that night. Kaita saw us off as we left the next afternoon when the Goose took us back to the airport. We flew into Seattle that evening and back to Moab the next day.

About a year and a half after this, Texasgulf scheduled a trip to take a look at this mine. I was glad to see the ship come out of the fog after we landed in the amphibian and were taxiing into the inlet on Prince of Wales Island where the ship was anchored. We off loaded our gear and I looked around to see if Kaita was coming to greet us. There was no sign of him and I asked the mine manager where he was. The manager said that Kaita was dead and nobody wanted to get another dog yet. It seems that about a year after my first trip there, the men got up one morning to find a 300 pound black bear trying to climb aboard the ship via one of the large hawser ropes that tied the ship to pilings on the shore. These bears were savage, as bad as a small grizzly once they went into attack mode.

Kaita smelled or saw the bear, leaped over the side of the ship and swam to where the bear was hanging onto the hawser. Kaita started biting and snapping at it until it fell into the water. The men on the ship were getting a rifle, but by the time they had one ready for use, both the dog and the bear had made it the 50 feet to shore and had begun a ferocious battle. The outcome was what no one wanted. Kaita injured the bear severely, but the claws and teeth of the bear were too much for him to overcome. The bear was shot and killed when he charged the men getting out of the boat to get the dog hoping to be able to patch him up.

Kaita was buried beside the landing dock with a cairn of stones mounded over his grave. A simple split log stood watch with "Kaita, our dog" chiseled into the face. Before we left, I went to the fishing skiff and took a trolling jig from a box of lures. I walked down to say goodbye to a very special dog and placed the lure with several others that had already been put there by the men on the ship. Such totems go with life in Alaska. It is a hard life and good friends and good dogs are not easily forgotten.

There was lots of flying, lots of weather challenges, lots of yo-yo trips to Salt Lake and Denver—sometimes three roundtrips in one day. Things were rolling into high gear on the mine project; consultants, Utah State mine inspectors, United States inspectors. We had a weekly parade arriving in Moab. I picked up most of the Texasgulf people in Denver or Grand Junction, transported them to Moab and then returned them to their departure airport when they were finished. One day I had taken three passengers to Grand Junction to catch a flight to Denver on Frontier Airlines and as I always did, if possible, waited until they had departed on their flight before leaving for home.

Well, this time the Frontier Convair 580 blew a tire on touchdown and limped into the gate, but was stuck until repairs could be made. I called the boss in Moab, told him what had happened and got permission to take our three passengers to Denver to catch their connecting flights. There were two other passengers who were also trying to make Denver connections. They happened to be members of the family of one of our Moab employees. I asked his permission to take them also and he said that by all means take them too. I had the Frontier Station Chief get their luggage out to our airplane. I told him if they needed to get a mechanic or parts back from Denver, I could drop them off on the way back to expedite getting the trip on its way.

We got off the ground in short order, were in Denver in one hour, taxied to a Frontier Airline gate at the terminal, with permission from Frontier and Stapleton tower, dropped the passengers and they all made their connections. Frontier's Station Chief said that he had three boxes of parts, which were necessary to repair the Convair in Grand Junction, ready to be loaded aboard if that was still possible. I told him that I had the company's permission to help them out, in order to expedite the stranded passengers, and to get the boxes on board. They did and an hour and 8 minutes later we were unloading them in Grand Junction. I flew home, cleaned and fueled the airplane and got ready for the trip the next day. The Manager's office received two nice letters from Frontier Airlines and ALPA, the airline pilots union, thanking the company and me for doing this. My boss was very pleased with the good P.R. work.

The telephone can change your life in an instant. On August 27, 1963, at 5:05 PM, my phone rang at home in Moab. I thought it might be my wife saying she was leaving work and would be home shortly. It was a female voice, but not my wife. It was a terrified, crying voice, the voice of my boss's secretary, Marge Phillips. "John, John, something terrible has happened in the shaft. Mr. Tippie wants you to stand by the phone until he has something to tell you. You might have to go get somebody—just stay by the phone." I told her I would, she hung up and I sat there thinking all sorts of things; wondering if one of the people might have fallen into the shaft or the cable on the lift might have broken. It was nearly two hours before the phone rang again. It was our assistant manager. He told me there had been an explosion in the mine and there were thought to be thirty-three men trapped at the working level. He said that no one was sure of anything right now, but we might have to fly at any time and would I go to the airport, wait in my office by the phone and be prepared to stay all night.

On the way to the airport I listened to our local radio station. They were trying to get information, but all that was being released was "It's too soon to know anything; we'll let you know as soon as we have anything definite." I pulled into my hangar, went over the aircraft thoroughly, checked the tire pressures, checked cabin supplies, made sure the Jeppesen manuals were up to date, cleaned all the cabin and cockpit windows and a lot of other nit-picking things to stay busy. I was about half asleep in my desk chair when the phone rang. It was Mr. Tippie, my boss. He spent about 5 minutes filling me in, but there wasn't much to tell. There was a major explosion which was probably a pocket of methane gas liberated by the mining into the walls in the lowest level of the mine. Several men had been brought out of the area in good condition, but the majority of the miners were somewhere behind the blast doors with no contact at the moment.

I would need to be in Denver to bring a team of our mining people to Moab at 8:30 AM tomorrow morning when they arrived from Newgulf, Texas. He gave me some more details and I told him I would be at the airport, in my office, and would leave about 6:00 AM and I would call in from Denver after I arrived there. When we got back to Moab the first reports were coming in. So far, seven miners were dead. During the next five days the rescue effort became a body recovery. At the end of a week the results were made public. Of the thirty-two men in the mine, eighteen had been found dead and fourteen in different areas of the upper mine workings survived, mostly with no serious injuries. No one on the two lowest actual mining levels survived even with the best emergency equipment available at this time. The report came in. Methane gas, mixed with oxygen from the atmospheric air in the mine, exploded having been ignited by an unknown source.

Some of these miners were from Canada and some from Utah and other places. Over the next two weeks, I flew our top people from Moab to funerals in Utah, Idaho, Colorado, and New Mexico. Blackie Eslick, who was in a deeper part of the mine, was the only Texasgulf employee in this area, but escaped without significant injuries. All the men who died were the employees of Harrison International, the shaft excavation contractor.

We all wondered if the project would survive after this accident, but it did and with much more stringent controls to prevent methane problems. Life goes on.

We had one trip early in the project, in November of 1963, that I remember very, very well. My boss asked me if we could fly four engineers into Leadville, CO. I told him that we could unless the airport should be closed with snow on the runway. The weather was no problem at this time and two days later at 10:00 AM we landed in Leadville, which is the highest commercial airport in the U.S., the elevation being 9,927 feet above sea level. We were taken to an old mining camp at over 10,300 feet elevation to look at a 122 foot high smokestack at the mill. Texasgulf was thinking of buying this smokestack, cutting it into sections, taking them to our mine site and making an air entrance into the deep mine so plenty of air could be pumped into it as needed.

What was needed now, however, were exact measurements of the thickness of the iron at the top of the stack, 122 feet above ground. There was a rickety looking iron rung ladder running up the side and the man who picked us up at the airport said he had climbed up there a week or so ago and the ladder was just fine. The wind was blowing about 15 mph. It was nippy at about 40 degrees. The head of the engineering department asked each of the three engineers if they would go up and measure the lip at the top which should be about 20 inches of concrete and between 3 to 5 inches of iron boiler plate. All of them said not me—not in my job description, I get vertigo, and I have a fear of heights, why don't you go? The chief guy said, "Well, you cowards, I'm the boss, so I don't have to go." I asked him if it was really necessary to do this and he said yes, and that the thickness of the iron had to be known to 1/8 of an inch all the way around the 22 foot diameter at the top.

I said "We flew all the way here to do this specific thing and nobody will do it?" Everyone shook their heads no. I was now steamed. I said "Tell me exactly what you need, how you want it measured and I'll do it so we can get the hell out of here!"

So I took the clipboard, a small steel tape, calipers, borrowed some heavier gloves, stocking cap and scarf from among them. Everything was clipped to a heavy leather belt leaving both my hands free to climb with. I went up 60 feet on the diving board in the Marine Corps Sea School and survived. I figured this would be about like that and I had the safety harness to clip onto the side rails as I climbed. What I always remember about that 10 minute climb was how much harder the wind was blowing around that stack than on the ground. I think the wind moaning and howling was the scariest part of the whole thing.

I got to the top; measured and checked with the calipers, "scootched" around the lip with one leg on the inside and one on the outside. It was actually less windy on top. I took my time and made it around in about 20 minutes. When I finished I made damn sure I had the notebook with all the data zipped up inside my jacket, because there was *NO* way I was going to go back up there again.

Actually, on the top it was a marvelous view toward Aspen and all around, surrounded by the Rocky Mountain range with the Collegiate Range to the south and west. It was not like flying though where you have that feeling of control. This was my Mt. Everest experience. Coming down started with difficulty because I didn't want to leave the lip for that puny ladder again, but after the first 10 feet it was easier. I took my time and didn't look down. When I got to the bottom the guys unloaded the gear, swapped our garments around and we headed to town for a late lunch.

After we got in the air on the way back home, they all said that this was the most boneheaded stunt they had ever had pulled on them. The head engineer said "Yeah, what if you had fallen off, how the hell would we have gotten home?" The company bought the smokestack and had it shipped in to the plant in sections after the railroad was finished and it did exactly what they wanted it to do. I never said a word about this trip to anyone but my wife. She heartily agreed with the engineers.

1963 came to an end. The mine explosion, the worst in Utah mining history up to this time, was behind us—not forgotten or put aside. We all lived with it in some way almost daily. Even in this short time the healing process for us, the Texasgulf people who had to pick up the pieces, had started working. This was the way of the world. We provided help and comfort to the families of the victims in every way possible. Texasgulf was a company with a heart, but also with a mission. We had stockholders, large and small investors, people who trusted us to continue to operate profitably and to help secure their future. The potash that would be produced from this property would be used in the production of foodstuffs for hundreds of millions of people around the world. The tragic death of these eighteen men was a stroke of particular bad fortune for men who were supporting families, paying taxes, planning for the future for themselves and the children they had and would have. There is no guarantee that life will be fair or that being honest, hardworking, responsible and morally upright conveys any better chance of survival to enjoy the bounty of life than the criminally minded, vicious, truly evil person has.

There was an expression I used to hear in Texas as a kid that rather sums up my thinking about fate. "You pays your dollar, and you takes your chances." I'm not a fatalist, since I believe good planning and preparation, attention to detail and an honest desire to do the task correctly, to the best of your ability, will produce the best result the majority of the time.

1964 was a year of many changes for me. My logbooks show that I flew 223 days, 603 hours, 927 landings and 107 hours of instrument time. The Potash project was getting into full gear again with ever increasing manpower and shifts working. We also planned to start researching a new mine possibility in southern Wyoming. This would be a trona mine, better known as soda ash, and would involve quite a bit of participation from the Moab operation. Just after the first of the year my status changed within the company, as my boss finally prevailed upon the C.E.O.to facilitate my employment with the Aviation Department. The Manager of Aviation had been reluctant to address this issue, saying they didn't have an airplane and pilot available that could be stationed here at this time. Being told by the top official in the company to hire me and get a proposal in for an airplane in the near future really did not make his day.

It came down this way. The pilot is in, the airplane is out and we would continue to lease the Aero Commander until a company aircraft could be made available, probably within a year or two. I was made a full time employee of the Aviation Dept., status Aircraft Pilot-fixed wing. I was also given a nice raise. I said nice, not big, and signed up for health insurance, savings plan, social security and the retirement plan after the first year. I received a call from New York in short order, telling me the good news which I had already heard from my boss, I mean the project manager. I learned right away who the real boss of anything to do with aviation was and heard in no uncertain terms that *everything* in aviation goes through the Manager's office at the White Plains, N.Y. airport hangar. *Period. No exceptions.* Thus, I joined the real corporate aviation world.

I almost left the corporate aviation world before my business cards got printed. My private life was going to hell in a hand basket; drinking, smoking, gambling, writing checks for gambling losses I couldn't cover. I was very fortunate to have a banker who would lend me the money to cover them. But I was told the last time I went in for another loan in early April that this was it, the well had run dry. I was sliding down the slippery slope of uncontrolled drinking, just as my father had.

My father had a drinking problem that went along with his gambling, womanizing, bad check writing, and poor husband problems. I'm not sure if there was any direct link between him and me and the drinking of alcohol—genes, heredity, whatever. But I know that we both suffered greatly because of it. I came very, *VERY* close to repeating his life. Dad died in 1970, at the age of fifty-nine. When I went to bury him in San Antonio, I thanked the doctor at the hospital for doing what he could for him. The doctor shook his head and said "Sadly, there was nothing I could do for him. Your father was one of the most used-up human beings that I have ever seen. There was not an organ in his body that wasn't totally worn out."

Dad had been drinking daily for years. He was 60-70 pounds overweight, he covered his food—mostly fried in fat—with a layer of salt. He smoked one or two packs of cigarettes a day. He was on his third wife; my mother had been his first. He had lost his musical career, the good job with Service Life Insurance Co., the assistant manager position of a Handy-Andy grocery store and had finally ended up running a pawn shop on Military Highway in San Antonio. This is not much of a eulogy for a great jazz piano player who once played the piano for Bob Hope on one of Hope's USO tours of 8TH Air Force bases in England and Scotland. Skinny Ennis, the band leader and piano man for Hope contracted pneumonia. Dad filled in and Hope was delighted with his work. This was in WW II.

My total estate was a $50 overdraft at his bank. His brothers, sisters and my wife and I paid for the funeral. We scraped together several hundred dollars for his widow to get her to her sister's place to live. I looked at him in his coffin at the funeral home and felt like I had failed again. I had been sober on the AA program for six years. I had tried to get Dad interested but he was unreachable.

I had come so close to destroying my career by hidden drinking, lying, all the misery with my marriage that comes with gambling, other women, financial problems. My employer had said that if I showed up one more time for a trip smelling like a brewery I was through. Now that is *the* kiss of death in the corporate flying business and almost all commercial aviation. I've seen it happen many times in the 48 years of my career.

Somehow, a friend of mine, the same J. W. Holland that rode to Salt Lake with me to pick up the blood, managed to catch me in a moment of weakness and trouble and against all odds got me to go to an AA meeting with him. I almost talked myself out of it, but he knew how I was thinking, because he had been through all of it himself so he *handled* me! To make a long and continuing story very short, I went to the meeting. I walked out the door after that meeting in April 1964, and I have never taken another drink. It was not a miracle. It was a lot of people helping me and letting me find my own way little by little.

Believe me, when I say this is not an advertisement for Alcoholics Anonymous. I don't mind anyone knowing I'm in the program and I don't mind them knowing that I think it has tremendous value for me. But I cannot and do not speak for AA. I would hope that others have success with it if they decide it could help them, but that's strictly up to them.

Some steps in this program of 12 steps advocates that we be as honest as we can be, admit our mistakes promptly and be willing to live our lives one day at a time. I managed to do this for a year, but I was physically sober and mentally drunk lots of the time. However, my flying got better, my attitude greatly improved, my boss was happy with my performance and my home life was now worth going home to. One day on the way to the airport I realized that I was content, even happy.

In early 1965, we changed project managers putting V-P Van Donohoo in charge, a very capable and brilliant engineer. One of the first things he asked me on the first trip was whether there was any word on the replacement aircraft for this operation. I told him very truthfully that the head of the Aviation Department had been saying for a year that this was a future project. The way he had put it to me, it was code for "Don't hold your breath." I had no reason to think this would change. I had had my tail chewed not long before this for allowing Win Eckland, the King Air salesman for Combs Aircraft Beechcraft Sales, to give me a demo even though I had told him I had nothing to do with the selection process. When I reported the demo to New York, the Aviation Manager who was also the Chief Pilot told me to call him if anything like giving a demo was requested and he'd take care of it. That pretty much told me I was still in the doghouse. I really didn't understand why.

In later years I found out that the Manager/Chief pilot had always handpicked the pilots and only selected ones he thought would be loyal directly to him, more so than to the company structured chain of command. This was the way it had been since the late 1940's, when he was hired by the company to set up and run the Aviation Department. In my case he had had no direct part in my hiring since I had been a lease pilot and was a Texasgulf pilot in name only. The money that paid the lease for the aircraft and pilot came out of the Aviation Department budget, but was paid through the development budget for the Potash project. I was the only one who authorized the maintenance, necessary supplies and other costs arising from the lease operation. I approved the bills. They were made part of the monthly lease billing and paid by the Potash Division. The Aviation Manager was cut out of my operation from the start and that was the problem. This was partially solved when I became a Texasgulf employee, as I now sent everything in the way of bills and expenditures to New York. My paycheck came out of New York and the flight department policy manual was the Bible for our operations. And now the Manager/Chief Pilot could fire me in an instant if I screwed up.

1965 was another busy year, especially with adding the Trona Project in Southern Wyoming at Green River. We flew into Rock Springs as it was the only all-weather airport close to the developmental site, had airline service and lots of support infrastructure for personnel in town. Near the end of the year, I was informed that Texasgulf was buying a corporate jet, the North American NA-265

"Sabreliner." This aircraft would be delivered about the second quarter of 1966, and was priced at somewhat more than $500,000 with all equipment included. *Wow!* Half a million dollars for one airplane. This was the same basic model that the U.S. Air Force was using for a small personnel transport, but would have a non-military cabin interior and paint job.

I was told that this jet would be based in New York as the Home Office aircraft. This would release the Lockheed L-18 Lodestar with the "Learstar" conversion package. Some aircraft shuffling would probably occur. At this time the company had two Lodestars, a Beechcraft E-50 Twin Bonanza and two helicopters that were being used in exploration duties, along with the leased Aero Commander. There had been some talk of basing one of the Lodestars in Moab. With us now flying out of the new airport, Canyonlands Field, it would be a fine aircraft for our use. There was one very small insignificant problem, however. It was too big to fit in the hangar we were leasing at the new airport and it was the largest hangar on the airport. The wings were about 12 feet wider that the door opening. No matter how I tried with scale cutouts, I couldn't get it in. About half of it inside was the best I could do. When I mentioned possibly building a new hanger to house it, it was as the Italians used to say "La bacio di morte" (the Kiss of death). I had already flown the Lodestar based in Houston, N508S, (*Photo #26*) 36 hours to get ready for my type rating ride, but it came as no surprise that this wasn't going to happen after the hangar problem. You couldn't leave a big airplane sitting outside in the kind of winters we had in Utah.

We kept going with the Commander with lots of flying. We were interviewing miners for employment as far away as West Virginia. We made almost daily trips to Rock Springs, WY, and support flights for engineering to Denver, Salt Lake and Phoenix. We were piling the hours on the Commander—getting a 100 hour inspection done about every six weeks. Fall came in gently with long easy days and the old timers said this was the "false spring" that usually preceded a fairly hard winter. In November, the White Plains office told me to pack up, take the Aero Commander to Combs in Denver, leave it there and catch the airlines to La Guardia Airport to do some flying out of White Plains for a couple of weeks. I had no idea what this meant exactly, but I felt that there was a change coming soon.

When I walked into the White Plains hangar I saw the other Lockheed Lodestar we owned, the one based in Raleigh, NC, the one I hadn't flown on. It was a Dee Howard conversion, called a Howard 250 model. It was the same exact type Charlie Steen had operated out of Moab. I was very familiar with all the changes and cockpit installation. I was informed that I would be the copilot on N505S for the next two weeks. Jim Markham, who was now designated Chief Pilot and flew the Saberliner Jet as a captain, told me that we were terminating the lease on the Aero Commander and I was going to get a company airplane to take to Moab in its place. When I asked which one Jim laughed and said "Beats me. The manager hasn't made up his mind yet." Jim was a really fine young man, about ten years younger than me and a very, very good pilot and a good fit for Chief Pilot.

I told him that the Saberliner would fit into the Moab hanger just fine. He said "Don't push your luck. Just be glad the boss is in a good mood lately, take what you get, make it do the job. I'll keep working on an upgrade for you."

I flew for two weeks and one day we flew down to our hangar in Washington, NC, where our Phosphate mine airplane was kept. Jim Markham went along on this trip. When we got out of the airplane he pointed to an aircraft parked in our hangar and said "meet your new Potash Division airplane." Well, it sure wasn't a Lodestar. It was a Beechcraft E-50 Twin-Bonanza, (*Photo #23*) the big brother of the C-50 that I had flown years ago before taking the Moab job. It was painted in blue, white, and gold, our company color scheme, and had a radome instead of a nose cap. It also had stairs to load into the cabin instead of steps on a pole like the earlier aircraft had.

I knew this model had the Lycoming GSO-480B1B supercharged engines, developing 340 hp a side. It had complete de-icing equipment for the props, windshield, radome, fuel vents, wings and tail. It had six individual cabin chairs and had a super soundproofing package, which this airplane needed since it had augmented exhausts to maximize the power output of the engines. That means it wasn't all that quiet in the cabin until you got to cruise altitude and set cruising RPM. Then it wasn't that bad, but to call it a quiet airplane, no way. It could take on the weather though and that was worth some noise. The flight manual said it could go to 30,000 feet. I believed it, but never had it over about 19,000. It had a good oxygen supply, but everybody hated to use the masks so I limited that aspect to only when absolutely necessary. The little ARC radar worked quite well and the 80 mile range was plenty for the speed of the aircraft.

The instrumentation was good with a Collins small flight director, a Lear autopilot and a duplicate set of instruments on the copilot's panel. All in all it was a good step up from the Commander as far as safety was concerned. But the Commander was one of the smoothest, quietest aircraft I was ever given to fly. Later in my career I would fly the 685 Commander and although not turbine powered, but being pressurized and with a great engine power package, it was like driving a Mercedes-Benz 450SEL sports model. Even the jets weren't as smooth as that aircraft.

For a week I flew the Beech all over the east coast on short runs for the phosphate division getting it shook down before I headed west with it, as it had just come out of an inspection at Greer Aviation in Spartanburg, NC. I had Greer fix a few things that I found and on December 10, 1966, I landed in Moab. The aircraft fit in the hangar. In fact, it looked rather lonely in there.

We went right to work on the standard runs. All the guys wanted to ride in the new airplane, but it was all business. Texasgulf didn't fool around very much. If I was scheduled for a trip, it came directly from the boss or his secretary. Even if I got a call from New York headquarters, the airport or home office, I had to run it through the project manager's secretary and get his okay, especially if it meant a conflict with our schedule. It was rare that this came up, but when it did, it was usually easily resolved.

The T-bone, the nickname for the new aircraft, broke in well and as it was winter, the heater made it toasty in the cabin which the ladies really appreciated. Some days I had to load passengers when it was −10 degrees on the ramp with a 10 to 15 mph wind and a chill factor of about −20. As soon as I got one engine running, I could start the heater and in 30 seconds it would be blowing fairly warm air out and hot air within 1 & 2 minutes. The coldest I ever saw it in Moab was −23 degrees one morning. It was so cold the starters on the Aero Commander wouldn't spin out and engage. We had to delay the trip for two hours while we got the engines warmed up to about −5 degrees. Then I went ahead with the trip climbing up into an inversion layer after takeoff, not unusual in the west, with the air warming up to −14 degrees. Rock Springs, WY could be one of the coldest trips we made during the winter, just staying below zero day and night for a week or two. I flew sixteen days in January 1967, making 38 legs, 9 hours of instrument time and about 21 instrument approaches, mostly ILS or VOR. We were back home every trip but three—one RON at Denver, one at Salt Lake and one at Rock Springs. If necessary, we could get the engines preheated at DEN and SLC, but at RKS we had to hope Frontier Airlines could let us use their equipment, engine heater and battery cart, which we paid a fee for if they were working.

The one thing you did *not* want to have was an engine problem and have to try to work on it on the ramp. If you couldn't get it into a hangar or a sheltered location, you had one tough day ahead of you. Hopefully, there would be an air service of some kind with a mechanic, but many of the small airports I used had gas and oil, a telephone and a rest room. Many problems you might possibly have would let you fly on to a larger airport, but most engine problems would nail you in place. You get to know your airplane, it grumbles and gets sulky at times and it might have nagging bad habits, but if it says "Uh-oh, it's the big one" you'd better listen. This is one of the major differences in the lives of Airline pilots and corporate, business, or private ones. The Airline pilot writes up the discrepancy in the logbook and leaves it on the seat. The mechanics check the plane overnight and fix or solve the problem.

One supposedly true story from Frontier Airlines from their DC-3 aircraft days has a young pilot making a write-up in the log "Something loose in left wing." He came in the next morning to continue his trip in the same airplane and upon checking the logbook found that the mechanic had worked on his problem. The mechanic's write-off in the log book said "Tightened something in the left wing."

The FAA would not be amused at all with this in these super-critical modern times and a lot of the fun of the early days has gone the way of all flesh. We'll talk about the modern era in the last part of the book, but right now let me see if I can get through the T-Bone era and into more modern times.

Winter finally broke and a beautiful Rocky Mountain springtime got everyone in the right frame of mind after a tough winter. My flying schedule stayed about the same, flying about four days a week. The T-bone ran fine, the weather was good, our projects in different areas were progressing well and the only crisis that arose was just enough to be a giant headache for me one day. I show in my logbook a trip on March 14/15, 1967, to Sacramento, CA and return. Time flown: 7 hrs. 35 min., instrument time 20 min., night-time, 7 hrs. 35 min. At 7:30 PM on the 14th, the phone rang. It was Tony Fratto, the Potash plant chief engineer, calling me direct because the boss told him to deal directly with me.

It seems that a special type water pump for the main power generator for the interior of the mine and the shaft had fried itself and was beyond repair. The closest available one was in a warehouse in Sacramento; could I take the plane and go get it? The company in Sacramento said it would take at least two days to get it here by road and we needed it ASAP. I asked Tony about the general size of it, how much it weighed, what were the dimensions, was it in a crate and a couple of other things. I told him our problem was the baggage door and if we could get it through that door, no sweat.

He had all this information and it was bad news; the pump was bigger than the door on one measurement. I asked him if the pump could be broken down into the motor and pump assembly and he said that it could be. I told him to tell them to break it down. We could get it in and back to Moab and our shop could reassemble it and put it to work. I also told Tony he had to go with me to handle things in Sacramento and to meet me at the hangar after he called the pump people and gave our plan to his shop at the plant. I rushed to the airport, took out the two rear seats to have enough room for the cargo and the aircraft was ready to go. At 9:00 PM we lifted off, filed a flight plan to SAC which had a low ceiling with fog, but was supposed to stay at minimums or above.

At 1:00 AM I was shooting the ILS approach into Sacramento International Airport. They had a 300 foot ceiling and ¾ mile visibility. After landing we pulled off the runway into Sacramento Flying Service. The truck with the pump was standing by and the fuel truck pulled up to fuel us. I rushed in to file a flight plan, went to the head, picked up some hot coffee in my jug, paid the bill and checked that everything was tied down. Tony said we had all the parts and gaskets we needed. I thanked and tipped all the guys there for helping us out. We started the engines, called for our clearance and found out that the airport was closed because the weather was now below landing minimums. I asked what San Francisco had, 90 miles to the southwest, and they were 600 feet scattered,

900 feet overcast, visibility 2 miles, and forecast to stay that way for the next two hours.

I then asked the tower for a part 91 departure (Part 91 allowed non-commercial aircraft to operate without takeoff minimums) with SFO as an alternate. We would be ready for takeoff at the end of the runway in 5 minutes. Once we were airborne I would request radar vectors to intercept the departure airway and have center issue my IFR clearance for my flight plan to CNY, Moab, UT.

The tower asked me specifically "You are operating part 91, is that correct?" I said yes, and he cleared me for takeoff under the pilot's authority of part 91. We had about 100 feet visibility so I did a localizer heading control takeoff, head-in-the-cockpit, zero-zero all the way. We lifted off, reported leaving 200 feet, 500 feet, then was given a radar vector to a N.E. heading to intercept the departure route, went over to ATC center, got my clearance, went home to Moab, visibility 50 miles, and landed. We put the pump pieces and parts boxes in the truck and at 5:50 AM they were on their way to the plant.

I heard from the boss that afternoon after I got out of bed that the plant was back in operation before 9:00 AM. He said "How do you feel?" I said I was fine and just a little groggy. He said "that's good, because I want to leave for Denver this afternoon with three of us for an early morning meeting tomorrow. Will 5:30 be okay?"

At 5:45 PM we lifted off for Denver. We came back late afternoon the next day. I got the airplane ready to go, went home and had two days off. Tony took me out that weekend for the full deluxe Hamburger Steak and a piece of the homemade apple pie ala mode at Milt's Stop and Eat. Tony said it was for me not killing him on that takeoff. I said "Oh well, maybe next time." He said "there ain't gonna be no next time." I had him on another flight to Wyoming about three weeks later. He asked "How's the weather?" I said "You don't want to know."

He said, "Yeah, you're right. I don't want to know."

The rest of 1967 was normal, flying up to ten days in a row at times. I once flew a fourteen and one-half hour day, which was the longest day I ever put in as a single pilot, and nothing very unusual happened which was really unusual. The potash and soda ash projects were coming along in good shape. We were going to put in a Western Division office in Denver, a new project might happen around Telluride, another operation started at Weeping Water, NE. Lots of things were happening in Canada, oil drilling platforms were coming along in the Gulf of Mexico, and a phosphate mine expansion was in progress at Lee Creek, NC. The *BIG* news was in April of 1964, when TGS announced the discovery of the Timmins, Ontario ore body. It was now in development and estimated to be worth *eight billion U.S. dollars*. The insider trading case against eight or nine top TGS executives, regarding their stock purchases, had gone through the court system and had been argued in the U.S. Court of Appeals on March 20, 1967, and was working its way through the appeals process. This was making most of us in the work force very uneasy, because we had been treated very well by the executive structure of TGS. A major disruption by the Court could not do anything but harm the operations of the operating divisions. Still, it wasn't something we had any control over and we kept things rolling, hoping for the best. The decision by the Court eventually was released on August 13, 1968. It was a very complicated legal document, and after reading it, I still had no idea what it said. But the good thing was that it didn't rock the boat so badly that we were hamstrung.

1968 was pretty much a rerun of 1967. There were a lot of very cold days in Wyoming and Montana. They seemed suddenly pretty mild when the schedule started to include very frequent trips to Calgary, Regina and Saskatoon the middle of February. The Canadians were good about giving us space in the hangars if they knew we were coming. A heated hangar meant it was at least 30 degrees inside, versus -30 outside. I flew or was out of town 43 days of the 59 days of January & February, but only 17 days in March. That was almost like a mini-vacation.

Finally spring came and then summer. The airplane ran well; the weather was normal with lots of short trips around the mountain west. Summer brought the thunderstorm season and the little AVQ–20 radar paid for itself over and over. All the passengers got a big kick out of watching me navigate between cells, a lot of the time in strato-cumulus clouds between the cells. I would point out what we were going to do on the scope and they were amazed at how smooth it was compared to the Aero Commander without radar.

The whole year ran by like it was on rails. The potash plant was making product and we started shipping potash the middle of the year, The Wyoming trona mine was being developed without any real difficulty so far. I guess the only real excitement of the whole year was when the Sabreliner came out on a trip from New York bringing all the brass to inspect the mine. After all the dignitaries had been loaded into company vehicles and headed for the mine, the pilot from New York fired up the jet and started for my hangar to park it inside for the night. I was on a trip and when I landed back in Moab there was our jet looking like a ruptured duck with one main landing gear tire and wheel sunk a foot into the asphalt ramp. The temperature was about 107 degrees and the paving from the edge of the main ramp to my hangar, about 120 feet of it, was only half as thick as the main ramp was. When it was this hot the asphalt really got soft and the Sabreliner was a heavy little plane and had a single high pressure tire on each main gear. It just didn't have enough footprint on the tire to keep it from cutting into the semi-soft asphalt. Fortunately, only one tire broke through, and they shored it up under the wing with lumber to keep it from going in any farther. We got it jacked up out of the asphalt, put planks underneath the tires and pulled it out backwards to the main ramp. We spent an hour with solvent and brushes getting the tar off the landing gear and brake. No damage was done, but that was just luck. Anyway, the mine tour was a big success and no one opened his mouth about the jet.

The weather finally cooled off, trees turned red and gold on the LaSal Mountains—a great fall season. Suddenly there was snow on the high peaks of the LaSal's; Thanksgiving, Christmas, and New Year's and 1968 was gone. Things were going so easy for me, my job was great, fine people to work with, my wife and I had gotten over our troubles from my drinking days and I had been sober over four and a half years. The Twin Bonanza was performing very well. The winter hadn't been brutal and with any luck at all, the prospect of a new and better aircraft might be in the offing. The Wyoming project was taking a lot of our attention now, being at a critical stage of mine construction. The last part of winter in Rock Springs brought some difficult weather to handle, but with the de-icing equipment on this aircraft it could all be handled. The Rock Springs airport was one of the few in the country that had a unique feature that allowed us to operate there at times when other airports would be shut down. This airport was built on a flat top mesa that rose up about 700 feet above the valley floor. It was possible to make an ILS approach to the west with a 200 foot ceiling and a very strong easterly wind, pull over to the north side of the airport after breaking out, drop down 150 or 200 feet below the airport elevation, fly around and line up on the runway, now flying easterly, hop up slightly and land visually.

I don't recommend that pilots who are not very familiar with Rock Springs do this; I'm only saying that it is a possibility here. What's that? Did I ever do this? Well, if there are no more questions ... Actually, the circling approach FAR is a little flexible, but I have no idea if it has a specific allowance where you can circle clear of clouds, at 300 feet below the airport elevation, then climb back up and land normally. Let us just say that I was lucky enough to be able to get in and out of Rock Springs through the winter.

Spring arrived and with it some fine weather, and to top it off, Christmas arrived a little early in 1969, also. In the middle of May, I was at home after a trip to Denver and back with nothing scheduled for the next few days. I was thinking of doing some odd jobs around the property the next day. The phone rang, I answered and the Aviation Manager/Chief Pilot's voice jumped out of the phone like a bull horn. "Dang" he said "That damn manager out there is a persistent cuss. He got Dr. Fogarty to okay that new airplane. Pack up everything for the Beech, spares, logbooks, whatever, and be in Ogden Thursday afternoon to turn it over to Sterling Meyers. Your airplane should be ready Friday. They're painting the N number on it right away. Call me when you get all set to leave with the 421."

I darned near dropped the phone. The Cessna 421A (*Photo #24*) was the perfect aircraft for us; pressurized, fast, good weather handling, and fast. But I really didn't think the front office would spring for a $100,000+ airplane, did I mention it was fast? And actually, they didn't. The 421 I was getting had been used by the President of Cessna, Mr. Duane Wallace, and had 100 hours on it. Cessna made us a very good deal on it, hoping to sell us some more.

And it worked. Within a year we bought two more, one for North Carolina and one for Newgulf, TX. Those two were air conditioned, while mine was not—but no argument from me. I was glad to take what they would give me. I called the boss at home and broke the news to him. He said "They made me promise to keep quiet when they called me yesterday. The Chief Pilot wanted to tell you himself. When do we get it in operation?" I said I should be home with it Friday afternoon and starting Saturday he could schedule it from then on.

I made my last takeoff in the Twin Bonanza at Moab, circled the field and made a low pass over the ramp, climbed out steeply, 60 degree banks to the left and right, and corkscrewed out toward the west. You hate losing old friends, but it's great to make new ones. We had transferred the N number, N517S, to the 421. It was already painted on when I arrived in Ogden. The 421 had been painted at the Cessna factory with our company color scheme—white, dark blue, with gold striping. It sat in the hangar like a predatory animal, raring to race away after its prey.

We flew an acceptance flight check, made a couple of minor adjustments, packed up all the spares and paperwork and Friday afternoon I went home. I climbed to 27,000 feet altitude on the way back to Moab. I could have gone higher, but that wasn't needed, I felt like I was with the angels already. I have flown Learjets up to 51,000 feet in the last part of my career, but nothing has ever given me such a lift as seeing the altimeter on the 421 reach that 27,000 foot mark. You never forget your first prom date. No pilot ever forgets his first pressurized airplane. For me, the only things missing were the tuxedo and the corsage.

Chapter 7 — Gee, This Thing Is *BIG*!

The new airplane was a great improvement in our operations. It was faster, had a better cabin arrangement, was quieter and we could usually be on top instead of in the clouds. We rapidly increased our working range to Calgary, Saskatoon and Winnipeg in Canada. Seattle, Houston, Los Angeles and San Francisco were all easy comfortable trips compared to our previous aircraft. Our Project Manager's wife was a lot more willing to travel with him now; having a "biffy" on board was his big selling point. The weather was a very formidable consideration for flight planning most of the year. We were now flying out of the new Canyonlands Airport north of Moab instead of the old unlighted field south of town.

The FAA had approved a Non Directional Beacon for navigation and instrument approaches for the new airport shortly after it was opened. This was necessary for Frontier Airlines to begin operating scheduled flight service to Moab. However, within a year's time the FAA installed a T-VOR (Terminal Omni Directional Navigation System) which allowed a much more precise instrument approach, navigation aid, airport beacon and lighting for night operations. This solved most of our operational problems, but we still had to telephone long distance to

Grand Junction, CO, to obtain a weather briefing from the Flight Service Station and file flight plans for trips.

Those guys were good! Over the telephone they could give me all the details I would need for a trip to anywhere. Remember, these were the days before computers, satellite pictures from orbit, radar weather observations and high speed networks for disseminating all this information in real time. These forecasters had telefax copies of dozens of maps, which many forecasters around the country had to prepare and then send along to everybody else every half hour. They analyzed and predicted the weather for the next interval. They went out with balloons, (for wind observations) read the instruments in the little vented boxes outside the weather building, recorded temperatures, barometric pressures and humidity. This had to be done to acquire the information. Then they had to get the information out on the teletype every half hour. No matter what the weather was like outside, every three hours the forecasts would be updated for all areas of the country and almost all major and secondary airports.

But the real key was that these guys in Grand Junction had been doing this for so long—20 to 30 years for many of them—that they used to claim they could smell a change in the weather coming in their sleep. They would say "Salt Lake says it won't go down before midnight, but if I were going there I'd make sure I was on the ground by 9:00 PM at the latest." Sure enough, at maybe 10:00 PM, the airport would be closed or flights delayed two to three hours by heavy snow or runway snow removal operations.

We once had a very important meeting to attend in Denver on Tuesday. The boss said we absolutely had to be at this meeting Tuesday morning. I called the weather bureau at the Grand Junction Airport. This old forecaster I knew real well said "If you're thinking of going tomorrow, forget it. Denver will up-slope between 3:00 AM and 5:00 AM, will go down to zero-zero, won't break out until 4:00 PM, maybe 6:00 PM, and then only up to about 400 foot ceiling, with ¾ mile visibility." I asked him if that was what

Denver was forecasting and he said "Nope, they seem to think it'll be a lot better than that, but all of us here think they got a hell of a surprise in store." I'd gotten years of forecasts from this bunch, and they were almost always real close on what they gave me and I took this to heart.

I called the boss and said "If you absolutely have to be at that meeting tomorrow morning, we need to leave here no later than 8:00 PM tonight." He said that would be hard to do, to get the engineers and their plans and things to the airport that quick. I broke in and said "You pay me to get you there, but I can't get you there if I can't land. Take it or leave it." He was not amused, but we did leave shortly after 8:00 PM, landed in Denver at 9:15 PM, went to the hotel downtown. They closed the airport at 2:00 AM Tuesday morning. They began operations again Tuesday night at 11:00 PM, and we left at 6:30 AM Wednesday morning. We landed in Moab at 7:45 AM, the boss was in his office at 8:30 AM, and life went on. The only repercussion of all this was that we had to make the trip again the following week because half of the people necessary for that vital meeting didn't show up. Their flights, airlines and company planes, were all stranded at Omaha, Salina, Grand Junction and other airports waiting for Denver to open up. The meeting eventually took place, contracts were signed, the mill at our potash plant got built and I got another star in my crown. From then on what I said about the weather was gospel.

Twice during the time I was flying out of Moab, I went against the advice of these forecasters and was fortunate to live to regret it. The first time I was young and dumb and I don't count that one. The second time I was pretty well experienced and dumb, so that one really stings to tell about, but I do count it. I had a trip out of Denver to Rock Springs, WY, at 7:00 AM on a Tuesday morning with four passengers from our New York corporate office. The trip was to tour the trona (soda ash) plant we were building outside the town of Green River, a short distance from Rock Springs. This was a high profile trip with two of our home office V-Ps, our Western Division V-P as host and a couple of others. This meant that I needed to leave Moab on Monday afternoon, spend the night in Denver, and be ready to leave at 7:00 AM Tuesday morning.

We were still operating the Aero Commander (*Photo #19*) at this time. I called Grand Junction for a weather briefing. The weatherman I got was one I knew pretty well. He said "I think Salt Lake has lost this cold front coming down from Idaho. It's got a lot of moisture with it and the temps are just right for possible mixed icing from the surface to the top of the clouds at about 18,000 feet. But they don't show the frontal location on the prog chart. I think it extends from Rock Springs to Aspen to Gunnison. Your best route would be from Moab to Farmington, NM, east to Pueblo, then north to Denver." I knew this would double the flight time for this trip, so I decided to go straight to Denver on V-8 airway (14,000 minimum altitude to the Eagle VOR, then 16,000 minimum across the continental divide to Denver.) I had flown this trip many times, but usually not with quite this bad a weather forecast.

I filed an instrument flight plan, took off, flew to Grand Junction at 10,000 feet, put on oxygen and climbed up to 14,000 in heavy clouds. About halfway to Eagle I started to pick up light rime ice, nothing to worry about. As I passed the Glenwood Springs area the clouds became thicker and wetter with the temperature showing a few degrees below freezing. In another 10 minutes the precipitation started falling much heavier, almost like a steady rain. I called Center and asked to climb to 17,000 feet. They cleared me to this altitude and I started my climb. Suddenly, ice was banging against the sides of the fuselage as the propellers slung the ice off the blades and the wings had about an inch of ice on the de-icing boots. I was being slowed down in airspeed so I pushed the props up to climb RPM, increased the manifold pressure to climb power and tried to hold 140 mph indicated air speed.

I toggled the wing and tail de-icing boots—the propeller electric boots had been on ever since I entered the clouds—and ice shelled off the boots pretty well. I was at 14,800 feet and climbing about 250 feet a minute. My air speed had slowed to 130 indicated and more precipitation was sticking as ice. Now it was mixed rime and clear. This was not good. Rime is very brittle because it has a lot of air mixed in with it so it breaks fairly easily. The airflow over the boots will take it off as it breaks so the buildup is held to a minimum—not so with clear ice.

Clear ice forms when supercooled moisture receives enough sudden shock energy to make it transform from the supercooled liquid state to an instantaneous solid crystalline state with virtually no cracks or weak spots like rime has. Rime ice has an opaque quality to it. It's cloudy and you can't see through it. Clear ice is pretty much just that. Clear. You can see through it, although it's distorted, and it has many times the adherence strength that rime has.

I'm passing through 15,200 feet, max climb power on both engines, and the rate-of-climb is showing a little less than 100 feet a minute. The heated pitot head keeps giving me air speed, but it's bouncing between 110 and 125 mph. The windshields are completely covered, except for about an inch at the bottom just above the defroster ducts. The angle of attack of the aircraft is about 4 degrees nose up which is as much as I dare pitch up while trying to climb. Any more nose up will probably stall the aircraft and then I'm really in trouble.

Five minutes later I'm at 15,500 feet, 110 mph airspeed, rate of climb, zero. She's all done. I'm about 10 miles west of the Eagle VOR and there's no hope of getting any more altitude. I'm in heavy precipitation with no visibility. I called Center and told them the story and requested a course reversal and a return to Grand Junction for landing. They cleared me to "cruise" Grand Junction which let me stay at my altitude and I could descend when I wanted to. I leveled the nose and picked up a little speed. The boots have taken off some of the ice, but they still had about 2.5 inches on them. The propeller spinners had 3 to 4 inches on them. I started a turn to the north very slowly, about 8 degrees bank, turning into the wind to try and stay as far north of the highest mountains as I can. I'm now slipping below 15,000 feet because of the turn. The engines are still running at max climb power, which has an unlimited time allowable rating. The cylinder head temps are high, but still in the green. The oil temps are right on the yellow warning mark, but still okay.

I'm through about 90 degrees of the 180 degree turn I have to make. I know I need to get back to V-8 airway to have a known altitude track. The altimeter now shows 14,000 feet and the rate of descent is about 30 feet a minute. I'm getting close to the radial of the airway so I feathered the turn onto the radial and now felt a lot better. The map shows that across the Glenwood Springs area, the MSA (minimum safe altitude, the lowest I can go and still have 100 feet of clearance for 5 miles either side of the airway radial) is 12,300 feet above sea level. It's about 20 miles to the Glenwood Springs area ahead of me. The ice on the boots is about 3 inches, airspeed 120-125 mph and 50 feet per minute rate of descent. At this time, my altimeter shows 13,300 feet with the descent increasing to 100 feet a minute. The ice is banging and the engines are surging a little. I see some breaks in the clouds and trees show up just under me in the breaks. Trees, there are nothing but trees about 600 feet under me in the breaks. My altitude is 12,500 feet as I cross Glenwood still shelling ice. I pushed the props up another 50 rpm. We're almost into takeoff power, allowable duration is 5 minutes.

The breaks in the clouds are getting bigger. I'm now halfway to Rifle, showing 12,300 feet. At Silt intersection the MEA goes down to 10,500. As I cross it I pull back the power and props to high cruise setting. At 5 miles past Silt I set up a 50 feet a minute rate of descent. The icing has stopped. Air temperature is up to 31degrees, I'm carrying between 3 and 4 inches of ice, air speed is building up to 130, 140, 150 miles an hour. Suddenly we hit some turbulence, shaking for 10 seconds, then whoosh! We run out of the clouds at 10,800 feet, visibility now is 15 to 20 miles through the side windows and the windshields are still covered with solid ice. I'm cleared for the ILS approach to Grand Junction, to descend and maintain 8,000 feet. I start down, the temperature is rapidly rising and suddenly all the ice lets go, off the windshield, the cowlings, and the wings. At 7,000 feet all the ice is gone and I get a normal landing clearance, land, taxi in, get the airplane fueled while I file a flight plan for Denver at 19,000 feet. I take off, climb to 19,000 feet in a circle over the Grand Valley and go direct to Denver on top of all clouds and land at Stapleton Airport. I get a good night's sleep and at 7:00 AM Tuesday morning we fly the trip to Rock Springs. Everybody has a good time and the tour is a big success. While we are loading to go back to Denver that afternoon, our V-P was looking at the airplane and said to me "What are all these dents on the sides? I don't remember them."

I said "You don't? It must be the way the sun's shining on the plane. We've had those for a while". "A while" in the flying business can mean two years or two hours.

Later that spring, I took that weatherman to lunch in the Airport Terminal Restaurant in Grand Junction. I also invited two other forecasters that had helped me a lot over the years. I put them down on my expense account as "Federal Aviation Safety Advisory Staff" which was damning them with faint praise. Besides, a lunch for the guy who had tried to save my butt was the best I could do for him—I knew I would never get away with putting a "Rolex" on the expense account. He had warned me and I didn't listen to him. After all, I was a big corporate pilot and I'd been flying this country for years. I'm a much better listener now.

Texasgulf Sulphur Co. was a great outfit to fly and work for. They had fine people upstairs, great skilled employees in the mines, plants, surface facilities and support staff. I had no problems with anyone as a division pilot. In Moab, I reported directly to the facility Manager, the top man in the Division. He was responsible for all operations in the mine, warehouse, processing plant, office, everything

... except the airplane. He made it very clear that it was under his supervision on the organizational chart, but that it was my responsibility to make sure that it did the job as I saw fit. The budget came out of the New York flight operations office. The Aviation Manager was the department head, but the division pilots were autonomous in their daily operations.

We had two airplanes in New York, one in Raleigh, NC, one in Newgulf, TX, one in Moab, UT, one in Perth, Australia, and five helicopters working on exploration projects, mainly in Canada. We also had railroad tanker cars for molten sulphur, barges, tugboats and two deep water sulphur tankers leased to deliver molten sulphur to chemical plants on the east coast from our gulf coast loading facilities. We lost one of these tankers in the Bermuda Triangle in February 1963. The name of the ship was the USS Marine Sulphur Queen. After making a radio position report 45 miles off the coast of South Carolina, it was never seen or heard from again. The only piece of wreckage found was half of the name board. None of the bodies of the thirty-eight crew members were ever reported found.

We also lost a Hiller 12-E helicopter in the deep woods of Central Canada in 1975, killing the pilot and a Canadian geologist. Apparently, the engine quit on top of 70 foot trees, after being refueled from gas barrels that had been contaminated with quite a lot of water. I'm not superstitious, but I do believe that you can do everything right and still have it come out poorly. That's why I prepare for every eventuality I can think of. That usually covers the minor things—sometimes not.

On August 9, 1957, I was flying the Steen Co. PA-23 Piper Apache, (*Photo #10*) a small twin-engine aircraft, from Moab to San Antonio, TX. I had one passenger, named Bill Lewis. It was a nice afternoon. I was about 25 miles from Wichita Falls, TX, according to the Distance Measuring Equipment in the airplane. I looked out of the side window for a moment or two and then back to the instrument panel. The DME now said "0" miles, and all the radios had the "Off" flags showing. I had oil pressure, air speed, altimeter, rate of climb, RPM and manifold pressure—nothing else. Everything powered electrically was *GONE*! No popped circuit breakers, no warning lights, no warning horns, nothing. My main fuel tanks showed about one-half full last time I had looked, so we had plenty of fuel even though they showed zero now.

I started descending, heading down the highway toward Wichita Falls and the Wichita Falls Airport. I found it and circled the tower with the landing gear, hydraulic powered, not electric, extended two or three times. They gave me a "Green" light, meaning I was cleared for a landing. I landed on the main runway, taxied off of it as rapidly as possible and followed an airport ramp vehicle to parking in front of the fixed base operator's hangar. I shut down the engines, hopped out and looked at them. There was no oil on the cowling, nothing looked wrong at all. I told a mechanic what had happened. He opened the cowling on both engines and they looked as good as they always did.

Ten minutes later, the mechanic came into the flight lounge and said "Tilt." The battery was burned out, both generators were burned out and all the heavy amperage fuses in the engine compartments were blown. He said "This is not supposed to happen." I had already figured that part out. I called the office in Moab, told them what had happened and that it was going to take some time to inspect and repair whatever it was that had gone wrong, but I'd keep them posted.

Late the next afternoon, as they pulled the aft nacelles apart—everything in the engine compartments had checked out okay—the two mechanics said "Wow" as the right aft nacelle was lifted off. One of the main DC power cables that ran from the engine generator to the main DC buss bar in the cockpit was welded to the frame structure and hidden by the wing on the bottom and the aft nacelle shell on the top. The cable had been incorrectly installed or had moved and chafed the insulation off over a period of time. It finally made contact with the aircraft frame grounding both generators and the battery with a dead short and very rapidly, in possibly one or two seconds, burning them out.

If this had happened in the middle of the night while I was on instruments with a low ceiling, both my passenger and I might have had a very wealthy widow in the family. The mechanics said this was a fluke and it should never have happened. Like I said, I had already figured that part out.

This was not a test from the Goddess of Aviation so much as it was probably an honest mistake by some mechanic who had moved the cable and fastened it out of his way perhaps. I didn't do anything but get the plane on the ground safely. I had plenty to work with. But, once again, good luck was the biggest factor in this scenario. The logbooks showed there had been some work under both aft cowls sometime in the past before I even started flying it.

I had, at one time in the past, landed this airplane twice in the same week with the left engine shut down and feathered because of no oil pressure. It was fixed, checked out and returned to service. Two days later the same thing occurred and caused another single engine landing. That is what training is for, but there is no training program that can adequately prepare you for every type of event. Being able to formulate a plan using what you have left to work with demands a cool head and rational thought processes. Like a mean dog, an airplane knows when you're running scared.

I once told a much older, wiser pilot about some problem I had had on a recent flight and what I did about it. I finished by saying ... "I did what I had heard would work, but to be honest about it, I was scared stiff."

He looked down at his hands and softly said "That's the only time it really counts."

The Cessna 421 really worked out well for us. It had the legs to go to Canada and most of the other places we were scheduled for. I would have rather had a Beechcraft A-90 King Air for passenger comfort and turbo-prop speed and safety, but I was grateful for what I had. The ability to handle weather with it having radar made it a day-in and day-out performer with very few maintenance problems between 100 hour inspections. But, to prove there is always an exception to the rule, a few times things happened that were new and different.

The winter of 1971-72 started off colder than normal in Utah. It was also colder than normal in Wyoming, Montana and, of course, Canada. So naturally Calgary and Saskatoon became two of our most scheduled trips during January and February. We had good clothing provided, goose down parkas, mukluks, gloves lined with wolf fur and so on. This worked well at −25, -30, and −35 temperatures as long as the wind was fairly light.

We had been in Calgary two days and I was notified that we would go to Winnipeg for a day or so before returning to the states. That afternoon at 4:30 PM we took off at Calgary with the temperature at −38 degrees. Sometimes in Canada you will have an inversion during part of the winter, with the air being warmer several thousand feet above the ground than on the surface. Unfortunately, this was not one of those times. The trip to Winnipeg in the 421 would take about two hours and five minutes. I climbed to 17,000 feet altitude for best speed and fuel burn performance. The temperature there was a crisp −58 degrees. I had the cabin heater on full hot, and it was giving us nearly warm air. The four passengers were huddled up with overcoats, gloves and scarves on. I looked like an Eskimo stuffed into the pilot seat with all my cold weather gear on. After an hour I noticed that the engines had gained some rpm's and were slowly inching up into the climb rpm range rather than the cruise range. I pulled them back with the prop controls, but they didn't respond. I looked at the engine oil pressures; they were down about 10 pounds each. The outside air temp now read −62 degrees, the oil pressures were slowly falling, the props wouldn't back off the increased rpm's and it was now dark. Winnipeg was still 30 minutes ahead and it would take about the same amount of time to go there as it would to turn around and descend into Regina which had an ice fog limiting visibility to less than a mile.

It suddenly hit me as to what was happening to us. These engines, the Continental GTSIO-520D series, 375 hp, (G=geared, TS=turbo supercharged, I=fuel injected, O=opposed, 520=cubic inch displacement) had an automatic oil cooling radiator system that was thermostatically controlled. This meant that as the oil got hotter, it was allowed to flow more rapidly through the oil cooler at the front of the engine, letting cooler atmospheric air cool the oil to its normal operating temperature. But now the oil was already cooled to the point that the thermostats on the oil coolers wouldn't let any oil flow through because it was already too cool. The engines were so cool that the oil was congealing, meaning it was getting too thick to flow easily through the oil bypass around the radiator or to work the prop control systems. So the props were creeping forward and would eventually increase to takeoff rpm which was limited to 5 minutes duration.

CARAMBA! This was not good, Amigo. If I pull the power back the engines will cool off so much the oil might quit lubricating the rods, the propeller gear box, and we will lose the pressurization from the turbochargers, among other things. If I don't get the prop rpms backed off, I might shell out the gearing (engine to props) and lose the engine(s). If I just jerk the power off I will probably crack all the cylinder heads and sidewalls—then we're really out of business.

I called Winnipeg center and requested an immediate descent to 8,000 foot altitude and it was approved. I am 25 knots below the maximum indicated airspeed landing gear extension speed at this altitude. I immediately dropped the gear, pulled the power back about 5 inches of manifold pressure, dumped the nose over to descend at 1,000 feet a minute, pulled the prop controls back to the stops, which decreased their rpm slightly, and as I descended, balanced out everything to stay within airspeed limitations. As we got down under 10,000 feet altitude, the outside air temperature was up to −52 degrees and the oil pressure had come back to about normal. The props didn't come back and I am now in feather range with them which brought them back into the yellow warning range, but I can live with that. Winnipeg tower cleared me for a straight-in approach. I landed and taxied up to the Field Aviation hangar. When I shut down the engines the airplane suddenly dropped about 6 inches with a clang. I opened the door and we are almost on the ground. All the nitrogen in the three landing gear struts escaped because the seals were so shrunken up by the cold temperature and the airplane was 8 inches lower than it normally is.

What a night. We got the airplane into the heated hangar which was heated to 35 degrees. As we went to the hotel in a cab we saw that every car on the streets was plugged into an electric socket for an engine heater and at least half of them were sitting there idling. The temperature was −49 degrees. It was −52 last night with some light wind. Tonight was dead calm, so there was no chill factor.

The next day, I went to the airport and had the airplane checked over, the oil filters and oil changed, the spark plugs cleaned, the air inlet filters changed and the strut oleo's filled with nitrogen. The check showed everything was normal. I also found out what the Canadian pilots with these type engines do in the winter to keep from having this problem. They fashion an air cover for the front of the oil cooler radiator that covers about half of it and that lets the oil stay warm enough to keep everything normal.

It had warmed up to about −39 when we left and headed south the next afternoon. I talked to one of the local pilots before the passengers got there. I said "How in the devil do you people manage to live here with these kinds of winters?"

He said "Oh, it's not so bad when you get used to it, Yank. We look on it as nine months of winter, and three months of poor sledding."

In late 1972, I convinced our Aviation headquarters that hiring a copilot/mechanic would be very advantageous to our operation. I had the backing of the project manager and there was a very good candidate waiting not 30 miles away. He was a tall lanky Utah boy from the Provo area and he was working for Jim Hurst at Green River Aviation, Green River, UT. His name was Shanley Scott Sorenson. He was about twenty-six years old, married to a sweet young blond and they had four young kids. They were a good Mormon family. He had a good background in basic aviation and I signed him up and started teaching him how to fly twin engine planes instead of Cessna 185's and 206's. He learned fast and he already had his A&P mechanics rating, a single engine Commercial rating with around 1,300 hours flying time. He was a quick study on the 421, and within a relatively short time got his multi-engine rating. Next he had to start accumulating enough hours of twin time to satisfy the insurance company standards. We had a lot of liability and passenger insurance on all our aircraft, so the standards for crew members were fairly high for background, training and experience. He had the same feelings about flying that I did so we got along very well.

I let Shan fly as much as possible from the left seat when we didn't have passengers and fly from the right seat with passengers if we didn't have any en route heavy weather to contend with. Our boss and everybody we flew out of the Moab operation liked him. I only had one gripe about him. He had such a great head of hair. I was shortly going to have my fortieth birthday and I was missing more of mine all the time.

The *Photo #25* in the photo section shows what a simple $20 nut and bolt can do to your day in this business. From left to right the people shown are Shan Sorenson, the copilot, me, Bob Curfman, Potash Project Manager and two Monarch Aviation mechanics. Please notice that the propeller blade at the top of the picture is in the "feathered" position, turned sideways to lessen the air resistance when the engine is not running while the airplane is flying. The black tube I'm looking at is the air feed tube from the turbo-charger air compressor that feeds air into the engine at high pressure, allowing the airplane to operate at high altitudes with normal engine power.

The trip that this *Photo #25* is part of is what began as just another run to Denver for some meetings and back home to Moab late in the afternoon. We climbed out, leveled at flight level 210 (21,000 feet) on an IFR (instrument) flight plan. About 20 miles east of Grand Junction, without a single spit or sputter, the right engine quit dead. This jerked the aircraft to the right sharply, disconnecting the auto pilot and altitude hold, and we immediately started losing altitude. The weather was good and there was no traffic in our vicinity, but it set off the altitude alert warning on the ATC center radar system before we got a call off to them. The engine was windmilling, the oil pressure was fine, there was almost no manifold pressure, the fuel pressure was okay, and there were no warnings on any of the ignition circuits and no response at all when we moved the throttle back and forth. It was just gone. We switched tanks, boost pumps on, nothing happened. I requested a reverse course track back to Grand Junction, which was given. I'm flying and Shan has gone through all the procedures on the checklist. I told him to shut it down, feather it, run the clean-up checklist, and to then call Monarch Aviation in Junction and tell them we have a problem that needs immediate attention.

The Grand Junction tower had been alerted that we were coming in single engine. This gave them a chance to get the emergency crews out for some practice and also to be ready if this doesn't turn out like it usually does. We made the single engine approach and landing with no problems, limped off the runway and a Monarch tug hooked right on to us. They towed us up to their hangar/ shop and by the time I got everybody off the airplane they had the cowling off. This was a Cessna dealer and an approved Cessna service center. In 30 seconds they had the problem pinpointed. A mechanic was already on his way to parts to get what was needed to fix the problem. In 5 minutes he was back, the problem was repaired; the engine had a quick inspection and in 20 minutes was ready to be started. It checked out completely normal and 35 minutes after we landed we were rolling on takeoff.

We landed at Stapleton Airport in Denver, put the passengers in a cab waiting for them at Combs Aircraft and they got to the meeting at the appointed time. I always build a little fudge factor into the schedule so in case of traffic, or weather delay for landing, we have a little slack in the schedule—and once in a while it really helps, like this time.

What happened was that the black round tube in the picture carries high pressure air from the supercharger compressor of the turbocharger to the distribution system on the top of the engine case. It is held on to the outlet of the turbo compressor (which is glowing red hot at altitude from the heat of the exhaust gases going through the compressor to spin the turbine which compresses the air) by a special stainless steel clamp. That clamp has a special steel nut and bolt designed to resist the high temperatures and should not fatigue and fail. Our problem was that this special $20 nut and bolt *did* fatigue and break, allowing the rubber boot end to blow off at the high pressure end. Thus the engine was getting almost no air. And they won't run without air, believe me. With the new nut and bolt and with Combs Aircraft in Denver changing the left engine nut and bolt while we waited that day, just as a precaution, we never had this problem again.

I've used a lot of words on this one incident and there's a reason for it. I have been told by several pilots that this engine will run without the turbocharged air supply. I usually ask them when was the last time they had tried it. Then it's, well, that's what somebody told me. True, the engine can be started on the ground and will idle with the boot off, yes. But getting 375 HP at 3,400 rpm, with 39.5 inches of manifold pressure out of these engines requires quite a few hundred pounds of air by the time both engines get you off the ground and on your way.

And, sadly, a number of crashes have occurred while the pilot is trying to get an engine restarted and forgets to fly the airplane. The three rules of survival in this kind of problem are:

#1. Fly the airplane.

#2. Fly the airplane.

#3. You want to make a guess? Fly the ___Airplane!

The 421 is still one of my favorite airplanes. I flew three different ones for TGS and had a few minor things like this happen. My logbooks show that I put in 2,237 hours flying them, with something over 700 hours of instrument time. I only log instrument time when it's solid instrument conditions. Many pilots log every flight they fly on an IFR flight plan as instrument time, even though there is no weather at all on the trip. The FARs specifically prohibits this, but it looks great in their logbooks. The bad thing about this is that they become convinced that they are great instrument pilots. If it never comes to "Put up or shut up" for them, they get away with it. I don't care so much about what happens to them, but the people riding with them have no idea that they could be in serious trouble, sitting in an aluminum tube with someone who has built up a reputation in his own mind that is totally made out of hype. I have broken a number of pilots in check rides and have been broken several times myself. Under the right conditions almost any pilot can be broken, but the true professional can come back rapidly. He will usually simplify things, go back to "needle, ball, and airspeed," get the aircraft back to as much of a stable platform as he can and go from there.

I'm about to continue on with my career story line, but before I do I want to say something about this last paragraph. I was flying out of Moab and we had a new pilot come into the area to fly and make money. He had a good aircraft for flying canyon tours and trips like that, but he was a show off, like the cowboys who used to ride hell-for-leather down the main street to the saloon in the western movies. I watched him fly for nearly a year and his act got wilder and wilder. He pushed hard to establish his reputation of being the best canyon pilot around, according to his own testimony. One day he came barreling into the Moab airport about 200 feet off the deck, pulled the airplane up tight into a semi-stall, kicked it around and barely pulled out to get it on the runway. That was as much as I could take. When he got out of the airplane I jumped him. I said what I thought, that he was one of the worst pilots I had ever seen, and I would advise him to go get some instruction about flying the aircraft to get the safest performance out of it in this rough country flying. He told me to mind my own business and that I was just pissed off to see somebody who could really get everything out of the aircraft.

I told a lot of my friends around town that this guy was a self-made suicide bomb, don't ride with him. I was told two or three times by the person I was talking to that they thought this guy was the best pilot we had ever had in the Canyonlands country.

About four months later he did some work for a government agency. He was flying three government people to do some sort of observing in the wild canyon country, stalled the aircraft, dove straight in, and killed all four of them. The town was shocked. How could this have happened to such a skilled pilot, such an experienced pilot? To the ones that asked me what I thought had happened, I simply said "This is an unforgiving business in an unforgiving country. If you bet short odds all the time, when you lose, they can choke you to death." Only half a dozen people had any idea what that meant and they were in vocations where you paid a high price for doing things the wrong way. They all just nodded their heads a couple of times in agreement.

And if I were asked who the best rough country pilot, besides me, of course, was around the Canyonlands country, I would have said that we had several very good ones within a 100 mile radius, but only one great one. His name was Jim Hurst and he owned Green River Aviation in the town of Green River, UT, between Price and Moab. This is where I stole my copilot from, and Jim was still not over this theft. Jim was noted for having a short temper—about half an inch most said. He called me a bandit and several other western descriptive words they won't let me put in this book, but cooled down finally and asked if Shan could finish some work he was in the middle of. I told him sure, just send him down to me when he's done with it. Actually, he told me he had known Shan wouldn't be around too long, he was just too good a kid. He was a hard worker, good mechanic and flew the Cessna 185 and 206 pretty well for his level of experience. Jim also said if he had to lose him, he was glad to see him leave for a corporate job where he had an opportunity to get into the big time.

He looked me right in the eye and said "I've known you nearly fifteen years. You've done flying for me at times; you've had me work on your planes, sent me business, and brought parts back from Denver or Salt Lake if I needed them. When Shan came to me and said he might have a chance to go to work for TG and he would need a recommendation from me, I said you gonna work for Sparks and he said yes, so I told him I'd give him the recommendation and one word of advice. Do the best you can, but don't ever lie to him. He'll forgive a few honest mistakes and if you ask why about something, he'll show you or tell you. But that guy is an ex-Marine and he will strip the skin off your butt clear down to the knees if you lie to him. And most of the time you have used up all three strikes on the first swing with them damn jarheads. But he'll make you a hell of a pilot for that business flying. And make no mistake; you're trading greasy hands and coveralls for suits and ties. Handling the passengers is more important than the flying most of the time. But listen to Sparks. He'll know all the shortcuts. Them Marines always do."

I said "I'll take good care of him, and break him of all those bad habits he's probably picked up here and thanks, Jim, I didn't know you liked me so well." He laughed and said "Where did I say I liked you? I just wanted to warn the kid, he's never been around you gyrenes. But I know he'll do well with you. He doesn't know how lucky he is." This did not turn out to be true, but we couldn't know that then.

Of all the stories about Jim Hurst and there were a heck of a lot of them, the one that set the high water mark with me is this one. One really hazy summer day about 1960, Jim was working in his hangar shop at the Green River Airport. A call came over the unicom radio he had had about a year. A voice called out in a frantic tone "Help, help, can anybody hear me? Help, I'm lost and about out of gas. Help me, please." Jim quickly called out in the blind "Aircraft calling on unicom frequency, this is Green River Airport reading you loud and clear. What is your location?" The frantic voice said "I don't know, I can't see very much in this haze. Please help me!"

Over the next few minutes, Jim got the pilot quieted down, found out he was in a Cessna 172 flying from Nephi, UT, to Grand Junction, CO. After he crossed the Wasatch Range through the Salina Canyon pass, the haze became so bad as he headed into the barren country toward Hanksville that he had become disoriented. He had been wandering around for over an hour, flying in circles, unable to recognize anything on his map. Jim got him to calm down, and tell him what the compass heading was, and then Jim had him turn to an east heading and hold it. He asked what his fuel gauge showed. He had about 5 gallons of fuel left. Jim told him to describe what he could see ahead and to the sides. The pilot, who was a new, inexperienced private pilot, was getting more and more panicked as the fuel gage was now at the reserve mark—about 4 gallons left which was about 25 minutes of fuel.

The pilot described a butte and a valley. Jim asked if he could see a big canyon to his left and in a moment or so the pilot said he did see it. Jim had him turn and fly toward it, told him to look on the near rim, that there should be a long, straight road just back from the canyon edge a couple of hundred feet. The pilot said he saw it, Jim said that was a strip he used occasionally and it was wide enough and well packed. He told the pilot to land on it and to pull off at either end on the cleared flat spot. In 5 minutes the pilot landed and Jim could still faintly talk to him. Jim told him to relax and he would be there in 15 minutes with some gasoline.

Twenty minutes later Jim landed in the Cessna 180 and gave the pilot a cold bottle of water. He poured 15 gallons of gas into the tanks, was paid and he pointed out the direction to Grand Junction. He marked the route on his map, told him to fly this heading, and this heading only, shook hands, and away they went. The lost pilot was in Grand Junction before his flight plan expired, although it was close. Jim flew back to Green River, parked and went back to working on whatever it was he had been doing. In less than an hour, he had rescued a lost pilot, fueled his aircraft to reach his destination safely, directed him on his way, and was back at work—just another day at the office? Believe it or not, this was still pretty wild country in those years. There are still nearly a hundred airplanes lost and have never been found in Utah. Every western state has a higher number than you would think.

It was the end of July 1973. My boss, Rudy Higgins, asked me to drop by his house after work. I did, we sat down and he said "Guess what? The home office is moving me to Denver." I hated to hear that. He was a fine manager and a great guy to work for. Before I could say a word, he said "Oh, wait a minute, I got that backwards. They're moving *you* to Denver."

I said "Oh gee, I don't want to go back to Denver, I like it here." He said "Okay, stay here then. I can put you in the warehouse moving barrels around or something like that, but the airplane is moving to Denver and I thought you might want to go with it." Now, he had my full attention. The company had been putting a western division office in South Denver for the past two months. It would handle everything in our four or five operations in the west, plus exploration, western Canada and the mine we were starting up in Green River, WY, a trona (soda ash) property. I had heard that in the future we might base an aircraft in Denver, but it had sounded like an additional plane not a transfer of this one. "So, you're not going then?" I asked him. "No, I'm staying here. You'll be working for Jim Estep, a V-P and a great guy. You two should get along fine." He was right, we did.

That evening, I called Shan at home. He and Judy had rented a little house in Moab and she was in the midst of getting it all set up the way she wanted it. When he answered, I said "Shan, guess what?" Well, the news that the airplane was going to Denver very shortly was a surprise. I told him that he had the choice of going with me or not. Think it over and let me know right away. He said he would be ready to pack up anytime. Judy wasn't that easy a sell. She was reluctant to leave Utah and her family in Provo, but she came around when she heard the company would pay all the moving expenses and help buy a house if necessary.

We were in Denver in a month, based out of Combs Aircraft, with space and an office in a large hangar, the old Continental Airlines hangar. We had barely gotten unpacked in our houses and at the hangar when the phone started ringing off the hook. There were trips to all our projects with every seat full, usually. On one of the first trips Jim Estep, our boss, took me aside for a cup of coffee and a chat. Things had changed already. Jim had gotten the okay from Dr. Fogarty, the C.E.O, and the man who ran TGS lock, stock, and barrel, for a bigger, faster aircraft that could be used by our division and also for the Sales Division to handle customer trips. Jim said the Aviation Manager was talking about getting one of the new Learjets, but it only carried five passengers and he wanted something with ten to twelve seats. He asked me what I thought would be a good aircraft. I was able to briefly describe most of the airplanes that fit that requirement and said that we could get along with any of the five on my list.

About a month later a call from the Aviation Division Chief Pilot dropped the other shoe. I was to prepare for a change over to a Grumman G-159 Gulfstream, (*Photos #27 & #28*) a fourteen seat aircraft, powered by two Rolls-Royce RDA-529-8X turbo prop engines, 14 feet diameter Dowty-Rotal propellers, 100 foot wingspan, 70 foot fuselage length and 25 foot height. It weighed 36,000 pounds for takeoff, had a speed of 350 mph and would have 12 passenger and 2 crew seats. It held 1,792 gallons of jet fuel, 1,550 gallons in the standard tanks and 242 more with the Grumman Service Change #125. It had a range of 2,700 miles with 45 minutes reserve fuel. We could hardly believe it. Stepping out of a Cessna 421 with a max gross weight of 6,840 pounds, 40 foot wingspan, 34 foot fuselage, 9 foot high, 240 mph, and 4 hour fuel range was David and Goliath in reverse. This aircraft was being acquired from another major corporation and would go into a service center for a complete inspection, new cabin interior, new standard company paint job and updating of the avionics systems. This would take approximately four months and in that time I had a lot of things to do. The first thing was to find hangar space for something this big. Fortunately, Combs was swapping things around and by October would have enough space available in the hangar we were already in.

Our insurance company wanted the pilot flying this size airplane to have an Airline Transport Pilot license (ATP). I had a Commercial, Multi-engine Land, Instrument license and all the necessary time and experience requirements to take the written test for the ATP. I went to a weekend written exam prep course in Denver given by John Darley, a very well-known pilot examiner and teacher in the Denver area. In two days we did a week's work. The following week we took the written exam at the FAA offices. This is an 8 hour time limit exam, in 4 sections. 70 per cent is the minimum passing grade. It isn't unusual to take it more than once. I felt very lucky to pass it the first time with a score of 84. It took me five and one-half hours to complete the exam and two more hours to go back over it twice. Believe me, I was glad that this was a "Once in a lifetime" exam.

I also had to find an aviation rated mechanic to work full time for TGS Aviation. He would be doing all the line maintenance and leading all the scheduled hourly and cycle required inspections and operations on the computer maintenance program, as specified by Grumman. We would use Combs Aviation mechanics under the control of our mechanic. I was going to have Shan control the maintenance operation since he was a licensed A&P mechanic. He would be flying a lot, but would have a reasonable amount of time off this way.

After making the best preparations I could for what was necessary in Denver, Shan and I hopped on an airliner and headed down to see what we were getting into. The airplane was in Ft. Worth, TX, at Meacham Airport. A company named Ward International Aircraft had made a contract with the New York Aviation office to do all the required work and paint on the G-1, as it will be called from now on. There was also a G-1 instructor pilot in the area who would be giving us our ground school and flight training in preparation for our type rating check rides, as required by the FAA, to be legal to fly this model aircraft. The Manager of Aviation was sending one of our Sabreliner pilots to get rated on the G-1 also, so there would be a backup Captain available if needed.

Jim Markham was that pilot and a fine young man he was. He was intelligent, capable, and was moving up in the Aviation Department very rapidly. He was in his middle twenties, but already had a Sabreliner type rating and was flying as a first pilot on it in New York. He was in Ft. Worth and met us when we got there. After getting settled in the motel we went over to see the G-1. It looked pretty bad. It had been torn down into a few hundred pieces, had no interior, the instrument panels were empty, it was up on jacks, no wheels, and a scabby look from paint that had been mostly removed, but not completely.

I walked around it, peeked inside and Jim walked up and said "How do you like it?" I said, "Is it too late to talk about a Learjet?" Yes, it was too late. I went to bed with a sick headache that night and the next morning we went into phase 2. We met our instructor, John Hollingsworth.

John Hollingsworth was about sixty-five years old, shaped like a dumpy barrel, a cigarette chain smoker, gruff and no nonsense guy. I thought to myself is this the best they could do for an instructor for us? I had thought maybe the instructor would look a lot like Chuck Yeager. At least he had an office with some tables, flight manuals and a blackboard. We started ground school. The flight manuals were 6 inches thick, with maybe 300 pages of text and about 60-70 charts. Jim starts whipping right through it, looking at charts and asking John questions. Shan and I are up to our neck in alligators. I had previously studied the Lockheed Lodestar manual which was about a quarter of the size of this one and even that one was hard to get into. Two or three days went by, Hollingsworth had put our feet in the fire the first morning and it wasn't getting any cooler. The fourth or fifth day, during a coffee break, I'm wandering around his office looking at pictures of early Pan American Airway's planes. I came to a certificate in a glass framed holder about 7 x 9 inches. It was headed Dept. Of Commerce, Civil Aeronautics Administration. It then said: AIRLINE AIRPLANE PILOT LICENSE, Issued To: John Hollingsworth, CERTIFICATE # 0007, SIGNED: Orville Wright, Dated: 1929.

It turned out that John Hollingsworth could fly the G-1 better standing between the pilot seats with one hand on the control wheel, the other holding a cigarette, than any of us could with both hands and both feet any way we tried. He was so good and he made it look so easy. The airplane just purred like a Siamese cat when he had it. With me at the controls it snarled like a Tasmanian devil. Jim Markham did pretty well, but Shan and I struggled. We were behind the airplane about 10 seconds and this is not good in the flying business. The Flight Manual charts were eating my lunch and page after page of detailed information and instructions made me hate to even open the damn thing. Shan had a valid excuse as he was just beginning. But, try as hard as I could, I couldn't find one. I had 9,000 hours in different airplanes and I was whipped. I was at the point of saying "Guys, I think I'll take a hike and go back to the small twins."

Hollingsworth caught me alone, sat me down, and said "They tell me you were a Marine, is that right?" I admitted it was. "You know you act more like the guys I used to see on the chain gangs down here. Where do you get off saying you can't do it, when all you *do* do is sit around saying it's too hard? Hell, even the tall skinny kid is catching on because he's not afraid of the airplane. Sure, it's big, but it can be had. Get your head out of your ass and you might see the light. It's just a *BIG* 421!" I should have been boiling mad. I should have got up in a huff and stalked out.

Instead, I looked at John and asked "Is there any chance you were ever a D.I. in the Marine Corps?" He laughed and said "Naw, I was too mean for 'em." He hustled me out to the airplane in the hangar, stuck me in the left seat and we spent 3 hours while he taught me the difference in little twins and big, complicated twins. He actually cut the airplane down to size. The next day on my turn at bat, he held out the training checklist to me with Jim Markham in the copilot seat and said "I'm going to sit in the last chair in the cabin. For Christ's sake, try not to make me airsick."

For the first time that morning, I started doing what the airplane wanted to do, instead of trying to force it into doing what I wanted it to do. It was a long way from perfect, but it was good enough to make me want to get back into the left seat my next session that afternoon.

A week later we flew the G-1 to Tulsa, OK, to the FAA General District Offices to get our ratings in the airplane with the head examiner in the region, General Ball, USAF, Retired. Since I was going for my initial ATP (Airline Transport Pilot), along with a type rating for the

G-1, I got to go first. General Ball welcomed us, took me into his office, examined my logbooks and paperwork and said "Everything looks okay so I'll just ask you a few questions, then we'll go fly."

The first question he asked I will never forget. It was: "Define the concept of transport category." This is the FAR that describes the requirements for operating large, transport aircraft, weighing over 12,500 pounds. After that, they got hard. I got through it and all of us went to the G-1. Again I was lucky enough to get to go first. I got through the check ride pretty well, but one of the holding pattern entries and one approach weren't quite what the General wanted, so he told me to take a break, gave Jim his ride, which went great and Shan did a good S.I.C. (second in command) ride since he couldn't go for a rating yet, but the S.I.C. would satisfy the Insurance company for now.

Ball put me back in the left seat; I did the holding pattern entry in good shape and then when he said we'll do one more approach and call it quits, I asked him to let me do the outer locator compass (ADF) approach to the ILS runway. This was the most difficult of all the approaches to do right since it is non-precision, but it's the type of approach I cut my teeth on in instrument training and I was good at it. He said okay. I shot the approach to minimums under the hood, nailed it to breakout and made an 8 out of 10 landing. General Ball smiled, slapped me on the back, signed off my paperwork and handed it back to me and said "Good luck, Captain Sparks." We went back to Meacham field and I got stuck for the dinner since I was the ATP newbie. John Hollingsworth and his wife went with us. He got up and said "Well, you guys did better than the bunch I had from New Guinea awhile back. Those bones through the nose and the feathers in the hair, I could take that, but those little heads hanging around their necks—that was a bit much." This was high praise indeed.

John Hollingsworth probably saved my career, or at the least with TGS. He was an early pilot for Juan

Tripp, who founded the airline running to South America which eventually became Pan American World Airways. John, along with many of the early jungle pilots in South America, pioneered the routes through the Amazon delta and forest which became known as the "off track navigation system" and made it relatively safe to travel across the featureless jungle. All of us in modern aviation owe these early trailblazers a debt we cannot repay. We can tell the young pilots about them and that it meant a lot when that was all there was, a bunch of guys with a desire to do things that had never been done before. Truly, there were giants in those days.

Chapter 8 — The Crash,
And Then the Crash

We flew the G-1 to Westchester County Airport (HPN), White Plains, NY, (*Photo #29*) with Jim and me swapping the left seat, while Shan held down the copilot side. We arrived and showed off the new bird to all the staff there and got thumbs up from everybody. We had a few items the mechanics had to work on, but that's what a shakedown flight is for. Shan got to ride the Sabreliner to Toronto and back that evening when it took some Canadian office staff back home and dropped them off. That was his first ride in a jet. He said it seemed a mite small after being in the G-1 for the last week. After two days we said farewell, you Yankee flatlanders, we got to get back to the west and the high country.

The next three years flying out of Denver were probably the most enjoyable in my entire career. I'm not sure I can adequately express it in words, but here goes. I had been given a wonderful aircraft, the Grumman Gulfstream. I had a fine young copilot rapidly developing into a captain. I had been given the go ahead to hire a full time qualified mechanic to support this operation and for a boss, one of the top people in TGS. Vice-President Jim Estep (*Photo #24*) was the personification of a totally alert, quick thinking, highly skilled and trained engineer. He was employee oriented, reasonable, and gracious with all the people he dealt with, company or customers. He was the poster boy for the boss a corporate pilot wanted to work for. Don't get me wrong, he wasn't soft. You did *not* want to equivocate or double-talk to him. He understood inadvertent mistakes, but there was zero tolerance for attempting to escape your responsibilities or escape them by distorting the actual facts. I never heard of anyone trying to do this with him more than once.

Having been told this by my boss in Moab as I was leaving for Denver, I never tried to find out if were true. There were times when I hated to walk into his office and deliver news that was not good, but I was never afraid to do it. It was a part of my responsibilities, but for instance, the day I had to tell him that by accident our mechanic had hooked up the new $3,800 heated pilot side windshield wrong, the replacement for the one that had cracked in flight a few days before. It then cracked when power was applied during the functional test and it would have to be replaced. He definitely was not amused.

And neither was the Manager of the Aviation department in New York. When I told him the story, he said "Fire that *SOB!*" I told him no, I wasn't going to fire him. I now have the most cautious, intensive maintenance manual reading, double checking mechanic on the airport. And so he stayed, doing a fine job, right up to the day that the entire company was bought by foreign interests (France and Canada), and the Aviation Department disappeared in a puff of smoke or in one week, whichever you prefer. But this was still far into the future.

We had been back in Denver a month and flying steadily. I talked to the aviation department head in New York, Lefty Gregory, and suggested that we should put on a third crewmember, who could be Captain rated rapidly, to back me up. Shan was doing fine, but it might be a year before he had the ATP requirements fulfilled and the only back up was Jim Markham. Jim was based in New York flying the Sabreliner and was preparing to go to school at Flight Safety to start training on the new four engine jet we had purchased, the Lockheed L-1329

Jetstar. This meant it was not reasonable to assume he could come to Denver and back me up in case of injury or other factors that meant I would be out of action for some time period. Also, there had been mention of a possibility of stationing one of the three 421's in Denver, since one was being replaced with a Cessna Citation. This would certainly require additional flying crewmember support.

The 421 was approved for Denver to take small passenger loads, shorter trips and replace the G-1 when it was in maintenance. Also, if two important trips were needed at the same time. I had a very viable candidate to interview. I told New York that and they told me to proceed.

There were lots of pilots looking for jobs in Denver in 1973. I had to have a pilot who could be checked out on the G-1 in short order as a command pilot and who could fly the 421 single pilot also. This eliminated a lot of potentially good pilots who were in the position I had been in seventeen years before. As badly as I felt about it, I had to exclude every one of them that did not have the required background and experience to fill this slot— not only for me, but for the Company and our insurance carrier qualifications. As luck would have it, I had one who qualified in mind.

I mentioned that I went to ground school in Denver to prepare for my ATP written exam. This was one weekend with two 10 hour days, run by a friend of mine and a super training pilot, John Darley, who worked as an instructor at United Airlines ground training, and was known as a superb ATP written exam instructor. We knuckled down and worked, I kid you not. This coming written exam was the top and the bottom of the iceberg, so to speak. I did pass it. Once more John Darley had made a silk purse out of a sow's ear.

In this class I had met a young Naval Aviator, who had been flying the Lockheed P-3 Orion 4 engine turboprop subhunter out of Rota, Spain, before he got out of the Navy. He also was carrier qualified on the Grumman S2F, the "Stoof." His name was Lynne Hobson and he was now out of the Navy and flying a light twin for a Denver Helicopter operator. Coincidently, he lived only two blocks from me in South Denver. He had asked about job opportunities with TG, and once the word came down to find another pilot, I had him fill out an application for employment. I also interviewed three other pilots, but Lynne was the only one who could be fast tracked into the left seat. The only problem was that in military flying you learned different navigation and approach procedures (Vortac and ILS for civil operations, Tacan and Radar for the military) so Lynne was still getting used to this changeover.

I hired Lynne as I felt he was our best choice and he fit right in with Shan and me. I started both of them off training for the left seat on the G-1 and alternating flying the 421. When they had the experience on the G-1 they needed to be rated, we sent them off to Flight Safety, one at a time, and they both did very well. I had applied for a PIC (Pilot in Command) Designated Pilot Examiner rating from the FAA, had passed the check ride on 11/24/1975, and received my designation. (*Photo #30*) Now I could give our G-1 pilots their 2 year required proficiency check ride and other G-1 pilots as well, as required by FAR 61.58. Both Shan and Lynn became rated in the G-1 and they did a great job for our flight department.

Lynne Hobson had an excellent background with a diploma from the University of Colorado. He enrolled in the AVROC (Aviation Reserve Officers Corps) in college, and then Naval Flight School, patrol duties in the Mediterranean, aircraft carrier duty, and now was flying for a major international mining company. He would soon do something that earned him his pay from TG for the rest of his life, and it earned him a place in my heart forever.

In the early spring of 1976, the New York office gave the Denver flight operation a high profile trip to accomplish. We were to pick up two of our TGS Directors, who were Canadian, and their families in Aspen and return them to Montreal. There would be four adults and five children and the usual amount of vacation luggage. The G-1 had just returned from a major inspection in Dallas a few weeks before this and had been flying almost daily. Lynn and I were on the G-1 for this duty period with Shan flying the 421. We picked up the catering, fueled up so that we wouldn't need to add fuel at Aspen and left in late morning. It was a nice day for this time of year in the Rockies. It was Sunday, the ski season was winding down, so there shouldn't be any difficulty going right in, getting the passengers and flying on to Montreal. I was flying the leg to Aspen. Lynne would take us to Montreal and then it would be my turn back to Denver.

There was some low level turbulence climbing westbound out of Denver, but once we crossed the continental divide at FL (flight level) 180 (18,000 feet), it smoothed out. Visibility was 60 miles, and we were the only flight inbound for Aspen. We started letting down about 40 miles from the airport and as we descended below 12,000 feet, it got pretty bumpy. I slowed down about 30 knots as I turned south toward the Aspen airport which was 7,815 feet above sea level. I stayed a little higher than normal, making a steeper approach and slower to keep the turbulence light. We dropped the landing gear, put the flaps down to approach and reduced the power back to about one-third of normal. The tower had cleared us to land and Lynne was finishing up the landing checklist. When we were a mile out from the fence, still about 400 feet high, nose pitched down about 10 degrees, I started putting nose up trim in since I was in the high end of the groove, backed the power off again to reduce speed, took my hand off the power levers to roll more nose up trim in, since the nose hadn't come up any. It still didn't come up. I pulled back on the control wheel to bring the nose up quickly. No response. It wouldn't move.

I couldn't believe it. I'm now looking straight at a large field of very big rock boulders just outside of the airport fence. Some of the rocks were the size of Volkswagens. This is where we are going to touch down at 120 mph. I had both hands on the wheel, pulling as hard as I could. The control is locked, no movement at all. *We have about 10 seconds left to live.* I shouted and I mean *Shouted,* "*Full power!*" and in ½ second, Lynne had slammed the power levers to the forward stops. (*Photo #31*) The Rolls-Royce Dart engines screamed with acceleration, going to 17,000 rpm, 2,000 rpm over red line and then smoothly backing off to 15,000, normal max power. This additional thrust increased our speed and lifted the nose 2 degrees, 3 degrees, finally 4 degrees, and now we could make the runway. We did, touching down only 200 feet past the threshold at about 20 knots faster than our normal landing speed.

I taxied in and parked. Each of us tried the elevator controls from each side. The yoke would go full forward to the stop (down elevator), but when we moved it back (up elevator), at about 2/3 of its normal travel range, it stopped. *Completely.* We got out and ran around to look at the tail. The elevator was hanging down just as normal as it could be. We got the line personnel to bring us a tall ladder. I climbed up on it and pushed the elevator upwards. At about one-third of its up travel range, it hit something inside the tail and stopped. I could feel it hitting. We had a little more than an hour before the passengers were due. It was Sunday; no mechanics were available on short notice. We got our airplane tool box, removed all the screws holding the tail cone on and took the tail cone off with two ramp personnel helping us. This tail cone was big, heavy, and awkward. When we slid it back and started to pivot it downward, we could see that the Doppler radar antenna was gone and not in its mounts just below the bottom of the rudder. We carefully put the tail cone down on the ground and there was the missing antenna lying inside it.

To make a long story shorter, when the work was done on the aircraft in Dallas, this antenna was removed and later replaced. It was put back in its circular mount below the rudder and the mount clamp ring that holds it in place was attached with a bolt and nut. This nut was supposed to be secured with a piece of stainless steel safety wire making it incapable of backing off, thus loosening the clamp ring and releasing the antenna. The wire had not been replaced. The clamp released the antenna after the vibrations in the tail cone area caused the nut to back off and the antenna, which looks like a medium size 18 inch flower pot, made of a thick ceramic material, dropped off into the tail cone in flight. So when we started the steep descent into Aspen, it slid forward in the tail cone, up against the bulkhead and stopped in such a way that the "up" elevator control horn mechanism was blocked and could not continue past a certain point, giving us only partial up elevator movement. A 4 inch piece of wire nearly destroyed a two million dollar aircraft and killed the crew.

But fortunately, there was no actual damage done. I reassembled everything in proper order, got a piece of safety wire from our tool box, made certain that the safety wire was now done properly, put in 150 gallons of Jet-A fuel to thank the aviation service for their help, and tipped both the line men $20 each. Without their assistance we would not have been able to affect the repairs, get cleaned up and be standing by when the passengers showed up right on time. We stowed the luggage, loaded them on board, off we went, and 4 hours later landed at Montreal. "Great trip!" they all said, shaking our hands. "Glad we could do it for you." we said.

It wasn't our turn. Lynne's Navy training kept us alive. If he had hesitated or questioned that full power command, it would have been too late. All over. Navy training kicked in, instant reaction. *GO NAVY!*

The G-1 had worked out so well in Denver for the western division that the decision was made to acquire a second one, to be used out of New York operations. The Chrysler Corp. Flight department had a G-1 that was being replaced by a G-2, the pure jet powered replacement for the G-1. The G-2 had the same basic fuselage and seating, but was about 150 mph faster. We bought this Chrysler G-1 aircraft, had it re-painted and I was moved to New York to fly it in May 1976. Jim Markham called and told me to get everything in order in my operation, because I was coming to HPN and Shan would take over the management of the DEN operation. Lynne and Jim Lard would remain in Denver, but I would be re-located to White Plains (HPN) to fly the Chrysler G-1 we were buying. And also I would be phased in to the Jetstar operation as soon as possible. I told him I would just as soon stay in Denver.

He said "Okay, but next month your paycheck is coming to the hangar at HPN. If you want it, you'd better be here." He was a hard bargainer. We sold our home in Denver, found a nice place in Connecticut in a little town called Ridgefield just across the New York State line. It was 23 miles to HPN, but we didn't want to be near the NYC metro area if we could help it.

We lived there six and one-half years and it was enjoyable. New England's beautiful woods, the history, the small town setting and the people were a new and happy experience for us. Ellie and her new friends had many excursions to the "city" to shop and enjoy the Broadway plays. I didn't mind flying out of White Plains, but it wasn't Colorado or Utah. It's almost impossible to get the west out of your system.

Just before this happened, we had the damnedest trip we ever made in the Denver G-1. We were asked if we could fly into the airport in Jasper National Park, Alberta, Canada, with two loads of our top people for a convention that was to be held there in April. I said I would get some information on the airport and let them know.

I got hold of the RCMP (Royal Canadian Mounted Police) in Edmonton, Alberta. They said that the Jasper airport was used by their Twin-Otter aircraft and had been used by DC-3 aircraft in the past. It was 6,000 feet above sea level, had a grass runway, 75 feet wide by 3,200 feet in length. The approach had to be made across a river canyon, onto the top of a flat mesa, through a stand of trees 75 feet high that had a 200 foot horizontal cut in them to get onto the runway. You landed to the south and made the take-off to the north. I looked up a map and saw that there were mountains in every quadrant, from 9,000 to 10,000 feet high. I looked at the Flight Manual charts, then called New York and told them if the weather was good, we could do it, but only this one particular way.

Since all our people were going to be at the company headquarters in Calgary for a day or two before going to Jasper, we would be bringing some of them in from Denver. The other division aircraft would be bringing in their loads also. For the trip to Jasper, we would leave with ten passengers; the trip would take 20 minutes. We would drop them off, come back to Calgary, pick up the second load and return to Jasper. We would be carrying only 3 hours fuel to keep the aircraft light enough to do this. The aircraft would stay in Jasper until the convention was over and then return the passengers to Calgary for departures to the U.S. But, if the weather was not suitable, there would have to be backup ground transportation available and allow 4 to 5 hours minimum for the trip either way.

Well, it's sure great when a plan comes together. We took off with the first trip, flew northwest up the east flank of the Canadian Rocky Mountains and turned west into the Athabasca River Canyon at Hinton. I flew under a high deck of clouds, found the airport, circled it, checked it out, set up for the landing, came down and through the 200 foot slot, plenty of room, eased it onto the grass and stopped with eight or nine hundred feet of runway left. The vans from the lodges were there to pick up the passengers. We told them we'd be back in an hour with the other load. We fired up, took off, pulled up to 300 feet, rolled east through the canyon, back to Calgary and loaded the other trip up. Slightly more than an hour later we were touching down again on the grass, but when we pulled off into the parking area, half the town of Jasper was there to greet us. This was the biggest airplane that had ever come in there and everyone wanted to stand by it and get their picture taken.

Going back came off without a hitch. Both trips got back to Calgary, thanked us and said it was a real experience to fly with us. The home office sent us a nice letter of thanks. Our boss, Jim Estep, said Dr. Fogarty, the top man in TGS, really got a lot of mileage out of hoorawing the officials of the other companies at the conference, saying "You had to drive up? Really? Too bad we didn't have room for you on our airplane; maybe next time." All these top corporate guys love to play "one-up-man-ship" whenever they can. I hear lots of them do it on the golf course every weekend.

Sometimes this gets out of bounds, though (a little golf humor, there). In the early fall of 1976, TGS had scheduled a Directors Meeting, along with a series of company division future planning meetings. These were booked to be at the Doral Country Club in Miami, FL. All our division airplanes were making multiple trips to get everybody there for this week of meetings (and golf). I was flying the New York G-1 and had made several trips up and down the east coast when I shut it down at Miami International Airport late in the day. When the copilot and I got to the Doral there was a note from J. M. Gregory, Manager of the Aviation Department, saying that he and I were going to fly a load of Directors and company V-P's to the golf course at Key Largo tomorrow morning at 9:00 AM in the G-1. I hurriedly looked up the airport there and found out it was a private airport owned by the Key Largo Golf Club. It was laid out in the center of the golf course from north to south, with aircraft parking on a ramp in front of the clubhouse.

I called Lefty's room and told him I thought it was going to require permission to use this airport. He said I was right and that our Chairman, Dr. Fogarty, had already arranged it. The next morning we went to the Miami Airport, got the airplane ready for the 15 minute flight to Key Largo and stood at attention as the limos drove up. Lefty has flown on the G-1s a few times, but isn't rated as a crew member. He usually flies the Jetstar and he can do a simple copilot gig like this, so I didn't say anything.

After all, he was the boss. I had seen that the runway on Key Largo was 75 feet wide, 3,700 feet long and was 12 feet above sea level. This was enough, but it meant I would have to use quite a bit of "ground fine" (a type of propeller reversing for stopping) and this would be pretty loud at close quarters. We loaded the golf bags and ten passengers. We were in the air within ten minutes and once out of the airport traffic area, I had Lefty call Key Largo unicom. They said we had permission to land; there was no other traffic and we could land straight in. I could see what had to be the runway running through the golf course. I set up for the landing and we made a 3 mile straight in. I had slowed to about 110 indicated airspeed, flaps and gear down and at about a half mile out, I could see palm trees on both sides of the runway, about 75 to 100 feet from the edge of the runway. That was enough, but they were high, maybe 60 feet. I saw people in golf carts on paths not 50 feet away from the runway. They were stopping to look and see what was making all this whining noise.

I know we looked big with the sun reflecting off our left side. I held it off about 6 feet above the ground just coming up on the end of the runway. It must have been an awesome sight to those golfers only 50 or 60 feet away, sitting there watching. Then I touched down, brought the power back, and pulled the props into full ground fine. They started screaming like banshees and pushing the air forward. I was holding the airplane right in the center of the runway with the nose wheel steering and putting in only about two-thirds braking action so that I didn't cut up the asphalt runway. Golfers are running away in front of us with their hands over their ears. Believe me it was really loud for these folks. We slowed down and I came out of ground fine. I carefully taxied into the parking area, turning the airplane around on the small ramp, enough so I could get back out. I cut the engines, Lefty let the airstair door down and we came down to the ramp with about five guys waiting for us, none of them looking happy.

I'm not going to get into this conversation since there might be some genteel ladies reading this at some time. They had expected a small light twin. Just let me say they gave us enough time to unload the passengers, the golf bags and pay a landing charge which seemed a little high, but this one time I could stand with my arms folded and let the boss do the haggling. We were told to never darken their golf course again and we could leave anytime we wanted to, as long as it was in the next 5 minutes. We left, eased over to Miami, landed and got a limousine service to handle the golf party's return to the Doral. During our stay some of our pilots played golf. I didn't do a thing for two days but lie by the pool drinking lemonade, reading a murder mystery and watching the scantily clad mermaids playing tag in the pool.

Providing transportation for the company directors to board meetings and other important functions was a standard duty for the flight department. It was a great experience for me, but some of the other flight group dreaded it. A screw-up on a normal flight could be handled relatively easily, but dump a cup of hot coffee into a director's lap and you never know how far up the food chain this is going to go. As you might expect, the planning and preparation for these trips was a little more meticulous than for a bunch of engineers in hard hats—but not always. One meeting of the board was to be held in Florida one winter—for some reason we never had them in Canada in the middle of winter—and after bringing in a group to Palm Beach, we took care of the aircraft. We then went to our assigned motel, checked in about noon, had lunch, and the phone rang— new orders. We were to proceed to Richmond, VA, and pick up Director George Bush and his wife, Barbara, and return them to Palm Beach. The G-1 was the only aircraft available at the moment and we took off for Richmond. We were supposed to meet the passengers at 2:30 PM and at 2:00 PM we were in position, waiting. At 3:30 PM, we were in position and waiting. At 4:30 PM, I called the Manager of Aviation at the motel in Florida and told him they were a no show, no message, now what? He called me back in 15 minutes, and it seems he had looked at his notes wrong. We were supposed to be there at 2:30 PM *tomorrow afternoon*. So, get rooms, stay there and at 2:30 PM tomorrow, bring 'em down. Simple.

What was not simple was the matter of having our luggage in a motel room 400 miles south of us. Summer weather on the east coast really uses clothes up in a hurry. We had no shaving gear, deodorant, mouthwash, etc. We got the aircraft bedded down, rented a car, got a motel, went shopping, had a good dinner and at 2:30 PM the following afternoon, in our brand new wardrobes, we welcomed George and Barbara Bush. We loaded up and got them down to Florida without putting a ripple on Barbara's hot tea. They were really easy to handle and enjoyable to have aboard. I had never met them before, so I felt obligated to tell Mr. Bush—he was a Naval Aviator in WW II—that I was a former Marine and had served aboard the aircraft carrier USS Philippine Sea as a Seagoing Marine. He sat on the jump seat for the takeoff and landing and this was his pattern for the later trips that I had him as a passenger.

In 1979, on the way to a director's meeting in New York in the Jetstar, Mr. Bush told us that he might be giving up his seat on the TGS Board and wouldn't be riding with us again if he did. I asked him why and he said that the RNC was pressing him for a decision on whether to run for president or not. He said this had to be decided shortly, and if he decided yes, then he would have to give up all his business connections. He said he would miss riding with us and that all our pilots and aircraft had been a pleasure for an old warhorse to be around. I assured him that if he did run, he had a lot of votes coming out of the flying business. After all, he was one of us. And the rest is history.

Probably the best liked of all our directors was the ex-governor of Texas, Allan Shivers. Governor Shivers lived in Austin. He had a G-1 of his own and a couple of dandy Texas pilots to fly it for him. When he was Governor in the '50s he looked like a movie star, was handsome, had a great head of hair, and the best political connections in Texas. I flew him and his great looking wife many, many times. Even in his seventies, he was one on the best looking guys we flew, although the hair had turned from midnight black to salt-and-pepper gray.

The Canadian directors were a different breed of cat. Most of the ones I transported from Ottawa or Montreal were basically of French origin. They were polite but aloof and a little removed from the everyday pattern most of us were accustomed to. A few of them broke out of the mold, though. They were down to earth and had a good time on the trips. However, we treated all of them with the proper deference. This paid off in the long run. When the French and Canadian governments bought out TGI and shredded it, the pilots were not the first ones thrown into the tumbrel carts and rushed off to "La Belle Guillotine." It took them over a year to get to us.

The G-1 sure wasn't a perfect airplane, but it was my favorite for handling about anything that came up. It was comfortable, roomy, with good amenities and reasonably economical to operate, but it had its dark side. John Hollingsworth, the instructor who checked me out in this bird, told me that all G-1 pilots have at least one bad landing inside them and it will come out eventually. Mine came out after six months of flying ours out of Denver and getting very comfortable in handling it. After an easy trip home one late summer afternoon, with eight or nine passengers aboard, I was in the groove for the landing, about 10 feet high flaring out. Without any warning, the damn thing reared up, quit flying, fell outa the sky, bounced 15 feet high the first bounce and less each time on the next three or four. After I finally got it under control and into the parking space in front of Combs Aircraft, Jim Estep, our boss, came up to the front to deplane. He laughed, shook his head a few times and said "Okay, okay, you guys can have the weekend off." He pretended to limp down the stairs, and yelled back "Next time, all you have to do is ask." I made it a point to really nail down the landings from then on and I never did ask for the weekend off.

It was March 23, 1976, and yesterday I had my forty-third birthday. We had just received word that a trip was planned for tomorrow to Chicago to remain overnight, then go on to New York the following evening and back to Denver after the passengers were finished at the home office. Shan and I had the G-1 duty this week. We loaded up six passengers on the 24th and headed east. After spending the night at a hotel close to Midway Airport, we had breakfast, had the hotel drop us at Butler Aviation at Midway and started preparing the plane for the afternoon trip on to New York. I saw a Jetstar sitting on the ramp down from the G-1, so I strolled down to see whose it was. I didn't recognize it or its N number, N1EM. One of the ramp attendants told me it was the "Black Muslim" aircraft based there, but it had just been sold and was leaving for the west coast sometime after lunch.

Shan and I finished our prep, and I found out that EM on the Jetstar stood for Elisha Muhammad, the head of the Black Muslim organization. This airplane had the same make of tires that we had had on our Jetstar when we blew two of them on takeoff at Denver a few months before, did $60,000 damage to the aircraft, and nearly ran off the runway which would have most likely destroyed the aircraft. I also noted that it had the -6 engines on it, so it was original. Our Jetstar had been updated to the −8 engines, which gave us more thrust and really helped shorten our takeoff distances. The two pilots for the Jetstar arrived just after lunch, and to my surprise, I knew them both. It was George Eremea and Jim Fugget. I knew George from when he was the instructor pilot on our Sabreliner after we bought it. Jim Fugget was a pilot from Denver who had worked for several corporations there as a company pilot.

I walked over and we chatted for a few minutes. They were taking the aircraft back to San Jose, CA, to get it ready to be sold by the sales company they worked for. I told George about the tires and that maybe they should check the pressure in them. Low tire pressure, below the normal 210 psi, down to 190 psi, is what blew ours out. George said the airplane had just come out of an inspection and was all checked out. The aircraft had been completely filled with fuel; all the spare parts that went with it had been loaded aboard. As it came close to the time to depart, two passengers, a man and a woman, and their luggage arrived. When everything was aboard, the engines were started and the airplane taxied down to runway13R. This was a relatively short runway for a Jetstar and especially since the temperature was up in the middle 60's. With seven of us corporate pilots standing under the wing of my G-1, out of the sun, watching, we knew this was going to be a very tight takeoff. I looked at my watch; it was 2:30 PM—this was just an old habit—as they started rolling. The acceleration was very slow and we thought they would abort at mid-field, but they didn't. By the time they did try to abort, it was too late. The official crash report read "The nose gear came up and settled back twice during takeoff. The takeoff on runway 13R was aborted but the aircraft overran at a speed of 60 to 80 knots. It crossed a perimeter road, struck a concrete slab and went through a fence and an ILS antenna array. Probable cause: Pilot In Command: delayed action in aborting takeoff; inadequate preflight preparation and/ or planning; lack of familiarity with aircraft." The aircraft then blew up like a napalm strike in Vietnam. It was 2:31 PM. No one survived.

In this business 1 minute can be a lifetime. I have had too many friends leave on their final flight plan, some self-induced as was this one, others merely drawing the short straw when the tests of fate are handed out. Tommy Munroe and Gene Shocker, pilots for Midwest Oil Co. out of Denver, were flying a beautiful Sabreliner 40, went to Midland, TX and never came back. They were as good a team of pilots as you would find anywhere. After letting their passengers off in Midland, they took off to return to Denver and on the climb out rolled over and dove 9,000 feet to crash into the ground. The reason for this crash is believed to have been a bolt on an aileron push rod end coming loose and locking the aileron into a deployed position, making the aircraft uncontrollable. I had said Adios to them as they were pulling the airplane out of the hangar that morning at Combs Aircraft—just another day at the office. See you tomorrow—or maybe never.

There was only one trip that the G-1 actually bit me and made me prove that I knew what I was doing when sitting in the front left seat in this airplane. It was the newer one, the Chrysler airplane we had put in New York. I had a trip to Timmins, Ontario, to pick up twelve of our Canadian miners and transport them to David', Panama. This was the third trip like this that I had made in the last seven months. TG was working with the Panamanian government to possibly develop a metals mine in northern Panama. I picked up the passengers in Timmins. We flew to Miami and spent the night. The next morning we departed on the trip to David' with our route taking us through the Girron Corridor across Cuba, east of Havana, then to the Cayman Islands. After crossing the Caymans we had a 750 mile leg over open water to Panama. It was 250 miles to Montego Bay, Jamaica. It was 350 miles to the coast of Honduras. I had lain out my "escape routes" when the first trip across here was scheduled.

About 15 minutes after we passed over Georgetown, Cayman, an alarm went off in the cockpit, alerting us to a problem and directing us to the master warning panel to see what it was. And what it was this time was not funny. The G-1 had only one big design flaw, but it could be big trouble. The designers had put only one main hydraulic pump in the system, driven off the right engine by a shaft and gearbox arrangement. The Rolls-Royce Dart engine was also unique in that it had all the burner cans mounted on the exterior of the engine core. What could happen if the shaft gearing became inoperative was that the shaft could twist out of its containment bearings on the top of the engine core, start whipping around and destroy one or more of the burner cans, letting 1,600 degree flames loose in the engine compartment. This could shortly catch the entire engine compartment on fire and it was sitting right on top of the wing, which was the main fuel tank for that engine.

The alarm readout was showing HYD PRES. I glanced at the hydraulic pressure gauge, and it was showing zero, no pressure. We looked out the right cockpit window. Skydrol hydraulic fluid was running, streaming out of the joints in the cowling. There was no doubt we had a major hydraulic emergency. I had Billy Warren, my copilot, check the amount of fluid we had left to use with the electric hydraulic pump for the landing sequence. He returned from the closet that had the hydraulic accumulator in it and said "Zero." All the fluid was gone. I had started a 180 degree turn as soon as the alarm confirmed that we had a major problem.

Georgetown International Airport was about 75 miles behind us, the closest possible landing field in any direction. I took 30 seconds to review our situation, our options and the resultants of any of our actions. One of the boss miners came up front to find out what was going on. I bluntly told him we had a problem and we're going back to Cayman Island, so keep your troops in their seats with their seat belts on, keep them calm and tell them my job is to prevent making a bunch of rich widows out of their wives. He said I hope you mean that and I told him "We'll have a drink in Georgetown tonight, get out of my cockpit, I got work to do, it's "Fire in the hole." He knew what that meant. He went back and we didn't hear a peep out of anybody from then on.

I told Billy to get the checklist, shut down the right engine and feather it. His eyes got kind of big and I said "Now, Billy." He ran the checklist, shut down the engine, took unnecessary electrical items off line and cleaned up the hydraulic emergency checklist also. I was on the radio, telling oceanic control of our emergency condition and that we were returning to Georgetown for an emergency landing. They advised Georgetown and let us know Georgetown was waiting for our call when in range and would have the emergency equipment standing by. We're descending through 10,000 feet, making 160 mph and still about 50 miles to Georgetown. I looked at the Georgetown airport chart. The runway was 5,400 feet long, 120 feet wide, with tall Palm trees on the west end, about 400 feet short of the runway. Just past the east end of the runway there is a cliff with a drop of 230 feet into the ocean.

As we got into radio range of Georgetown, we found out the wind was from the east at 10 mph, so we would be landing to the east, toward the ocean, across the 70 foot palm trees 400 feet from the end of the runway. I wasn't so concerned about that. My concern was to get things done at the right time and not ahead of time, or even worse, late.

First, with no hydraulic system, the gear would have to be blown down with the emergency air bottles. Once extended, it could not be retracted, and the gear doors would remain open, giving more drag and reducing our speed.

Second, we would have no flaps, since our fluid was gone, so the emergency hydraulic electric pump was of no use. This also meant the approach and touchdown speed would be about 15 mph faster than normal.

Third, we had no ground fine reversing until we slowed to 70 mph on the runway, since we had one engine feathered. This was a flight manual restriction.

Fourth, we had no normal braking; only air powered braking with the emergency air system bottle. This system progressively braked all four main gear brakes together equally, easily or hard, depending on how far out you pulled the T-handle. This bottle would give us four and possibly five brake applications so we had to use them skillfully.

Fifth, we had no anti-skid brake protection, so a hard application of the brakes could lock up the brakes, blow all 4 tires, and we would then have no way to brake the aircraft to a stop.

Sixth, we had no nose wheel steering, no differential braking to steer with and no differential engine power to steer with, so on roll out after touch down steering with the rudder was our only method and as the speed on the runway decreased so would the rudder effectiveness to steer the aircraft.

Seventh, when we did slow to 70 mph on the runway, if we pulled the operating engine into ground fine and applied power to spool it up for more reversing action, it would likely pull us off the runway. We had no way to counteract all this aerodynamic braking effect on the left side. We would put it into ground fine and let it idle, steering with the rudder, slowing with a slow, steady application of air brakes and at 20 mph, come out of ground fine and use full braking with air. The key to all this was: keep the air speed as low as safely possible, don't land long, get it on and decelerate deliberately—and don't clip those damn palm trees on approach!

Too fast? Too long? Too late? Too Bad! Well, wouldn't you know—it worked just as planned. We touched down 600 feet down the runway, used the techniques I outlined and came to a complete stop with nearly 1,000 feet of runway left. They had a tug and tow bar available and we were towed in to the main parking area. As we got out of the aircraft I learned there was an airliner coming through in a few hours that could take the passengers back to Miami, and there were seats available for them. That solved that problem. I had the flight service operator's mechanic open the cowling. We found the main hydraulic return line to the pump had split and had lost all the fluid. I called the White Plains hangar, gave them a brief report and they said to keep them informed. I called Grumman Aircraft in Savannah, GA, told them what happened and that I needed the parts and a technician down here ASAP—they said "That can't happen, it's designed not to happen."

It took two days to get them there on the airlines. I was able to rent equipment and go scuba diving the first day; walked all over Georgetown the second day and then I met the flight that afternoon with the tech and the parts. He worked into the night and said "That's not supposed to happen." We were running by noon the following day. He was still saying this is not supposed to happen as he was changing the parts. I gave him a ride back to Miami where we cleared customs. I told him to hop an airliner back to Savannah. He said "You're not going to drop me off?" And I said "That's not supposed to happen."

About this time the company bought an almost new Cessna CE-500 Citation (*Photo #36*) to replace the 421 in Texas. The little jet was set up for two pilots and five passengers, and at 400 mph, it could cut the time of trips in the 421 in about half. The Aviation Division decided that a number of our pilots would get rated in the 500. This way pilots could be shuffled around to cover nearly all our equipment for vacations, annual recurrency training, illness, etc. I was told to report to the American Airlines Citation School at the Greater Southwest Regional Airport, between Dallas and Ft. Worth. This airport is now gone, a victim of DFW, Six Flags Over Texas, and several other entertainment venues that now sit on that site. I was one of five TGS pilots to get the Citation rating there. It was like being on vacation compared to the schools on the G-1 and the Jetstar. It really went fast and easy for the three of us who were flying these bigger birds, but the other two pilots had to work at it, since this was their first turbine powered plane. We all sailed through it in a week and over the next two years I flew it 275 hours before I left Texasgulf Sulphur (TGS), which had been renamed Texasgulf, Inc. (TGI) for some Wall Street reason.

In late 1978, a decision was made to sell the Denver G-1 and handle the flight needs of that division by other means. As a result of this, Shan Sorenson was re-located to New York in early 1979. Lynne Hobson and Jim Lard were re-located to Raleigh and the western aviation division was closed.

Shan and his family settled in South Connecticut. He flew the G-1 and began preparing to move to the Jetstar in the near future. It looked like a bright future for all of us with the G-III and Challenger coming on line in a few months. But things have a way of setting their own agenda. We had a lot of surprises coming in our futures, none of which we had even suspected, and all of them life changing.

In late 1979, the company decided to sell the G-1 based in New York, since we were getting our two Lockheed Jetstars (*Photo #33*) upgraded with turbo fan engine retrofit packages from AiResearch Aviation in Los Angeles. We were also ordering a Grumman Gulfstream III jet for delivery in 1980, and a Bombardier Challenger 600 to be delivered a little later than the Grumman. This meant that the Jetstars would be phased out as these two new airplanes took their place. I had been made a captain on the Jetstars in 1978, (*Photo #32*) and had divided my time between all our aircraft since that time. Our first fan jet Jetstar (*Photo #34*) was completed and put back in service and all of us had to learn how to handle this airplane. There were numerous differences in almost all the operational procedures. We had a mach trim coupler added, plus now a stick pusher and a stick puller, and the airspeed max limits became very critical. We had AOA (angle of attack) indicators, true airspeed (temperature corrected), rudder bias and several other systems and instruments we hadn't had before. One of the biggest improvements was in having the single point fueling system. Now we could quick turn the refueling in less than half the time it took with over-the-wing fueling. We added about 100 more gallons of fuel with the dropped down slipper tanks and gained a little over 2,000 pounds of allowable maximum gross weight, but had increased the empty weight with the new engines and mods. Still, we picked up about 500 pounds of useful load.

But, the big item was in the reduction of fuel burn with the Garrett AiResearch TFE-731-3 by-pass fan-jet engines. They reduced our overall flight fuel burn by 35 per cent. That is a lot. We could now leave Westchester Airport in White Plains, NY, and fly direct to London with adequate fuel reserves. I flew several trips from Westchester to Los Angeles and then back home nonstop. (*Photo #35*) On returning on one of them I had 180 mph tail winds all the way at 39,000 feet, landing 1 hour and 20 minutes early on our flight plan. This got me a chewing out from our C.E.O. because he had to sit and wait an hour for the limo to pick him up and take him home. Any time we were going to be early from then on, I made darn sure I let the passengers know so they could bump up their transportation by calling ahead on our Sky phone.

The second Jetstar was getting close to being finished in Los Angeles and AiResearch wanted a company crew to do the test flights. The office selected me and Rich Williams, one of our young copilots to do this flying, so we packed our bags for two weeks in sunny southern California. We flew American Airlines out of La Guardia and the company put us in first class on the DC-10 we were on. We got settled in and as we were taxiing out, the cute little hostess (not stewardess, politically correct) got our pillows for us, a magazine or two and said in a whisper "The man sitting in front of you is somebody important, so please don't bother him." We took off and climbing out the seat belt sign went off. Immediately, the man in front of us jumped up, turned around and said to the four of us in this row—we were in the middle seat section—"Well, now it's time to bother you. Does anybody have something that really gets them steamed? I always like to start with them." Everybody in first class is breaking up, clapping and standing up. The "important man" is Victor Borge, the piano player from Scandinavia who does one of the funniest routines in music hall comedy, TV and movies. He is also one of the finest classical pianists to play in all the major concert halls across the USA and Europe.

For the next 4 hours, he kept the whole airplane in stitches. Even the cockpit crew came back one at a time to shake his hand and visit with him. On the letdown for LAX, the seatbelt sign came on and the party was over. When they opened the hatch to unload at the terminal, Victor got a 5 minute ovation from everybody, including the whole crew. He had his coat and hat on, standing with his back to the door and just before stepping out, he said in a voice you could hear all the way to the tail "What, no tip?" He waved and whirled out the door to face the cameramen and TV reporters. His concert later at the Hollywood Bowl was standing room only. I never thought to ask him for his autograph.

The AiResearch operation was really something to see. We went through all the mods with the engineers, watched as they put it all back together and started out with the static engine runs to calibrate everything. After a week we were ready for the first flight, after the engine team had trimmed everything to specifications. Each flight was carefully set up with specialist mechanics or engineers in the jump seat, recording data as I flew precisely the agenda that was required. After the flights, the aircraft would be towed into the conversion hangar and reworked as necessary. We flew over the mountains to the east and over the Pacific, offshore 10 miles or so. Finally, it was written off as completed. We received the amended airworthiness certificate and were cut loose to head back to HPN (White Plains).

When we checked in with the home office, we were told to come back through Denver, pick up some New York headquarters people and bring them home, which we did. We reversed on landing at HPN and when I came out of reverse, we got a warning on #4 engine. No oil pressure. Over the next year we lost two more engines on reversing and two others because of shearing an accessory drive shaft from the engine to the accessory gearbox. These were teething problems on this new AiResearch 731 series engine, but AiResearch kept spare engines at key depot sites around the U.S., so we usually had another engine in place within 24 hours.

What a fine aircraft this retrofit made out of an already good one—which was much more than just new generation engines. It tamed the thirst that the Pratt & Whitney JT12 (−6, and-8) turbo-jet engines had for jet fuel. It basically gave us 10 per cent more thrust while consuming one-third less jet fuel. The aircraft was a thoroughbred, but the checklist was a bitch to handle at first. There were so many items to contend with that a lot of companies compiled their own version of this checklist to get it fast enough for quick turnarounds, when you might have six or seven legs on a trip, one after the other. Finally, some electronic company came up with a simple program to put the checklist on the radar scope, like a TV screen, and either pilot could handle it with two buttons on their control yoke. This cut the workload in half and it became something standard on almost all larger type corporate jets, at least as an option.

We were now flying almost daily trips from HPN to Timmins, Ontario, as the mine development there kept gaining speed. There was not a hangar on the airport large enough for our G-1 or Jetstars. My first winter in New York I was outfitted with an Eddie Bauer goose down parka, snow boots, leather gloves with fur *inside* them and thermal exterior pants to go over the thermal underwear. I thought to myself, they're trying to tell me something. And it didn't take long for the message to get through. I had a trip to Timmins in December1977, on the G-1. It was a brisk −37 degrees when we landed in the morning and had warmed to a balmy −33 at 4:00 PM when we were ready to start engines. I had started the APU (auxiliary power unit) about 45 minutes before our scheduled departure time. It was reluctant to spin up to fuel cut-in rpm, but finally it did and with a bang it lit off and in 30 seconds was running very normally. I put the airplane batteries on charge and fed hot air at about 45 degrees into the cabin. When I turned on the electronic master switch, switched the inverters on to spin up and stabilize the gyros, the gyros just barely started flopping around. These were Collins FD-108Y flight director gyros and usually erected within 3 minutes. It had been 15 minutes and they were just starting to settle down.

When the troops showed up I found out we needed to drop off a few people in Toronto which was no problem. The cabin was now up to around 50 degrees; I closed the entrance door and even though we had the batteries charged up well, they were slow to spin the engines up to starting rpm and the whole engine start was slow compared to our usual start sequence. We went home with a stop in Toronto and I said to Jim Markham the next day "Damn, it was cold up there, 37 degrees below zero." Markham said "Well, that means it will be battery weather in another two or three weeks."

I asked him "What do you mean, battery weather?" All our pilots and mechanics in the break room where we were having coffee snickered and chuckled. I suddenly got a bad feeling about this. "Well" Jim said "It's going to be getting down to 45 or 55 below one of these days soon, and if we're going to be there more than 4 or 5 hours, or overnight, we have to take the batteries out of the airplane and put 'em in somewhere warm so we can get the APU started and then start charging the batteries to keep them warm enough to get at least one engine started."

I said "Take the batteries out? Are you kidding? Those batts in the G-1 weigh 80 pounds apiece, and it takes two guys to change one."

He said "The ones in the cabin floor of the Jetstar weigh 85 pounds each and you have to lift them up and walk 'em down the stairs." Well, that's what we did for three months, until it fell to a spring like −20, but that winter loosened up the purse strings. They decided to put a small twin up there to run short trips around eastern Canada and build a hangar big enough to hold a Jetstar and a light twin. Lifting and hauling two 85 pound batteries down the entrance steps of a Jetstar at 55 below zero, then taking them back up and re-installing them should be made an Olympic event. It would sure beat the hell out of skateboarding.

When they built the hangar at Timmins, they finally used their heads. It had doors on both long sides. You could open one set, taxi the Jetstar in and when you got ready to go, open both sets, start the engines and taxi it right out with the passengers, luggage and anything else already on board. This was really a great idea for a weather condition area like Timmins. Summers up there were fine and nobody complained about the schedule then.

The G-1 was sold in October of 1979. I flew it on the last trip to deliver it to the new owner in Wisconsin. After I landed and parked, I walked through it one last time, thinking of those Canadian miners, the trips to Bermuda with our salesmen and customers going to conventions there. I recalled a trip to Rock Springs, WY one winter when the plane was iced in and we bought all the isopropyl alcohol we could find in town to de-ice it. It took two days with hiring five guys in town to soak mops with the alcohol and wipe one area at a time until the ice was gone. Another trip that came to mind was flying out of HPN to Lee Creek, SC, to our company airstrip at the mine site on the Pamlico River and shooting the approach to it up the river on our weather radar and landing with a 200 foot ceiling and a half mile of visibility. Both G-1s had been great aircraft for us. I had over 4,000 hours in them and they always brought me home.

In the spring of 1980, the Grumman III was getting close to delivery. We sent four pilots to Savannah, GA, to go to school. I wasn't one of them. I was left on Jetstar duty. I didn't mind as I had more airplanes than I could fly at one time anyway and the two new ones would come along in due course. The first thing I heard from our guys down there at the school was that if the airplane flew like the simulator, we were all going to have to eat a lot more Wheaties. They said after flying the Jetstar, it was like trying to wrestle a farm truck around. The instructors gave them some tips which helped a lot, but I can't divulge them. They are a closely guarded secret, so secret that our pilots wouldn't even tell me what they were when they got back -- sort of a poor boy's "Skull and Bones Society".

The Bombardier Aircraft Challenger 600 was also coming along and would be delivered about six to eight months after the G-III. We had a setback when we were moved from delivery position 29 to position 31, and this delayed our delivery four or more months. This was because the certificate testing procedures on this new aircraft called for "deep stall" recovery tests. While doing this set of tests in the test aircraft, the "stall recovery parachute" snapped off and the airplane crashed and was destroyed. Bombardier took two finished aircraft off the line for test aircraft and we, among others, were bumped back on our delivery dates. The aircraft was also having a lot of teething problems requiring dozens and dozens of modifications, known as "Service Changes". This is not abnormal with a new production model aircraft, so nobody got too excited. We all regretted the crash that caused the delivery delay and more so because the chief test pilot for the program didn't get out. He made the copilot bail out, but he rode it all the way down trying to gain control and save the aircraft, to no avail.

The G-III was in the interior shop, then exterior paint and final tests. It was handed over to TGI the middle of 1980. This bird dwarfed the Jetstar and made a roomy, two aircraft hangar into a very crowded two aircraft hangar, requiring very careful handling going into or out of the hangar. We had added to our maintenance department to prepare for the two new aircraft and now had a director of maintenance, two mechanics and a general helper. The type of aircraft we were using required strict maintenance procedures, done at specific intervals, and reported to the manufacturer and the FAA. All the mechanics had to go to the approved factory schools, pass exams on the courses and have access to the correct tools and parts to do this computerized aircraft maintenance program, (CAMP) or else have a qualified and licensed shop do it for them. Any way you look at it, modern jet powered corporate aircraft involved a significant financial base in order to operate correctly.

Our Manager of Aviation Operations set the training schedule for the pilots. The first set of Grumman III pilots had gone and returned. The aircraft would be used in high profile trips, probably until the Challenger also came on line. The two Jetstars would probably be reduced to one shortly after the Challenger became operational.

Because both of them had been updated, they were a hot item on the used aircraft market and should be very easy to dispose of quickly and profitably. I was informed that I would probably go to Challenger school in early 1981, and later to G-III School. I was doing all the flying I needed—I flew over 800 hours in 1980—so it made little difference to me how the training schedule laid out. The G-III made a couple of trips to Europe and one to Australia, to show off its range ability and to inspect our iron mine in northern Australia.

We kept busy with the two Jetstars. The Challenger was in the completion center in Dallas and wouldn't be available for several months yet. We were having a problem with the second Jetstar, having to do with the handling of the generator control units (GCU) on the aircraft. Each engine had a generator and any one generator could supply enough power for the normal flight load needed to operate the essential systems. However, on a takeoff and climb at night out of Midway Airport, Chicago, all four generators came off line and would not reset. The aircraft returned and landed on battery power. This problem was apparently solved by the controls manufacturer, but kept coming back at intervals, dropping one, two, and once, three generators in flight. This last episode was on a flight that I was flying on February 5, 1981. While returning to HPN, in good weather at midafternoon, we dropped three generators in less than a minute and landed at HPN with one generator operational, crew only aboard.

The controls company sent out a team to work on the GCU's the following day and over the next several days. They worked on and tested the units and finally had all of them working by February 9th or 10th. The aircraft was scheduled for a trip to Toronto, Canada on the 11th, with me as the captain and Shan Sorenson as co-captain. I was bumped by the Manager of Aviation from this flight as he wanted to fly it for personal reasons and so I had no trip on the 11th. I was at home that evening and shortly after 7:00 PM the phone rang. It was Jim Markham, the Chief Pilot of the flight department. He said in a low, shaky, voice "They crashed—on approach to Westchester about half an hour ago. They're gone, everyone is gone." I knew without a doubt he meant our Jetstar and I knew he meant that no one survived. There were two pilots and six passengers on board. The C.E.O. of Texasgulf, Inc., Dr. Charles F. Fogarty, and five senior executives were killed instantly in the crash. The Manager of Aviation of Texas Gulf, Inc., James Morgan Gregory was captain on the flight. The co-captain was a young, tall, skinny kid from Utah, named Shanley Scott Sorenson. Both also died instantly in the crash. The only thing that gives me any comfort is the knowledge that no one suffered in this accident. The impact of the crash was so great that it produced a 20 to 25 "g" negative force in stopping the motion (deceleration) of the aircraft from 200 mph to 0 mph in 667 feet and all life function ceased in the first 2/100th of a second. There was no pain, no suffering, and no knowledge of death.

We all have responsibilities that come with being part of our society. Some are joyful, happy, uplifting, and cherished. Others are not welcome, dreaded, avoided if possible, but have to be done to keep our connection with the living, the beauty of friendship, the joy and love of home, family, and cherished memories. I had to do the thing that makes a wound that will never heal completely. I had to tell the wife of this young man—a young man that I had put into that airplane—that Shan would never be returning to his home again. Never would she hear his voice, feel the smoothness of his skin, the caress of his hand running through her hair, his laughter as he whirls his young daughter around the yard. All these things will be denied her throughout her life, because of me and aviation.

And because Shan Sorenson and John Sparks were different in some unfathomable way, we were flawed, or blessed, or cursed, with a desire that only flying could soothe and make bearable. It is not the mechanical act itself, no more than the canvas and tubes of color was painting to Vincent VanGogh. It is not the completion of the act, for it lives only inside us for a brief few moments after that completion and then fades to anticipation of the next flight. But, it is as real to us as the knowledge that it demands a terrible price for failure. And striving for success is as much a driving force as pain, or hunger, or the desire to create beauty.

The aftermath of this crash produced many stresses within the families of the victims, even more so within the control structure of TGI. Richard Mollison, the president of the company, was given complete control to restructure and repair as necessary. The first thing he did was to have myself and the other pilots fly him and his team to all our branches and divisions as soon as the funerals and memorial services were concluded. This was as much to exhibit confidence in the flight operation as it was to assure the TGI workforce that the company would continue to operate with the same standards that it had before this tragic event.

The National Transportation Safety Board (NTSB) investigation was ongoing for many months. The final determination for probable cause read: *NARRATIVE*:

"A major electrical system failure during a runway 16 ILS approach distracted the pilot. The Jetstar descended into a heavily wooded area, 6,000 feet from the approach end of the runway."   *PROBABLE CAUSE*:

"A distraction of the pilot at a critical time as a result of a major electrical system malfunction which in combination with the adverse weather environment caused an undetected deviation of the aircraft's flight path into the terrain."

Many of us in aviation believed this was not the whole story, but it was the official report from the federal government. I testified before the NTSB investigation panel in New York. My segment took more than 3 hours, since I had been the last pilot to command the aircraft on a trip before the crash. The electrical problems I had experienced on that flight were significant to the final report and of special interest to our Liability Insurance carrier. I had to return to New York City in 1983, after relocating to Florida in 1982, to testify. The several teams of lawyers representing plaintiffs in the numerous damage suits arising from this accident nearly stripped the skin off of me trying to get me to say what I thought was the principle cause of this accident. I stubbornly told the same story eight or more times over the three days I was under oath at the preliminary discovery session. I simply said "Nobody knows for certain." When pressed further, I then said "If the NTSB can't come up with a more positive cause than they have, how would I be able to? I wasn't there." Finally they got tired of hearing this and sent me back to Florida. I was never called to testify in lawsuits, so I assume the insurance companies must have settled out of court.

Jim Markham was made the Manager of the Aviation department and all us pilots approved of this choice. Jim was a very fine young man, and even though several of us were older than him, he was as good a pilot as any in the company, and better than all of us in his ability to deal with the ramifications of this disaster. He had been Chief Pilot for several years and knew the ins and outs of the complex arrangements jet aircraft required to satisfy the FAA and the manufacturer's maintenance programs. He proceeded with the phasing in of our two new aircraft. These were done deals as far as contracts and other obligations for the company were concerned.

By this time, about the first of May, the Challenger was in completion in Canada, and the G-3 was flying the long leg trips. The Citation was operating in North Carolina and the Jetstar was scheduled for most of the domestic trips. A new wind was blowing from the north, however, and it was disturbing in many respects. For some years the government of Canada had been investing in TGI. They had accumulated a considerable amount of the common stock of the company, something around 40 per cent. This resulted in our board seating a number of Canadian nationals on the board of directors. We had significant operations in sulphur recovery from sour gas in western Canada, producing sulphur and sweet gas for the natural gas market. We had a viable potash mining operation at Saskatoon, Saskatchewan. There were also several small stand-alone operations in western Canada. But the jewel in the crown was the multi-billion dollar metallic ore body being developed in Timmins, Ontario. It had been estimated to be possibly an eight billion U.S. dollar deposit and that was in 1980 era dollars.

The Canadian influence on the board had been minimal before the Jetstar crash, but in the chaos that followed that there were undercurrents that were disturbing. Many of the executives who had been promoted to take charge of the vacant posts found that it was more difficult to work with the Canadian interests within the company than previously. There were also signs that other players were entering the market, using the Canadian wedge in the company as leverage. All of us pilots knew something was up. We pilots were too close to the executive suites to not feel the atmosphere becoming more charged on the return from Canadian trips. We were smart enough to keep the barrier between us intact, however. Our responsibilities ended when their feet hit the ground at either end of the trip.

In July, 1981, it was suddenly announced that about 83 per cent of the common stock of the company was now controlled by the French oil conglomerate, ELF Aquitaine, and the Canadian Development Corporation (CDC). They would be taking control of the company in September 1981. The flight department, along with many other departments, was told that in order to be paid for our vacation time and severance package, etc., we would have to let the personnel department know in 48 hours whether we would remain and hope for the continuance of the operations, or take the severance package. My wife and I discussed it and for a number of reasons decided to opt out and take the package. This I did, but because the flight department needed a Jetstar captain for operations while the new aircraft were phased in and crews trained, they asked me to stay and fly that aircraft on a monthly contract, which I did until June 30, 1982.

This last year of flying for the company I had been part of for twenty-one years was bittersweet. I knew I would be hard put at my age to get a ride in another first class corporate flight operation. You usually grow up in the department, just as it had been at TGS. I owned 10 acres of land in Dade City, FL, just north of Tampa. My wife and I decided to relocate to there, build a log home and semi-retire. Her sister and husband lived across the road from our property and that was one of the factors· that made this an easy decision. (*Photo #37*) The day I cleaned out my desk at the Westchester airport hangar and said goodbye to all of those who were left (about half) of the flight operation, I wondered if I would ever sit down in the left seat of a jet again.

Chapter 9 — The "Mouse" Trap! In Italia ...

The move to Florida took three trips, since I moved myself. Interstate I-95 had good stretches and lousy ones, especially through Philadelphia. Our house in Connecticut sold rapidly and that meant getting out in short order. It took a month of hard work and our planning was not as good as I had hoped, but finally we had everything stacked up in a storage building in Dade City. I drew my own plans, had a local lumber mill cut and shape the logs, hired all the major contracting done and was smart enough to get a local architect to finalize the plans in order to get the county planning department to approve them and let me have the building permits.

I hired labor at the local labor office every morning. I was amazed at how many skilled people they had to choose from. These were fairly tough times in Florida around the central part of the state, especially before the orange harvesting and processing began. I had about six workers I used every day, half of them white and half of them black. All were good hands and I paid a small bonus at the end of the week if we had made good progress. These men worked and took orders very well. I was working right beside them and this made a team out of us.

Ellie and I were living in a mobile home trailer on the land next to our property. This belonged to our niece, Toni Hill, so we were only 3 minutes on the commute. I had done some wood working at one time, a few small projects, and wanted to build a house like I wanted it. So I did. I made the cabinets, put down the pine floors and did it very well with the help I had. It took 5 months and I got that out of my system once and for all. Okay, now what?

The closest airport of any size was 23 miles south at Tampa. There were a few small ones scattered around, but not much in the way of flying jobs, except for Zephyrhills 7 miles south of us. There was a flying service there that catered to the sport parachuting enthusiasts. They had some decent sized aircraft to haul jumpers in, but they had plenty of skilled pilots that lived in the general neighborhood who had been flying for them for some time and didn't have any turnover. It was time to clean up, head for Tampa and see what the pilot market was like there. Also, the St. Petersburg-Clearwater airport across Tampa Bay might be worth checking out. The last close possibility would be Lakeland and I had no idea what they had there.

In Tampa, I dropped into the flying service at the Tampa Airport first since I had made a few trips in there with the Jetstar. They usually remember big airplanes that buy a lot of fuel. They didn't remember me all that well—I found that strange, but they did remember the TGS Jetstars and that made a decent contact. The problem always was that there were dozens or hundreds of pilots looking for a seat in the south and for various reasons. Some had retired from the airlines at age 55 and wanted to continue in flying (I don't find that strange), some had come from situations similar to mine, and many had had enough of snow, subzero temperatures and flying in airframe icing conditions. If they do relocate for those reasons, they will quickly learn that it is a tight market and no one area is that much better for job possibilities. Many have brand new pilot certificates and don't want to leave their home areas. The difficulty in finding a pilot position for these pilots is one of the main reasons that so many have been recruited into the illegal drug activities and other illegal activities. Stealing aircraft, flying illegal immigrants, and flying courier runs to off-shore banks with cash for the drug cartels, are just a few of the activities that need desperate pilots. Many of these pilots disappear into this lifestyle and are never seen again. It's a big ocean and a single cartridge is quite a bit more economical payoff to a pilot than a grocery sack full of hundred dollar bills, especially when there are so many more pilots available.

I did find out that there was a little airport north west of Tampa that might be a good place to make a contact. It was named "Topp of Tampa Airport" and it was a private field owned by Pam and Jamie Jordantopp, which explains the name. There were a number of twin engine aircraft based there, with some being business owned and might need some help. I went out and looked the place over. I was impressed by the cleanliness of the field in general. In the office I asked a young lady if there were any positions available for pilots on the field. She had me wait for a moment while she checked with Mr. Jordantopp. He came out, we had a cup of coffee and he poked around in my background. To my surprise, he (Jamie) said that he had a customer that was looking for a part time pilot to fly his Piper Cherokee 6 and might I be interested in something like that?

There's an old Texas saying that says "You can't git a job unless you got a job." That means that it's a lot easier to see what's available in your work area if you are around it every day, than if you're sitting at home, whittling on a stick on your front porch. I told Jamie that if the aircraft was in good shape and legal, and the pay was average for the work done, I had no problem at all with flying a single engine aircraft. I had done it many times in my career. He made a phone call and sent me a few miles down the road to visit with the owners, Mr. Bill Wylen and his wife, Liz. He was a businessman who had interests at Lake of the Ozarks, MO, and other areas up and down the Florida coast.

Bill had a single engine private license, but had had a mild heart problem recently, and was wise enough to listen to his doctor who forbade him flying himself. Therefore, a pilot with experience was the thing he had in mind and one who could work as needed. I had looked his plane over at the airport and could see two or three minor things that needed to be worked on and I told him he should have them resolved. I suggested we should take a kind of a "Honeymoon Trip" to see how we got along and then talk about it in more depth. He was delighted with this approach, so we set up a trip for the weekend to West Palm Beach and back with him and Liz. We made this trip, everything went fine and I quite enjoyed being back in an aircraft that was more like a vacation than a fire breathing 4 engine dragon to be slain every trip.

We flew a few trips to Missouri and one day after we returned to Topp airport, I was introduced to a really nice looking guy named Ben Jarrett. Ben and his wife, Sarah, had a title company and a very nice Piper PA-34 Seneca twin engine aircraft. Ben had a fistful of ratings, ATP on down, but he needed someone to do some flying for him since his business tied up so much of his time. We made a deal. I would fly all I could for him. For the next 8 months, I flew the Seneca off and on and put about 68 hours on it. I was also flying occasional trips for Bill Wylen around Florida, so I wasn't exactly getting rusty. Then the Seneca was sold and I was only flying for Bill Wylen occasionally. But, in two months, something really great came about.

I was recommended to a pair of Tampa business men who had purchased an Aero Commander 685 (*Photo #38*) aircraft and were in need of a pilot. They were in the real estate business, dealing in commercial properties. They were avid fans of the University of Tampa basketball team, since one, and possibly both, had played on this team when they were in college some ten or twelve years ago. They traveled to every "away" game they could. I was also asked to transport the five first team starters to several games to avoid a long bus ride. This I did, after I figured out how to fold them up to get them in the cabin. The partners also did some flying in the Bahamas to evaluate properties and so had a travel necessity for an aircraft. They bought a beauty. This was an 8 place, twin engine, pressurized, and very well equipped Commander. Since I had nearly two thousand hours of time flying this basic model aircraft, I was the perfect candidate for the pilot and I got the job. I flew this little jewel for 5 months, about 230 hours of flight time, just happy as a clam. Then one day, one of the partners said "We've sold the Commander and we're buying a Swearingen Merlin IIA. (*Photo #39*) You can pick it up in Memphis this weekend."

This was not the best news I'd had lately. They couldn't have known that I knew Ed Swearingen personally, during the period when he had worked for Dee Howard in San Antonio, at Howard Aviation. I was crew on a Howard 250 Lodestar conversion, and later, on a Howard Super Ventura and Howard 500 (re-manufacture of the Ventura), all for Charlie Steen in Moab. Ed Swearingen, along with four or five other brilliant engineers, had helped Dee design and build these aircraft into a very well-known and viable segment of corporate aircraft. Ed Swearingen was one of the most innovative design people in the engineering department. Eventually, he left Howard and went out on his own to develop some of his ideas that had no place in Dee's plans.

The aircraft that the partners were looking at was the first big project that Ed had started up, after working on some smaller projects to get his operation going. The Merlin IIA, model SA26T was a hybrid, using the wing and tail components of the Beechcraft Twin Bonanza Queenair series aircraft, and then building a new tubular fuselage and equipping it with Pratt & Whitney PT-6 turbo-prop engines. It was pressurized, relatively fast, and comfortable for the passengers. The thing that kept it from being a big contender against the Beechcraft King

Air turboprop was the number of system changes that Ed designed and installed in the IIA. These were notorious for being headaches in operation and maintenance parameters. Especially the cabin door locking pin system which had a tendency to bind up and refused to let you in the airplane when you wanted to get in and preflight it for a trip. The way this ended most of the time was that you drilled out specific rivets on a specific cabin window, swung the window in, crawled in and released the door mechanism from the inside.

Afterward, you could fly the airplane normally until you got to an operation that could re-rivet the displaced rivets, but this was a pain. I know I went through it a couple of times on the aircraft that I brought back from Memphis. It had more space in the cabin than the Commander and a small toilet compartment. It was heavier on the controls than the Commander, but still a good aircraft to fly. I didn't say anything to the partners, it was a done deal, but if they had asked me first, well ... Ed Swearingen continued to work on this project and the next model, the IIB, was a vast improvement and well received. Then, the Merlin III and IV became the definitive aircraft of this series. The Merlin IV was made into a commuter airliner and did well. This was known as the Metro IV, SA226-TC.

I flew this Merlin IIA aircraft slightly more than seven months and put about 150 hours on it. Other than being locked out of it twice, having some interesting system problems, it did the job fairly well. The passengers liked it, it was quiet, and the Bahamas trips were the only ones I kept my fingers crossed on. Nothing happened on them, however, so we came out well on those. But sooner or later the bills came home to roost and when the projected maintenance costs came up, the goose, as they say, was cooked. After returning from an overnight trip to Key West on November 3, 1984, the partners shook my hand, paid me off and the aircraft was sold to a dealer. I wound up having November, December, and January off with my beautiful wife and some time to enjoy our house.

The Christmas morning freeze that killed practically every orange tree in Central Florida was a shock, but no two feet of snow to shovel was alright with me.

February to July of 1985, was a mixed bag of airplanes, from the Cherokee 6, small Cessnas, a few trips on a Cessna 421-B and a Beechcraft BE 65-80 Queen Air. One evening in middle July, I got a long distance phone call from a pilot friend of mine. We chatted for a few minutes and he said "By the way, the reason I called you was to tell you some scuttlebutt I heard today, I thought you might be interested." I said "As quiet as my life has been lately, anything would be interesting. Spill it." He told me that he had heard at the airport where he was based that the Disney Company was moving the G-1 from Burbank to Orlando, since they now had a G-2 in Burbank. They were going to be interviewing for a pilot starting next week in Orlando. I said "Yes, that is interesting, I will look into it and you have a free cheeseburger coming next time we get together" I still owe him, our paths haven't crossed yet. I called the Walt Disney World main number and finally reached the secretary of one of the vice-presidents. I inquired about interviewing for the pilot's position and she passed me through to someone who was working with this project. He took my name and contact information, my basic background, and said they would call me when the interviews were scheduled in about a week.

The next week they called and gave me an appointment for two days later which was agreeable with me. I was at the interview at the home office building at Lake Buena Vista Village at the appointed time. I was interviewed for about an hour by five men and told that if there was further interest, I would be notified very shortly for a second interview. That notice came at the beginning of the following week. I was told to pack an overnight bag and be prepared to stay over at the park. At this next interview, I spread out all my G-1 documentation, including my FAA paperwork designating me as a G-159 Pilot Proficiency Examiner in the Rocky Mountain Region and later in the New York Region. I had approximately 3,400 hours of command pilot time in G-159s as my logbooks stated. I was asked numerous questions for over an hour on the aspects of operating a G-1, and then was asked the final question. "If we operate this aircraft 50 hours monthly, 600 hours a year, with three pilots as staff, what would be the approximate cost per hour of operation?"

I took a sheet of blank paper from the pile in front of me, and without hesitation, wrote $1,200 per hour, $720,000 annually on the paper and held it up for the entire panel to see. The main person said "Where did you get that number?" and I answered that after operating two of the aircraft for a period of seven years and formulating the budgets for the aircraft, I would certainly be remiss if I didn't know what the average operating costs were. The main official said that's remarkable, because Grumman Aircraft had given them a figure for the 50 hours monthly, and it was $1,187 per hour. I broke the board up when I said "They forgot to factor the shrimp trays in with the catering costs."

The next day they informed me that I was being offered the position of Chief Pilot of Walt Disney World and that, with my approval, the runner up, David Howe, would be offered the copilot position. I met and chatted with Mr. Howe and other than his being young and handsome; I could find no objection to this. (*Photo #41*) I told them that with Mr. Howe's background and experience, he would be checked out as a command pilot, not a first officer (co-pilot), and that we would probably need a copilot also when we got into operation. We would start out operating as co-captains and go from there. I was led to believe that suggestions I had already made and would be making as we got into the actual operation of the aircraft would be implemented through the approved budget. My budget was evaluated and approved with minor modifications. I had had no answers in some areas yet, such as staffing of a qualified mechanic, starting a copilot search program, the timing for procuring hangar space and a few minor items.

In order to get the actual scheduling and flying started, I requested a meeting with one of the Vice-Presidents in charge of operations who I had assumed would be my direct contact within the organizational framework, like most corporate flight departments were handled. When I did get to see him, I was informed that my immediate superior was on a lower floor of the office building and I would report to him and no one else. The Manager of Transportation would now be my boss and would administer the flight department budget and policy. This was the man who bought the trucks for the park, had control of the trains, street sweepers, dump and trash trucks and now a multi-million dollar aircraft and its operations.

I went down to his office, his secretary had me wait a while and then I was admitted. The manager was cold, abrupt and not at all friendly. The first thing I found out was that it was his opinion that this aircraft and its operation were unnecessary. I asked him if he had any experience with aircraft and was he possibly a pilot. His answer was, "Hell no, I don't even like the damn things." I then asked him how it would be possible to oversee an operation of this magnitude with no practical knowledge of its operation and purpose. His answer was short and concise. He said "It's my job to see that you don't spend any money." I tried to point out as politely as I could that I already had a budget to operate with and the money had already been approved. His answer was chilling and it told me this was not what I had envisioned in a major corporation flight department.

He said "Just because it's in the budget doesn't mean we're going to spend it." I left that office with a sick headache and the feeling that all my sins had caught up with me. I went back to the Vice-President's office to try to get some enlightenment on this situation. After the secretary came back from asking if I could have a moment of his time, she said she had been instructed to tell me that I was not to come to this office again unless summoned. She was very nice, polite, and apologetic. I smiled, thanked her for her trouble and left. This had to be one of the longest afternoons and evenings I can remember. I wondered what the devil had I gotten myself into this time. Where should I turn, who should I consult and would it do any good to try to get some backing through the flight department in Burbank?

After a restless night, I got up and found that I was steamed. I was mad. I did call the chief pilot of the Disney Companies in Burbank and he said candidly that I better watch my step and my mouth. This was not the kind of company you can get out of line with and that he had no input whatsoever with the C.E.O. or the President of the Disney organization or about any other operation than the one in Burbank. I thanked him and decided to cool off over the weekend at home and see what I could come up with. This was it. I had never given up at anything in flying. I had too damn much Irish blood in my veins to quit before trying, so trying it would be. I called the Orlando office and got the schedule for going to the Disney University programs that all supervisory personnel had to attend and graduate from.

In short: I went through the Disney University programs, graduated, went out in the park for one day as a character (required to graduate), in my case as "Goofy." I went to Burbank, CA, on the airlines. One of the Burbank pilots and I brought the G-1, N234MM, back to Orlando where it went into the shop at Page Aviation for an inspection and paint work. Dave Howe and I went to Savannah, GA, to Flight Safety and got our simulator time and check rides accomplished. We went back to Orlando to get everything ready to start operations. I bought a Cessna 152 (*Photo #40*) to commute to Orlando from the little grass airport which was about a mile from my house in Dade City. The commute was one and a half hours by car or twenty minutes by plane. I did this for about six months, but we got so busy and as I couldn't land at the grass airfield after dark, my wife and I finally decided to buy a house in Orlando and sell the one in Dade City. So far I had done a very good job for Disney; we had lots of compliments and orchid letters from our non-Disney passengers. I thought that time would let me straighten out the difficulties I still had.

I couldn't get clearance to hire a full-time copilot. I made a deal with Ben Jarrett and another pilot named Dennis Kochan to put them on as part-time copilots when needed. They were both in a position to have the time off as needed for this, since they were both self-employed. I trained and checked them out on the G-1 and I have to say they did a very good job for us. Dave and I both enjoyed flying with them. The company did have four young ladies from the Guest Services Dept. go through the Eastern Airline Stewardess School in Miami, so we had a pool to draw from for hostesses. They were great kids, did a fine job, and got along well with everybody.

Page Aviation did all our maintenance work and I had a good working relationship with them. The only problem with this kind of a program is that you might get different mechanics every time work is required on the aircraft. Some of the supervisory staff was well acquainted with the G-1, but many of the mechanics spent a lot of time with the maintenance manuals, referencing and looking up methods of doing things on the aircraft. That didn't bother me to any great extent. It would have bothered me much more if they hadn't referred to the "Bible" and spent a lot of time and money doing it wrong. Still, a mechanic who works solely on one airplane and leads the maintenance in the shop work will get the work done quicker and usually cheaper. Having four or five mechanics standing around at $40 an hour waiting for someone to obtain the information, pass it along to them and tell them what it says in the maintenance manual, can sink a budget in a hurry. Page did as good a job as was possible under these circumstances. They had fine facilities, knowledgeable people, but with the extra expense I could have hired two full time mechanics.

N234MM was a fairly late production G-1, being serial number 121 out of 199 G-1s built. There was a fuselage (s/n 200) that was built, but was used as the test bed for the Grumman G-2, the first pure jet in the Gulfstream line. The Disney aircraft was purchased by Walt Disney himself, since his board of directors turned him down on his request to buy one for company travel needs. It had a lot of hours on it, but the maintenance had been handled by a company aviation mechanic and there were several good maintenance shops at the Burbank Lockheed Terminal Airport for support. We had a few problems with it, but handled them with no trouble. Both Dave and I had to land with limited hydraulic functions, because of a sub-system that had been installed in Burbank and was not part of the factory installed equipment, and so had no maintenance specifications on its upkeep. All airplanes are individuals and working with them is kinda like dating a pair of twin sisters. They look a lot alike, but have different personalities and different ways of getting even if you mistreat them.

I spent a lot of time on obtaining parts and supplies for the airplane from people I had known and worked with when I was with Texasgulf. I managed to buy tires, brake parts, spare wheels and many other replacement items at discounts, from 10 to 25 per cent off. I also had some of our spares from Burbank, which were run out, overhauled at shops that I could get very good service and warranties at and at a good discount also.

A year went by and still no full time copilot, no mechanic and no hangar, but lots of flying, though. I was called in for an annual evaluation by the personnel and budget committee. I sat down at a table with nine people, answered their questions as reasonably as I could. After two hours discussing my department operations, they said I would get an extremely good evaluation report. Then the budget portion came up. They congratulated me on my handling of the budget, the hours flown timeline completion of 92 per cent of the flights on time as scheduled. They then congratulated me on being 8 per cent below the estimated budget costs and told me that my budget for the coming year was being reduced by 5 per cent. I jumped up and said "Why would you reduce my budget after telling me I had handled it so well?" The answer was that if I came in under budget, it was obvious that my operation had been over budgeted to begin with; therefore, a correction was being made for the coming year, but with the same number of anticipated flying hours. I didn't yell and scream. I explained that I had used all my contacts and lines of supply to obtain the best prices, but this couldn't be guaranteed and that the unexpended budget was, in effect, a pad against possible unexpected but necessary un-budgeted expense. They said sorry, your immediate supervisor has agreed to these budget parameters, so it's a done deal.

Well, enough about life under Cinderella's Castle. Let's mention some of the bright spots that came with the job. The employees we worked with were the saving grace of the Disney organization. From the very young, working during the summer, to the old timers, many of whom worked with Walt himself in the early days and came to Florida when Disney World was being built. They were engaging and had a great attitude. Some of the foreign students from China, India, the Middle East and Europe were some of the passengers we carried. When we went on the press trips, State Fairs, promotions to give a Disney flavor to trade shows, we carried the actors who were the characters, their costumes, the P.R. people and lots of literature inviting guests to come see WDW and especially Epcot Center.

Everywhere we went, people at the airports wanted to get pictures of themselves by the airplane with the big Mickey on the tail. No one was allowed to go on board unless they were invited by the head coordinator of the team we had on that trip. All the local press and TV reporters, travel agents and travel writers were the people who had invited us to come, and all of us went to great lengths to make it enjoyable for them. After all, this was *Show Biz*, Kids!

During the second year I was there, we carried a team of hot air balloon pilots to State Fairs mostly. We carried the balloon envelope, which inflated to a giant Mickey head, in the aircraft rear cargo hold and were met by a Disney support team in a truck with the gondola and all the necessary equipment to make flights during our visit. The reason we carried the actual balloon was because it had a value of $75,000 and it got *VERY* special handling. It looked like a one-half size cotton bale when folded up and put into its travel bag. This was enjoyable work and the aircraft was a great promotional tool. Between trips of this nature, we made standard corporate type trips and sometimes we were sent to provide VIP transportation to selected people. There is a long list of celebrities that we transported, but some were special. My favorite passenger was the newly retired Chief Justice of the Supreme Court, Warren E. Burger (*Photo #42*). He was a prime example of a gentleman. He and his staff traveled from Washington to Orlando to give a series of speeches about the Constitution. I brought them down and Dave Howe took them back. Dave and I made a good team and our copilots did a fine job. Our in-flight hostesses were super and every "Orchid" letter the company received about a flight always mentioned them especially. I also had to transport Dick Cavett and his production team from Newark to Orlando to put on some TV specials.

When we loaded the Cavett team on at Newark, I noticed that Dick was stiff, pasty faced and appeared to be in some sort of discomfort. I asked his manager if he was ill and was told that Dick did not enjoy flying and that he might become tense and to please try to have a flight without turbulence if we could do that. I told him we'd do our best. Once we were at cruising altitude and had the seat belt sign off, I gave the copilot the cockpit duty and went back and kneeled down by Dick's seat. I told him I was the Captain and I needed him to help me out with something. I got him to come forward with me to the cockpit and I took my seat. Then I had the copilot go check with the hostess and make sure everything was running smoothly. When he left, I pointed to the right seat and said "Dick, it's your turn. Please get in that seat while I talk to you."

Well, he didn't like it, but he did it. The next half hour I explained what was going on, what the crew and the flight controllers did to ensure safety, how the radar showed us any weather of consequence, how the autopilot was merely doing what the crew told it to do. I took it off autopilot and made a few slight turns to left and right to show him how smoothly the aircraft responded and that the crew and plane worked as a unit. Finally, I had him put his hands and feet on the controls and just follow through with me while I moved the airplane around a little bit. We were at 29,000 feet with no traffic near us, so this was no problem. After about 10 minutes of lazy, easy movements, I took my hands and feet off the controls and said "Try it yourself." He said "Are you sure you want me to do this?" I laughed and said that's the only way you can find out that *you* have control of what's happening. He took a deep breath, eased the controls very slightly as I directed him to do, and in 5 minutes he was smiling. He went back into the cabin and the hostess came up and said "What did you do to Mr. Cavett? He's talking to everybody back there, telling them how much fun it was to be in the cockpit."

When we started off loading everybody at Orlando, the manager came up and shook my hand. He said that this was the first trip he had ever seen Dick smile and be casual about getting off the airplane. I told him that Dick wasn't the first nervous passenger I had ever had and that this job involved more than just getting from point A to point B. My job also involved trying to make sure the passengers enjoyed the experience. I still have the Cavett program that he sent me with these big printed words on it, "John, you did it! Dick Cavett."

One of the few perks that came with this job was in having my office at Orlando International Airport, at the Page AvJet Services fixed base operations flight lounge and offices. Just about everybody who was anybody who had an airplane came through this lobby right by my office—Arnold Palmer, whom I had met several times before, Jack Nicholas, and many other sports notables, movie and TV personalities and so on. But at the top of this list was the NASA astronauts who flew in from Houston quite frequently to do some training at the naval facility in Orlando. They were John Young, Gene Cernan, Roger Chafee, Mike Collins, Charles Conrad and maybe a half a dozen more whose names I didn't write down or can't remember. I had a deal with Gene Cernan and John Young. Every time they came to Orlando and I was in town, I would pass them, their families and any of the other astronauts into WDW as that was another one of my perks. In return, they got passes for me and the other pilots and our families, to the VIP area at Cape Canaveral for a couple of the early shuttle shots. This was about four or five months before the Challenger disaster on January 28, 1986. I saw that explosion from my front porch in Orlando about 30 miles away. As soon as I saw the exhaust plume split and the trails start spreading apart, I knew it was blown. I was hoping the crew escape container system would work, but unfortunately, it didn't.

We struggled throughout 1986 with no hangar, in the rain and hot weather, with the G-1 sitting on the ramp. We didn't make a lot of friends by running our aircraft onboard APU (Auxiliary Power Unit, and *extremely loud*) wide open on the ramp in front of the Page AvJet customer lounge to try to get and keep the interior somewhat cool for passenger boarding. Rain was also a pain, but at least we had big golf umbrellas to help with that. The crew usually wound up pretty well soaked by the time the luggage had been loaded aboard through the rear luggage door. I always hoped we didn't smell like a pack of wet hunting dogs. Also, we had no mechanic, so we sometimes had a Page mechanic standing by with us in case of a minor glitch coming up at the last minute. But the job got done. We flew about 600 hours in 1986, and took nearly 300 duty days to do it. (*Photo #43*)

Summer arrived early in 1987, especially the humid, heat soaked conditions. The park was adding a new feature at Epcot Center. It was to be called "*The Living Seas*" and was to be a super aquarium. With performing dolphin shows and possibly orca whales, it was supposed to be a "Sea World" competitor and draw off some of their market. Disney had a dolphin training facility established down at the south end of the Keys, close by Marathon Key. We had flown a couple of day trips down to take design teams, etc., to see what facilities would be necessary for handling these very smart dolphins.

Word came down to prepare for a trip to Marathon the next day, as some of the Disney Studio's top brass wanted to see the dolphin setup there. I flew them down and in mid-afternoon we took off to return to Orlando. As we leveled out at cruise altitude one of the Disney executives came to the cockpit and asked me how everything was going in my operation. I was hot, sweaty, had been having some real battles with my department "Manager" concerning things about the airplane and its operation, so I thought to myself "Self, maybe this is the break you've been waiting for." I looked at him and said, "Well, to be truthful about it, almost none of the things I was told would be part of this aviation operation have happened, the hangar, a mechanic devoted to this airplane full time, access to the V-P of park operations and authority to run my own operation as I thought best for the Disney interests due to my experience and background. None of this has been made available to me. I have been under the control of a person who buys your ground service equipment and has no knowledge of or interest in the Aviation Department. I have to hire copilots by the trip. I have to fight constantly with my supervisor about the use of our budgeted funds to keep the aircraft in a legal and safe condition. That's how it's going."

I rapidly learned one thing. The Disney brass liked responses such as fine, great, swell, terrific, couldn't be better, etc. I'm not sure he ever wanted to hear the words that I used. He said, slowly and distinctly "I don't want to hear complaints that should go up through the proper channels to your manager to be dealt with. If you feel that you cannot do your job as instructed here, keep in mind that you *don't* have to stay here."

I nodded my head in acquiescence and said "Sir, that's one of the few really intelligent remarks I've heard since I've been in Disney's employment." He turned around and went back to the cabin. I finished the trip; he and his retinue got into the limos and zoomed off to do the Studio's work. The next week I went into my manager's office and placed a brief letter of resignation on his desk. He had already put me on his black list because I had made a decision on my own, as he couldn't be reached to okay or deny it, a few days earlier on a trip. He had said that this insubordination would probably be grounds for my termination. I saved him all the hard work. If anyone had said "Let me look into this" I would probably have done something different. I might have decided that maybe they had no idea of what was happening here and that there could be a remedy. And indeed, there was a remedy. They brought in another pilot and in a couple of years the airplane was an exhibit in Epcot Center at Walt Disney World. It had become un-airworthy and therefore legally unflyable.

It's said that as one door is closing, another is opening. The trick is not to stand and watch the one that's closing, but to continue straight on and head for the one that's opening. Sounds fairly easy, but like most everything else in this life, it's not. However, it gets easier with practice. I had to re-align my career after Charlie Steen, but that open door was only a step away. Then, after a stable and wonderful twenty-one years with TGS, I literally had to run to get through the door before the French welded it shut. Well, again, whether I had pushed the door to start it closing or it was the winds of fate that did it, it was time to jump through and not look back at The Magic Kingdom. Now, where was that opening door?

It turned out to be 100 yards away to the north in front of the Page AvJet maintenance hangar. Or 4,700 miles, whichever way you want to look at it. A month before I resigned, I had done a favor, for a fee, of course, for Dexter Cox, an old friend of mine from Denver. Dexter was now working out of Dulles airport with a large aircraft sales operation and he needed a G-1 crew to fly some inspection flights for a G-1 customer. I flew these two flights for him with Ben Jarrett as my copilot. This aircraft was still in Orlando being worked on at Page AvJet. The buyer's representative was Augusto Lama from Italy. This was one of several G-1s that were being turned into 24 passenger seat aircraft for an Italian airline named Mistral Air based in Rome.

A few days after the word that I had resigned from Disney was spread around, Dexter Cox called me and asked whether this was true and I said "Yes, indeed, I am now what you call in show business, at liberty." He laughed and said they still needed crop dusters in Georgia. Then he got serious. He had spoken to the principal owner of Mistral Air, an Italian film actor named Carlo Pedersoli, stage name, Bud Spencer. (*Photo #46*) He needed a crew to bring the airplane to Italy after all the work at Orlando and Millville, NJ, was finished. Would I be interested? I said if they would pay in dollars instead of lira and give us tickets back to Orlando, yes. I had a valid passport and could find a copilot that had one, but they had to know that this airplane didn't have the legs to go straight across the Atlantic. It would probably have to be to Goose Bay, Iceland and then Rome.

The next day I had lunch with Augusto Lama, the airline rep. We worked out a timetable and a list of things to go with the aircraft. He would handle the customs on both ends, so all I had to do was get it to Rome in one piece. First, it had to have some engine hot section work done in Millville, NJ, about five day's work. I planned to take it and leave it there, come home on the airlines and return when it was ready to go. This is what Dennis Kochan, the copilot I was taking on the trip, and I did. On June 19, 1987, we left Millville, (*Photo #44*) flew to Goose Bay, Labrador, and shot a radar approach in fog to a landing with about 100 yards of visibility. We fueled up, took off and landed in Reykjavik, Iceland, 5½ hours later. We spent the night at the famous Loftleider Hotel at the airport—great food, good looking blond waitresses—and still daylight when we went to bed.

The next morning we had an early takeoff to Scotland, across England, over the Channel to Paris, down to Nice, across the island of Elba, direct to Rome, to Ciampino Airport on the south edge of the city. We landed 7 hours and 10 minutes after takeoff with an hour and 20 minutes of fuel remaining. When we taxied up to the Mistral hangar, every one of the 53 employees who were at work that day were standing in front, waving ribbons and cheering. I felt really glad that I had made the trip. The only previous time I had been to Europe was directly across the North Atlantic to Luton Airport in North London in the Jetstar. We sure didn't get a reception like this. The Operations Manager of the airline brought the customs men out and in 5 minutes we were cleared into the country. Carlo Pedersoli himself met us in the lobby and whisked us off to a late lunch at his favorite Café in Castel Gandolfo.

At lunch Carlo asked me if I would like to work for him at the airline as the chief instructor pilot to phase in the G-1s and help with the transition in six months to the BAE-146 four engine jet airliner being produced in England. He made me a very good offer, covering all my expenses relocating to Italy, a company car, and other nice features, including a good salary. I told him I would see how my wife felt about it and let him know tomorrow. She was a little shocked when I outlined this on the phone that night, but when I got home three days later we talked it over and said "Why not?" You only live once. So we did it, sold the house, put a lot of things into storage, and sent some to Italy via an ocean shipping container.

I went back to Italy while Ellie finished things up in Orlando. Mistral put me up in a nice motel until I could find a small villa to rent. At this motel, I met a lady about sixty-five years old who spoke very good English. Her name was Rella Hard and she was a survivor of a Nazi death camp in Central Europe during WW II. The rest of her family had perished and she was only a teenager when the war ended. She met and married a Canadian officer and went to Canada to live for a number of years. She was widowed and returned to her home country and immigrated to Italy with her two young daughters. She met an Italian man who became a significant other in her life and they were now living in Castel Gandolfo where she had a small shop for women who knitted, sewed and made clothing. When we became acquainted, she helped me find a small villa about 5 miles from Castel Gandolfo in a gated community of private homes overlooking Lake Albano. The airline had given me a little Fiat Panda, a small car with a motorcycle engine and I could drive up the mountainside from Rome to my villa, a distance of 12 miles, in about half an hour.

It was, to a great extent, like living in a giant amusement park. Since I was teaching the ground school at Ciampino airport daily and commuting to another nearby town called Albano to teach a class also, I was driving in city traffic daily. It was like the Bumper Car track, only scarier. They had a saying about driving in Rome traffic. "If you fail your driving test in Rome, you emigrate and become a taxi driver in Mexico City." Anyone who has ridden in a cab in Mexico City would go along with that after driving in Rome for a few days. I had to go to the Italian Civil Avia, the equivalent of our FAA, to get my paperwork done and get my Italian Pilot License issued. I learned that they had no flight inspectors with G-1 experience and therefore, they asked Mistral Air to let one flight inspector go through the class with the Mistral pilots I would then give him a check ride, sign him off, if he passed, and he would then be rated to give the necessary check rides for ratings in the G-1. I told Mistral Air I had no problem with this arrangement, so the Civil Avia inspector sat in the front seat of the class and was the first one to receive the flight training from me after the ground school tests. He was a good pilot, had a good background and I had not a minute's trouble with him.

But the Mistral captains were a different matter. Almost all the captains had been in the military or pilots for the Alitalia National Airline in some cases. They treated the young first officers (copilots) like serfs most of the time. Carlo Pedersoli told me one of the main reasons he wanted me on board was that they were losing the young copilots because of this treatment by the captains. He wanted someone to make the captains and copilots work as a team, and give the copilots some feeling that there would be a future with Mistral Air. Dexter Cox, my friend from Combs Aircraft in Denver, had recommended me because of my experience with these aircraft. Also, I had the designated authority of an examiner for the PIC bi-annual check ride FAR, and this gave me standing in Italy where position is nearly everything. But last, I was an ex-Marine and could be very hard-nosed when necessary.

Even after much studying, my Italian was poor, but good enough to get by. I was walking down the hall to the classroom when I heard two or three captains talking. The gist of the conversation was why did the company bring a "gringo" in to teach? I knew if I let the first few days get away without doing something about this, it could turn into a cat fight. I decided we would start off with a little humility lesson—something between Marine boot camp and John Hollingsworth's motivational chat with me about the G-1. I entered the classroom, went to the desk at the front of the room, looked at my watch and at exactly 8:00 AM I slammed my flight manual on the desk hard enough to make everybody jump. I said, in English, "Everyone stand up. *Now!*" I put the Civil Avia pilot at an end table on the first row.

"Now, who is the senior captain?" The short, grey haired captain I had seen in the hall raised his hand from the back of the room. "Captain, you will come to the front and sit here at this first table in front of me." I then asked for the senior first officer and put him beside the captain and the head of the maintenance operation on the other side of the captain, who was looking very stony faced. I had all the captains and first officers alternate their seating at the tables with the mechanical staff at the rear. There were 42 students total and four rows of tables. There were 12 captains and 22 first officers, 1 Civil Avia pilot and 7 mechanics. I waited until they settled themselves. I stood in front with my arms folded across my chest, and one by one, I slowly looked everyone in the eye for a few seconds, taking about two minutes to do this. Then I walked around my desk and stopped in front of the senior captain.

"Captain, as senior flight officer of Mistral Air, I am giving you the honor of answering every question first, so the junior pilots can benefit by your vast knowledge. All mechanical questions will be answered by the head of maintenance. This is the way it works. I talk, you listen." I pointed to a first officer I had put at the front table. "Flight officer Rebecchini speaks excellent English, so any questions that are very technical in nature will be translated into Italian by him so that there will be no misunderstanding. This course will take six days and then flight training will start with the Civil Avia inspector, then the captains, then first officers. With two aircraft and once the Civil Avia pilot is certified, he will be giving rating rides to captains in the second G-1 while I am instructing in the first one. The company needs to have four crews ready in thirty days. That should be no problem since we will be working 10 hours a day. Classes start at 0600 in the morning and should be through by 0430 PM."

"This is a fine airplane. It is rugged, honest and has no really bad tricks. It does, however, take a firm hand and the knowledge of what to expect from it. This, I will teach you. You *will* ask any question about anything you don't understand and I will answer it. But, you *will* do what you're told. *No exceptions*. Now, we start. Oh, by the way, I heard that some of you have referred to me as a gringo. It isn't unusual for Americans to be called gringos in some foreign countries to make fun of them. I don't mind it at all. I just want to remind you that a few thousand "Gringos" beat the hell out of the French and Mexican armies in the Mexican-American war. We won".

The training went well after I thoroughly made the senior captain a little humble. Then I brought him back in line by telling him that I needed him to be an example for the younger pilots on how to act like a top pilot. I told him that he would be guiding them and he should remember when he was first learning how much he disliked being made to feel inferior. He came around better than I thought he would. Still, the Italian male ego is 2,200 years old and doesn't have much flexibility.

In thirty days, at the end of the first class, they were calling me "Comandante Sparks." This helped a lot with the second class. (*Photo #45*) They listened, they worked hard and they absorbed the information as fast as I could get to it. The man who ran Mistral air for Carlo was Werner Romanelo, who had been with TWA in Rome for many years and really knew the ins and outs of the airline business in Europe. He was a delight to work with. He gave me all the room I needed to get the work done. I made a number of small suggestions that would help with the handling of the aircraft. Every one of them went down to the head of maintenance and was implemented. This was an easy organization to work with once you learned a few rules of procedure.

When we had finished all the classes on the G-1 for Mistral Air, Carlo asked me if I would teach another airline the ground school course. I told him I was working for Mistral Air and if they told me to teach some other airline pilots the course, that's what I would do, provided I had control of the training. After a month of line checks flying out of Milano into France and Germany, I went to Bologna, commuting by train for a week at a time, then home to Rome on weekends. I set up the training there for TAS (Trasporti Aerei Speciali), a small feeder line flying through France and into Birmingham, England. They had one G-1 in their fleet and were planning on adding two or three more in the near future. I worked with their most experienced pilots, eight of them, and ran the other less experienced ones through a second course after the first class was finished. This took a total of seven weeks and some hairy flying in some of the smaller airports in France and England. Finally, I had everybody signed off, we had a small farewell dinner and I went back to Rome. I told Ellie we were going on vacation for three weeks.

After we arrived in Rome, we bought an Opel 4 door sedan. I told Mistral I would be gone for three weeks and would be back to start the new ground school for them in June. We packed our bags and drove through Switzerland to Paris. We followed our map to the Arc de Triumph, parked and walked to the Seine River, strolling along the bank toward the Eiffel Tower. I thought about Gene Kelly and all the movies I had seen about Paris. It was late spring, the air was fresh and there was only moderate traffic in the streets. At the Tower, we went about half way up and looked over the environs of Paris. When we came down we found a telephone booth and I called the Mistral offices in Rome to check in, as I had promised to do. Sure enough, there was a change. They wanted to start the ground school a week earlier. I said we would cut the trip short. We still had time to do what we wanted to do, but we had to keep moving. So, instead of a couple of days in Paris, we ate, went back to the motorway and spent the night in one of the motorway hostels. It was nice and clean—about like a Motel 6. The next morning, after a quick breakfast, we went on to Calais. Then we took the auto ferry to Dover, into London and up through the Avon district to Birmingham. I went there to talk to Captain David Roberts, Manager of Flight Ops., and Liz Law, Personnel Manager, at Birmingham Executive Airways. They had contacted me in Rome to ask if I would be interested in a position in their training department as Assistant Chief Training Pilot.

I was interested in this as they were bringing in DC-9s to replace their turbo-prop equipment and my wife and I loved the Midlands south of Birmingham. After a few days touring around, I had the job offer in my briefcase and we went back to London to talk to the CAA of England to see about getting an English Airline Transport Pilot Certificate. I met with this agency in their offices in downtown London in the Aviation House Building. I laid out all my records, log books, documentation, etc. The six or seven board members examined it and all concurred that I was highly qualified to be in anyone's training department. Then the chief official said "We're sorry, but we cannot issue you a CAA pilot's license. You may start flight instruction here and work up through the ratings if you wish. That will take 500 flying hours and about two years. However, there is no guarantee that we will issue you the certificate to work as an instructor pilot for a British Airline even after you obtain your British ATP license." I was stunned.

"You say I'm extremely qualified, but I can't get the necessary certificate from you? May I ask why?" He said "You are not from a common market country and we have no reciprocity agreement in place with the United States. Therefore, we are not compelled to issue this certificate." I was mildly upset to say the least.

"So, if I were from Kenya and had a license typed with a typewriter on a piece of plain white paper, you would give me the certificate?" He said "Of course, you could have it in hand before you left the building, but, you are not from Kenya, are you?"

And now you know why I am writing this from a small town in Kansas, instead of from a thatch roofed cottage in the middle of the Avon River district, perhaps in Stratford-on-Avon, just a stone's throw from Anne Hathaway's cottage. We toured around London for several days and saw Buckingham Palace, Whitehall, Trafalgar square, Westminster Abbey and most of the other standards. The one I liked best was "The Olde Curiosity Shoppe."

We went back to Birmingham and told them the story. They said that this was not totally unexpected as this happened quite often when they attempted to hire in expert help. It was "English jobs for English lads!"

There was still a lot of sightseeing available. In the Midlands we enjoyed seeing the ruined castles, stone circles, the famous churches and other sights. Then it was back to the continent via the car ferry to Calais, across France north of Paris and on to the town of Bastogne, Belgium. Here the "Battle of the Bulge" was fought to its conclusion in WW II. I had two friends who were in this battle and survived. Of all the turning points of the European campaign, this was probably the most significant and best remembered. The American Patton tank that was "killed" by a German 88 artillery cannon round was still where it was destroyed—on the edge of the main square of Bastogne. The round that penetrated the front armor and killed the crew left a gaping hole. It was still as it was that day in December 1944; the tank, the hole in the armor and the track blown off. The soldiers who died in it were buried in a military cemetery. The tank will stay where it died, a lasting memorial to duty, honor and sacrifice. This was the bloodiest battle fought by U.S. troops in WW II. From December 16, 1944, until January 25, 1945, the American and British Armies had 22,400 killed, 51,000 wounded and 25,500 captured, missing, or unaccounted for. The German forces losses were roughly the same.

Upon our return to Rome a week later, I set up the next ground school and had a few days to do nothing. I had brought my bicycle to Italy with me and I biked around the towns close to where we had our little villa. One day I went to Castle Gandolfo to see my friend Rella Hard, who helped me so much when I first came to Italy. I stopped at her shop and she and her significant other, Sabino, were just leaving to go down a block to the square and have an espresso. We sat down at a table in front of one of the five or six "Bars" on the square and ordered the espressos' and a cappuccino for me. Suddenly, the big gates of the Pope's summer castle were thrown open and the Swiss Guards with their Lances and flags, in the Striped Livery and tall hats, came striding out. In the center of the square they formed, the Pope, John Paul II, dressed in a white cassock and white skull cap, came walking briskly down the ramp into the square. He began stopping at the tables where everyone was standing. He would speak to the people briefly, smile, and move on to the next table. In five or six minutes he reached our table. He clapped his hands and said (in Italian), "Rella, Sabino, how are you?" He looked at me, and said (in perfect English) "Ah, I think you have an American with you, do you not?" Rella replied (in perfect English) "Yes, Papa, this is a friend of ours who is living in Monte Gentile and he came to visit with us today."

The Pope said to me "What do you do in Italy? Are you on vacation?" I replied "No sir, I am working in Rome, flying an airplane for an Italian movie star." That was true as Carlo owned the company and I flew him on trips occasionally. Pope John Paul said "Ah, which one do you fly?" and I said "Carlo Pedersoli." The Pope threw up his hands and smiled broadly. "Ah, Bud Spencer! I like his movies. How is he?" I said that he was well and very busy making a movie in Spain at the moment. The Pope said "Tell him Papa said hello and come see me sometime."

He also asked me if I were Catholic, and after I had said no, he asked if I had some Catholic friends? I said yes, I do. He told me to get some articoli de religiousi (articles of religion), crosses, medals, etc., as he would be coming back by shortly and blessing them as they lay on the tables. I could give them to my catholic friends. I bought eight pieces at the little shops by the Bernini Fountain in the main square. Soon the Pope came by all the tables saying the blessing in Latin and making the sign of the cross over them as he gave the blessing. After he blessed the items on our table, he said to me "I hope your time in Italy will be enjoyable. You have been fortunate to find Rella and Sabino to be your friends. I hope to see you again. Ciao."

After he finished his walk and was back at the castle door, he turned and waved to us. There were about a hundred people in the square. He and the Swiss Guards marched inside and the gates closed. I said to Rella "I can't believe that he would come out without some real protection after Ali Aga shot him in St. Peter's Square a few years ago." Rella made a very small motion, pointing up and over her shoulder. I glanced up and saw that there was a balcony with iron railings running down both the long sides of the square. Just leaving their posts on this balcony were forty or more Carabinieri, with rifles and scopes and some with automatic weapons. I was glad that I had been very polite and had not tried to slap the Pope on the back with a Texas style greeting.

When Ellie and I went into Rome for the day, we would drive to the Castle Gandolfo railroad station, park and lock our car, and travel into the Rome Termini on one of the trains that ran almost every hour. From the Termini we would walk or take a cab or the subway which would take you to any quarter of the city in a reasonable amount of time. We did not drive into the city proper if it could be avoided. Even walking was a hazard with the traffic. There were more than three-hundred pedestrians a year hit and killed by the city buses alone. Most of the automobiles had some light damage from fender benders, but you almost never saw a really serious accident in the city.

Occasionally we would drive down to Anzio and Nettuno on weekends. It was a nice walk on the beach between them. This was one of the landing beaches that were heavily defended by the Germans during the amphibious assault to gain a foothold in 1943. The American Military Cemetery entrance lies just 100 yards from the edge of the beach sand. Inside this beautifully laid out final resting place for our American warriors are the graves of 7,890 men and women of the U.S. Military commands of WW II. There are 23 sets of brothers buried side by side. In one area all 10 crew members of one of our bombers lie side by side. In the chapel, on all four walls of beautiful Italian travertine marble, are carved the names and ranks of all the service members missing in action and that were never found. They were members of all five of our Military service forces in Africa, Sicily and Italy. I walked up to the U.S. Navy wall and saw a name I had known since I was a child in Ennis, Texas. The name was Guy Youngblood, a young man who lived down the road from us, and would hang around my aunt Billy Jane when they were both in high school before the war started. Guy enlisted in the navy, was on an ammunition supply ship off shore during the Salerno invasion in September 1943, and was killed in action when the ship was bombed and it exploded, taking the entire crew to their deaths. His body was never recovered.

The British Military Cemetery is just north of the US one and is beautifully done also. The British-Polish war cemetery is about 20 kilometers north of this one. In Pomezia, 50 kilometers up the coast from Anzio, is the German Military Cemetery, holding German soldiers from North Africa, Sicily and Italy. There are more than 39,000 buried here. They are buried five deep in each grave in order to contain them all. There are several more cemeteries in Italy for Italians, Germans and other combatants in many battle areas. This was a massive campaign in the "soft underbelly of Europe" as Winston Churchill referred to it. The number of military cemeteries provides proof of that.

One other special place we would take all our visitors to was the hilltop town of San Gimignano which was about a three hour drive northwest of Rome. An American couple living in Arricia had taken us there on a sightseeing trip and it was amazing. Five-hundred years ago, the Guilds of that era had competed with one another to show their wealth, power and control. In this town the various guilds built towers on the city walls and in the city proper, each new one higher than the others to show their superiority in their trades. At the "height" of this competition, there were seventy or more towers built, some to heights exceeding 300 feet. Today only twelve remain. The tallest one is nearly 250 feet high. All of these were constructed with stone and masonry, as there was no structural steel in those days.

Well, back to work. I started the ground school and put some time in each day working with the pilots who were already licensed to fly the new 4 engine jet transport built in England, the BAE-146. These pilots had been through the simulator and flight schools in Scotland and they brought the first aircraft back to Rome. They had the basics down fairly well, but some of the procedures in the flight manual (in English) were giving them trouble. Werner Romanelo asked me if I could give them some help on this. This kept me plenty busy for a couple of weeks.

At the end of the ground schools, I was called in by Carlo and told that the movie company needed to use one of the G-1s and pilots to do a scene for the movie he had been working on for the last few months. It was an all ground action scene at Ciampino airport with no flying involved, but because it was in tight quarters with lots of camera gear and people involved, he wanted me to do it as I was the most experienced pilot he had. I told him as long as I got my name right below his in the credits, it was no problem. He said something in Italian that I deciphered as "In your dreams" and there went my movie career down the drain.

Our niece, Toni Hill, was touring Europe and was staying with us for a while. I invited both my wife and Toni to come out and watch the scene being shot that afternoon. I went to the Ciampino airport, got fitted for my costume and watched the special effects team change the left side of the G-1 into a beat up hulk with dents in it, the cabin windows glazed and cracked and black streaks of oil all over everything. This was all done with aluminum cooking foil, water based paint, etc. It looked terrible. They had taken the first six rows of seats out to make room in the cabin for the actors and props. The airline name on the fuselage was in Arabic script. Carlo had them put my name in Arabic below the left cockpit window. "There, you're in." he said.

The assistant director briefed me on the scene and how they wanted it done. I said (in perfect Italian)"You gotta be kidding!" He assured me he was not and to save the humor for the scene. The time comes with lights positioned and cameras on the dollies. A lot of airport people came out from the offices and hangars to watch the show along with my wife and niece who are right in front. I stride onto the set in costume, a heavy Arab robe covering my clothing, a black beard in place, heavy black sunglasses and a white burnoose on my head. The copilot, actors and props are all aboard the aircraft. I powered the air stair door up into place, got in the left seat, started the engines and we taxied out toward the run-up ramp beside the runway. I'm watched for the signal from the assistant director. He waved the green flag. *Action!*

I taxied up toward the ramp, cut off the left engine and pulled up in front of the cameras to where there were chalk marks to stop. The right engine is cut off and I go back to the air stair door. When the right engine prop stopped, I popped the door open and it folded out and down toward the ramp. As it does about a dozen chickens flew out, flapping all over the place, squawking and clucking. Then, an Arab man comes down the steps pulling a goat and Arab children ran down the steps, strewing paper bags and clothing. Next the women and men in robes, rags and bare feet tumble out along with more goats and some small sheep.

All this time I'm standing at the top of the door waving my arms, yelling in English, get off the damn airplane and other tidbits. It doesn't matter what I say. It's all going to be dubbed in with Arabic anyway. Finally, all twenty extras are off the plane and I'm still throwing bags and boxes off onto the ramp and the director waves and yells whatever "Cut" is in Italian. Man, I'm thinking am I glad that's over. That's what I thought. That's not what the director thought. We finally got it right on the third take, nearly three hours later. I was so drenched with sweat I could hardly walk.

This movie, a comedy, was being made for distribution in the Middle Eastern Arab states. Apparently they do a good business with them in Egypt, Tunisia, Saudi, Yemen, etc. I got my paycheck from Carlo a few weeks later. L30,000 (thirty-thousand lira), or $24 U.S. I wasn't in the union or it would have been double that. I made up my mind if something like this came up again I would ask to re-negotiate my contract.

I had been busy training two young copilots to get them ready to go to school on the BAE-146 and also training a ground instructor to teach re-current training after I left. It was the first week of July and Carlo called me into his office. When I got there, Werner was with him. Carlo said "Your contract is up this week. We would like to know if you are going home or want to stay on. We can make a three year contract, but we have to know right away." I told them I would have to talk it over with Ellie and why three years instead of one, as before?

Carlo said that they had a chance to hire a good Captain and certified instructor pilot, but he wanted a three year contract. If I wanted to stay, they needed to know that I wouldn't be leaving before three years. If I wanted a one year contract, they would take the other pilot to make sure they were covered under the regulations. I told them I would let them know tomorrow.

I talked to Ellie that evening about this. She said that her mother was having difficult health problems and with her father no longer alive to help that she should be close enough to be of help if needed. She also said it had been a great year, one we would never forget, but she would like to get settled down for the long haul if we could.

I had to agree that she made a good case and after thinking it over for an hour or so, I said I thought that the best thing to keep us happy would be to go home and get settled. The next morning, I told Carlo and Werner that I liked them and Mistral Air, but I loved my wife who had been beside me for 32 years and since she wanted to go home, I would take her home. They said they understood, but they had kind of gotten used to having a "Gringo" around to keep things stirred up. I told Carlo with all the Westerns he had made, he could probably get the exact "Gringo" they wanted from central casting.

A year can seem very short when things go your way and it's exciting to get up in the morning knowing this is not going to last forever, so make the most of it.

The "Going Home" lunch the company threw for me the week we were heading back was almost painful. The people I had worked with stood up and drank a toast to Commandante Sparks. I waved them to sit down, stood up and said (in Italian) "All of us who do the flying are brothers, all who support us and keep our airplanes ready are our family. I choose you to be my family, as I want to be part of yours. You have earned my respect. I have tried to earn yours. We are all better because of each other. May we all have the best fortune."

As I cleaned out my office that last afternoon, everyone came by to say goodbye in their own way, the mechanics, the office staff, the parts men, pilots, Werner and Carlo. The three pretty and thoroughly married young office secretaries each gave me a quick kiss on the cheek. I told them that that was a heck of a lot better than the handshake I had gotten from everyone else. They laughed and said I had made them laugh a lot, they would miss me and my "sposa" was a lucky woman.

I turned in my keys, credit cards, my gate pass for the airport and my instructor license that had to go back to Civil Avia. I was now just another tourist.

The flight back to New York and on down to Orlando was long and tiresome. It seemed as though I had spent a lot of my life saying goodbye to people. Maybe it would be a good idea to come up with a plan for the next part of it that had some stability involved with it. I was fifty-five years old and no longer a spring chicken. No longer a boy wonder either and getting a lot closer to being an old timer. I thought of the retired pilots of all types, airline, corporate, private, who used to gather every weekend at the Front Range and Aurora Airpark Airports east of Denver and other airports west, south and north. They sat and drank coffee, walked around looking at the tied down airplanes and talked about the "good ole days" before all this complicated stuff came along; the times when you could fire up, take off and go wherever you wanted to, land at any airport, except military, without any fuss. You could fly any altitude you liked, the sky was free, the gas was cheap and things were pretty simple to understand.

After the war the boom came. Airlines sprouted up all over the place, the military had to have a lot of the sky to operate in and you had to *keep out* of their areas. You'd better have a radio if you wanted to get into a bigger airport. The tower wouldn't give you a green or red light at some of the big ones anymore. You had to fly at different altitudes depending on which direction you were going. As time went by you had to have more training to get that private license, the test got pretty tough compared to what it once was. Then, not too long ago, the FAA said you had to take a test every two years, something called a Bi-annual Flight Review (BFR), before you could take your own airplane and fly from one dirt airport to another grass airport.

The big thing about flying for so many pilots was the freedom you had in the early days. It was like the "old west" before barbed wire and fences. Back then you could walk to the top of a hill and look in almost any direction and all you would see were places to go that you hadn't been to before. In your airplane all it took was a little movement of the controls, no fording rivers and no trying to break trail to the top of a mesa. It opened up the world to you in a matter of hours instead of months. It was as close to real freedom as most pilots have ever felt or would ever feel. But this feeling is short lived. You have to keep your eye on the fuel gauge, your reality meter.

There probably never was an old west like we see it in the John Wayne movies. The extreme difficulties, the hardships, the sacrifice of comfort, the shortness of life for so many young innocents has been layered over with the thrill of adventure and the triumph of good over evil. The western has been made over into the modern version of the morality play of the middle ages. So what has all of this to do with airplanes? Good question.

It has virtually nothing to do with airplanes, but it has quite a lot to do with the age old desire to have the same power and freedom of action that the God's had. Almost all deities of the various early religious cult beliefs had the ability to move through space without effort, flying or simply moving from one location to another without limitation. Some had wings, some traveled in ships in the sky and there were many other manifestations. Almost all Paleolithic and Neolithic cave and stone wall art show figures with wing like appendages or in positions above the terrain surface. Roman, Greek, Asian, Chinese and Hebrew writings include descriptions of gods, angels, devils, genii and other forms of beings with this miraculous power. The search for this freedom, through magic and spells or adaptation (Icarus with wings of feathers and wax) has continued to this era, with the balloon, powered with hot air, being the most successful before Wilbur and Orville Wright.

The modern understanding of the basic laws of physics has led to the proliferation of "action at a distance" mentality. The first phases of this were the telegraph stations linking army posts and railroad operations with stationary lines and then the extension from one continent to another one with the undersea telegraph cable. Next came widespread two way contact via stationary wires with the telephone. Information was delivered one way via radio waves to a household receiver. Two way communication via radio waves, information of movements of objects in space (radar), video and audio transmission through space and later wires by television equipment. Then there was the development of mammoth size computer banks to handle complex mathematical equations. Now we have computers the size of a box of Kleenex and more powerful than any of the early IBM equipment. The thing that has transformed modern society and will very probably destroy it within a few decades are the wireless systems with information distribution, two way communication, the internet attachments and unthought of things yet to come. All society around the world could be brought to a total standstill with the detonation of 20 or 30 nuclear devices designed to "fry" the electric grid and it's components with neutron radiation.

Is this a real possibility? That's not the right question. Is this a real probability? That's the right question and the right answer is: Nobody Knows.

For the first time in recorded history, *everybody* has access to doomsday weapons. Thermonuclear is what we hear all the time, but that isn't what we should be worrying about. In all honesty, the one thing that can do the job relatively quietly, easily, and permanently, is some type of biological warfare. Airplanes will probably have some part in whatever happens in the world in times to come, whether good or bad. You cannot send Anthrax over the internet, the bubonic plague over a cell phone, wheat blight over a conference call, or the severe type of influenza that killed twenty-five million Americans at the end of World War I through television.

I brought this up to show that we people on planet Earth are connected, like it or not, and the largest link that we presently have in operation is travel by aircraft. Many more people travel by automobile and even trains, possibly, but to go any real distance in a hurry, which we seem to be in all the time, you must go to an airport.

The airplane can be a fantastic tool for promoting peace or a ravening Angel of Death in war. The weapons that it can now carry are insanely out of proportion to the amount of death and destruction they will cause in relation to their size and mass. One cargo aircraft can carry enough medical supplies to save the lives of tens of thousands of people in distress. Which way will our aircraft be utilized in the coming decades? Only our political leaders can tell us and they are constrained by events beyond our immediate control to a great degree.

These were some of the musings I had on the way home. The immediate plan has to be simple, like finding a job in a desirable place to live. I hadn't found Florida to be the place I wanted to spend the rest of my life. I don't play golf, I don't own a boat, don't care about fishing and I plan to take up shuffleboard when I'm 90. So Ellie and I talked it over and decided that to relocate to Denver one more time was the way to go. She would be fairly close to her mother and I had enough contacts there that I thought I could hook up with a job without too much trouble. We stayed with Ellie's sister Marge and her husband John for a couple of weeks. We got our junk loaded on a U-Haul truck and trailer and hit the road for Colorado.

A week later we've unloaded at a condo we rented and I started the airport circuit to see who's looking for a pilot. I found out pretty shortly that most of the guys I had known for the last 30 years have retired and are living in Florida, California or somewhere else. I did find two or three old friends and they told me that jobs were as scarce as hen's teeth. There are no corporate or company jobs open that they know of, but they'll ask around. One salesman at Combs on Stapleton airport said he heard recently that a little part 135 air freight Operator called Air Today might be looking for pilots. They were down the way from Combs to the east about a mile, so remembering the old Texas saying again "You can't git a job unless you got a job," I decided to check with them. When I did the Chief Pilot, Al Halbert, asked if I had any turbo-prop experience and I told him yes, some. They had two Mitsubishi MU-2s, two Swearingen Metroliners and one Cessna C-208A Caravan in the fleet.

I filled out an application, and under Turbine, I listed 8,900 hours (Turbo-jet 3,815, and Turbo-prop 5,085). He asked if I had flown anything like a Swearingen 4 and I said I had about 300 hours in a Swearingen 2A, with PT-6's. I got hired on the spot, had a check ride a few days later and flew my first trip September 29, 1988, after riding as an observer for a couple of days. I was put on the Cessna 208A Caravan (*Photo #47*) and flew the Denver-Casper- Rapid City-Denver run. After two weeks of this, I checked out in the Swearingen 4 Metro (SA226-TC) (*Photo #48*) with Air Research TPE-331 engines. The routes changed according to the season if it was a mail run or cargo run. We also flew charters to pick up and deliver freight to operators with breakdowns in the oil fields, etc. Then winter arrived.

We basically flew to airports in Wyoming, Montana, Colorado, and South Dakota on daily runs with mail or freight. We loaded the freight on board our three airplanes at 5:00 AM, getting off the ground by 6:00 AM. Sometimes it was all small freight, with boxes no bigger than 3 feet x 4 feet, and other times it was ugly freight for Casper or Billings—drill stems, a 400# transmission and small drums of special drilling fluid. We had a fork lift and five guys to load all this. The pilots were responsible for making sure the cargo was in the proper position in the cabin for weight and balance control and chained or secured properly. So we helped load our airplane with the cargo crew, then they went on to the next one and so on. We usually stayed at our farthest destination for the day and left to return home about 4:00 PM, picking up freight going to Denver and arriving home about 6:45 PM.

When the real winter started about the middle of October, it was very difficult loading on an open ramp at 5 degrees with 25 mph winds, chill factor –12. I had good arctic type gear and I could hardly get into the pilot seat with it on, but it was so cold you didn't take anything off until the cabin warmed up which was usually about 10 minutes after takeoff. We flew single pilot unless we were training someone or carrying a helper to help get some ugly freight off at a small airport. I see one entry in my logbook: SLC (Salt Lake)-BUT (Butte, MT)-HLN (Helena)-GTF (Gr. Falls)-HLN-BUT-SLC, Instrument time 3:45, Flight time 4:35, Night time 1:35, Inst. Approaches 5. This was a long, hard day and this was a scheduled flight that flew six days a week.

When Christmas started getting close, we were flying extra trips when needed. Sometimes we just bedded down in the hangars to get enough sleep to be legal. We rotated pilots with our two spare captains and the chief pilot, but that still meant when there was freight to fly, you flew. Well, hell, that was what we signed on for. I flew because I wanted to, not because I had to. There was a lot of weather flying this winter and lots of instrument approaches, but the Metro handled it pretty well. It was so cold we didn't have much icing problems, until January 4, 1989. The weather had set up an inversion coming out of Canada, with it being about 15 degrees warmer at altitude than it was on the ground which was about 14 degrees.

I had the DEN-CPR-BIL-CPR-DEN run this morning. The Metro (*Photo #48*) was full up on freight. I had George Graham, a retired Frontier Airlines Captain, riding in the copilot seat as an observer. He did PR work for us, making contacts with airlines and re-shippers and was good company to have along. I took off, climbed to FL180 (18,000 feet) and started getting ice about 11,000 feet. The engine de-ice was working fine on the props and cowl inlet heat, but I had to run the boots part of the time on the descent into Casper. We unloaded about 800 pounds of freight and added about 300, so we were 500 pounds lighter and had burned off about 250 pounds of fuel.

We climbed up to 16,000 feet for the 30 minute flight to Billings. The ice was moderate at this altitude. We had everything going—engine inlet cowl heat, prop heat, wing and tail boots cycling. About 20 minutes out from Billings, ATC cleared us down to 8,000 feet and as we descended through 9,000 feet the left engine quit dead without warning. I glanced at the warning readout and it said L ENG DEICE. George looked out the side window at it and said the ice had almost completely covered the air inlet. No air, no run. The circuit breaker on that de-icing system is popped out and won't reset. I was hand flying the aircraft against the pull of the windmilling engine, so I pulled the prop control back into feather. It feathered and the prop stopped in the streamlined feather position. I asked George to call Billings approach control and declare an emergency and get the weather for runway 9L, the ILS runway.

Billings Approach control acknowledges the emergency call and tells us we must maintain 6,500 feet until the 10 mile DME arc, then we are cleared for the ILS runway 9L approach, maintain 5,700 feet on the 10 DME arc until crossing the 271 degree radial of the Billings VOR, no procedure turn inbound. The current weather for Billings is indefinite 200 feet ceiling, RVR 2,500 feet, wind 120 degrees at 8 knots, 1½ inches of snow on runway, braking action reported as fair by airport vehicle. We're right at landing minimums, but with an emergency declared, I can legally land at zero/zero if I have to. I've practiced for that situation quite a bit.

George acknowledges the clearance and as I asked him to tell approach control to inform the tower that we *will* land and we cannot go around. We do the landing checklist, holding off on the flaps and gear until we are inbound on the localizer. We bend it in on the arc, intercept the localizer, call the tower, are cleared to land, and there is no improvement in the weather. I look at George and smile and say, "I always knew I'd have to do one of these ILS things someday." George laughs and says "I always had the copilot do 'em for me."

We finalize the checklist and I asked George to call the lights in sight. There's a space of about four inches high at the bottom of each windshield kept clear by the defrosters, enough to see to land once we get the lights. I have to keep the plane slightly slipped to the right to keep it flying straight. We're right on the localizer, on glide slope, right on airspeed +10 knots to counteract the drag of the wing ice. George calls lights at one o'clock, I look up and get my alignment set, 80 feet above the runway, power back, flare, solid touchdown, gentle braking, come back into idle reverse on the right engine. The braking action is good now and we roll to a stop just past the runway 4 intersection with 4,000 feet of the 9,000 foot runway left. The airport emergency equipment is standing by on the ramp, but we tell the tower all we need is a tow in. It's too slippery to try to taxi in on one engine. Fifteen minutes later we are parked at the air freight ramp and the unloading crew is preparing to unload us.

I went in and called the tower, thanked them all for a great job and had them thank the emergency team for coming out. Such a little thing as a thank you from the crew really makes their day. The mechanic from Billings

Aviation is looking at the engine with the cowling up. He checks with his meter and says "The controller for the left engine de-ice is shelled out. It won't take but an hour to replace it." I called Denver. We have a spare controller and they got it on the Frontier Airlines early afternoon flight; the controller was changed, the system was checked out and we were only a half an hour late on our departure time back to Casper and on to Denver—just another day at the office.

George shook my hand vigorously and laughed. He said "I've got to fly with you again sometime. This was the most fun I've had in a year. A time or two there, I almost thought you knew what you were doing" and he laughed again. I said "Captain Graham, you're welcome on my airplane anytime." A left handed compliment in the flying business is the best you will ever get, especially from a pilot who flew DC-3, Convair 340 & 440 aircraft for thirty years.

The weather in January was very cold, snow was about average and there was lots of freight. I flew fifteen more days, about 65 hours, after the single engine landing in Billings. On the evening of January 31, I taxied into the freight operations area and the crew car picked me up and took me to the company hangar on the south side of Stapleton. I took the log and freight manifest sheets in and put them on the dispatch desk in the tray for N752S Metroliner. The chief pilot called everyone in the office over and then he sat on the edge of the desk. I filled out the paperwork. He took it and said "I've got some news. Effective at midnight tonight, Air Today ceases operation. All of you pilots will get your paychecks tomorrow afternoon and if any of the ground staff work the next few days, you will be paid for it when it's all done." There was not a single word from anyone. The last few days there had been rumors that the owner of the airplanes might be trying to sell them, but there are always rumors flying around small operations, be it airplanes, truck lines, tugboats or what have you. We picked up our gear and were told to be at the office between noon and 5:00 PM tomorrow to get our check and final paperwork. The airplanes would be flown out in the morning, all five of them.

The following afternoon we seven pilots, three mechanics, two office staff and two freight handlers had a cup of coffee together for the last time. This had been an interesting four and a half months for me, something to put flying freight in perspective. The pilots for the big freight operations, DHL, UPS, AIRBORNE, FEDEX, EVERGREEN and others used to have a saying: Freight don't complain. No passenger squawks, no turbulence problems, no ground hold complaints, and so on. They flew the same equipment as the Airlines, made about the same money and didn't have a worry as long as the freight got on the ground undamaged. Freight don't complain—kind of a catchy phrase. If I ever start up an air freight operation, it'll be named FDC Airways.

Well, none of us saw the door closing this time. We all scattered like a covey of quail, trying to find another safe place to roost. The mechanics went to work right away. The shops for general aviation and sometimes even the airlines maintenance programs, always seemed to have a place for a skilled aviation mechanic. The office gals disappeared into the greater Denver labor pool. The freight handlers probably went right to work on the Stapleton freight ramp for one of the freight handling companies. That left the pilots, seven applicants for any seat in the front end of an airplane. I know that Al Halbert, me and at least one other pilot found positions in Denver, because I saw them from time to time. Later on Al and I were employed by the same company at the same time. As to the other four, I hope they found something they liked. They were good kids and pretty fair pilots from what I saw. You had to be pretty competent to stay alive in this kind of work in this part of the country at this time of year. Fedex lost a Caravan 208B on approach to Stapleton in Denver this winter in an icing situation, just 7 miles south of the airport, killing the pilot and narrowly missing a house as it went in vertically. The turboprop engine helps a great deal, but ice is a terrible foe to handle correctly.

I got a tip from a pilot friend that an FAR 135 charter operator called International Jet Aviation, located at Centennial Airport south of Denver, was a good choice to put in an application if you had some experience. They were operating a number of Learjets and some other types. They had at least ten to twelve airplanes normally and a very good operational history and background. I had found nothing going on in the corporate pilot market. It was time to explore alternates. I knew very little about the Learjet, other than a short ride in one once, in the back end. Still, I thought that if I could fly the Cessna Citation without too much difficulty, maybe the Lear wouldn't be that much harder.

I went to Centennial Airport to the hangar of IJA east of the control tower and walked into a very attractive set of offices with everything well set up. The hangar itself was clean and organized. My first impression was that this was being run more like a corporate operation than the average "Charter on the cheap" operation I had seen a lot of in my career. The young receptionist said that all of the top people were out, but I could fill out an application. If the Chief Pilot or the President of the company returned this afternoon they would review it and someone would be in touch to give me the results in a day or two.

I filled out the application, gave some Denver references, handed it to the young lady and went into the hangar to look at the Learjets. They were good looking aircraft—clean and looking ready to go in no time at all. Well, we'll see if they can use an old guy with a lot of miles, but all the gears still meshing smoothly.

Chapter 10 — Life in a Learjet

The next day the phone rang and I was invited to come out to IJA for an interview with Steve Parks, the Chief Pilot, and Lynn Krogh, a partner and the manager of operations. Would this afternoon between 2:00 PM and 3:00 PM be convenient? I said it would and the appointment was made. At the meeting I was introduced to Bill Milam, the other partner and President of IJA. He and Lynn Krogh had put this company together on more-or-less a shoestring and had made it into one of the best Part 135 charter operations in the western U.S.

I provided the information on my background and experience to Steve and Lynn. We discussed the general operation at IJA and the long-term outlook the company had for its continued operations. I told them that if they employed me and I proved satisfactory, I would be a long term employee, as that was what I was looking for. I wanted to finish my career in the western U.S. and would adhere to the standards and guidelines of IJA in such employment. Lynn said at the moment that there was no immediate opening for a Lear position, but this would probably change within a few months. However, they did need a well experienced Cessna 340 (*Photo #49*) pilot who could be put to work in short order.

I had indicated experience with the Cessna 310 and the Cessna 421A series on my application and this was what interested them at this time. With over 2,200 hours of time in the 421, which was a big brother of the 340, it should be no difficulty in getting me a part 135 letter in the Cessna. Then when the Lear position opened up, we could look at that. Would I be interested in this type of employment? And the answer was maybe. I asked about the pay for this operation, what other plans, medical, etc. would be included and said that I would stay for six months minimum if I took the job. However, at the end of that time, if no Lear position was in the offing and a better position came up from another operator, I would reserve the right to move on with two week's notice. I thought this was fair and it seemed to meet with their approval and we had a deal.

On February 20, 1989, I started my employment with IJA and on the 24th, passed the check ride and had my letter to fly Part 135 charter-on-demand in the Cessna 340. This particular airplane had several add-on maximizer kits that increased its ability to make short take-off and landing operations. We used it in small airport/high altitude airport operations with full passenger loads with no difficulty. Having pressurization made all the difference in comfort for the passengers and being fully equipped for de-icing operations gave me a lot of flexibility in flight planning. Telluride, Aspen, Durango, Steamboat Springs and other higher altitude airports were just right for the 340. I enjoyed flying this little machine. It was more like being in a sports car than a stretch limo and the Lear could wait its turn. When you're having fun making a living, you should make the most of it.

I never was an airplane snob and I'm proud of that. Oh, sure, I enjoyed stepping out of the Jetstar with a nice shirt and tie on, down the air stair door of that 4 engine jet with all the other pilots on the ramp standing by their King Airs and smaller airplanes. It's a one-upmanship world, after all. But I didn't think I was any better than they were, just more fortunate. I enjoyed stepping out of the old war surplus silver Twin Beech when I had one. At that time and that place, I was one of the fortunate few. Other pilots would come over and walk around it and go back to their Tri-Pacer, Bonanza or Cessna 170 after paying their respects to the "big iron". The radial engine was on "real" airplanes. The day I got checked out in the Cessna 195, with its 275 HP Jacobs radial engine was one of the best days of my young aviation career. I had arrived, I was flying radials now. I've been fortunate enough to fly thirty-seven different makes and models of aircraft. Sometimes I was asked which one was my favorite. I always replied "That's easy, the one who's keys are in my pocket right now."

About the middle of March, I was sent on a Lear (*Photo #50*) as an observer on a trip to Albuquerque and flew as the copilot on the way back to begin getting ready for the copilot rating. You need to get some time in the airplane to get to know it. You have to know an aircraft to some extent to be able to train in it and flying copilot with an experienced captain is the best way to go. It gives you some real good information first hand and gives him a reason to stay awake. I started jumping from the Cessna to the Lear and back for the next eight weeks. We were flying a lot with all the airplanes, and I do mean a lot. It was six days a week some weeks and the Lear was becoming pretty familiar. We also had two Mitsubishi MU-2s for freight hauling, but I wasn't interested in them and I got to bypass that part of the operation. Al Halbert came to work for IJA and he filled one of the MU-2 slots since he had a lot of time in them.

In June, I was sent to Lear school and simulator training at Flight Safety in Wichita, KS. I got along well there. They had good instructors and being able to spend time at the Lear factory watching the Lears being built was a valuable experience—then back to Denver, lots of flying, and getting ready for the check/rating ride in the Lear. On June 30, 1989, I passed the ride and got my new temporary license with the Lear type rating added to my other types. On July 2, I strapped into the left seat and flew a freight flight to Salt Lake City with a nice young copilot. I didn't tell him that this was my first trip as a captain, but he must have known it, because he watched me like a hawk. I was glad they started me out with a freight flight. Remember, freight don't complain.

Well, I wanted to fly Lears, and I got to fly Lears—and fly, and fly—and also the 340, to break the monotony. The first month I flew 70 hours on Lears and 21 hours on the 340. That's a lot of flying in this type of operation. I was only one of about eight captains and ten copilots. IJA was rolling and they kept the equipment maintained, clean and the crews were dressed in standard uniforms. Everything ran very smoothly for a charter operation. I got to see a lot of the Rocky Mountains again, usually from 41,000 to 45,000 feet high. We had contracts with several of the freight haulers, UPS, DHL and EMERY among others, and made daily flights to Albuquerque, El Paso and Boise on a scheduled run basis.

The flights that were extra important were the organ recovery trips for C.O.R.S. (Colorado Organ Recovery Service). These were usually at night and could be to anywhere an organ donor had become available. They were at night because the hospital operating rooms were available then and the surgeons we carried usually performed the actual surgery. We pushed hard on these trips, knowing that someone died to make these organs available to people who still had a chance to live because of them. Some organs and tissues had a lot longer window, sometimes more than 24 hours more than others. The heart trip was the most critical. From the time the heart/lung machine was stopped for the donor, until the heart had to be in place and beating in the recipient, 6 hours was the maximum allowable time.

We had a special flight plan "code" to let ATC centers and towers know that we were an organ medical flight and therefore received special handling to expedite the trip and reduce the time as much as possible. The heart recovery trip had the least number of trips. Kidneys, livers, eyes, and a half a dozen other types, plus skin, nerves, ligaments, bone (there's an amazing number of usable things that can be used from a cadaver) were the more usual items we brought back. The recovery surgeons were all young, highly motivated and very easy to work with.

But understand, although we pushed performance and operating standards to the limits much of the time, we never went out of bounds, taking chances that could have made all of us organ donors. The company insisted on this and the crews adhered to this policy. The one time I might have gotten one foot across the line, just a very little bit, was a heart trip from Oakland, CA, back to Stapleton on the night of January 6, 1992. This was a long leg, 1,050 statute miles direct or 915 nautical miles, which is used in aviation. We had landed in Oakland, the recovery team had been choppered (flown by helicopter) to the hospital while we refueled and prepared for the return trip to Denver. The weather was cold, but good the whole way, except for some light fog in Oakland. When the hospital called and said the chopper was leaving, we got everything ready for engine start. When the chopper sat down beside us the copilot helped them load all their gear in and closed the door while I was starting the engines. We were given taxi and take off clearance immediately and within 7 minutes were rolling on takeoff. As we were climbing eastbound, I asked the head of the team how much time we had left. He checked the paperwork and said 3 hours and 4 minutes. We had been flying 4 minutes.

The trip from Oakland to Denver will ordinarily take 2 hours and 20 minutes if there are no delays involved. The chopper from Stapleton to the hospital should take 10 minutes—chopper pad to operating room 10 minutes—heart prep and trim arteries 10 minutes—get operation performed and start heart 8 to 10 minutes—minimum total time required 2 hours and 56 minutes—total available time 3 hours and 4 minutes—extra time available 8 minutes.

I had filed for flight level 390 (thirty-nine thousand feet) in order to get the best tailwinds and was keeping the indicated airspeed at .80 mach. When I was 90 nautical miles out of Stapleton, I requested descent and kept the airspeed at 450 to 460 knots indicated. The air was smooth with no turbulence, so I could keep a higher speed in the descent. At 40 nautical miles from the airport, they sent me over to Denver approach control who told me we had no traffic for at least 20 minutes. I was cleared for the visual approach to runway 26 Left. I asked him if they were doing the radar maintenance tonight. He said yes, as a matter of fact it was just going out of service for the next few minutes while it was being checked. I thanked him, continued my descent at 350 knots indicated air speed, came down under 10,000 feet at 300 indicated and set up for a left turn onto final for 26L. At 8,000 feet I backed off the power and deployed the speed brakes, dropped the landing gear at 200 indicated, turned a 2 mile final at 150 indicated, went to full flaps, touched down at normal landing speed and pulled into Combs Aircraft where the chopper was waiting with the engine running. We rolled to a stop, got everything into the chopper and it lifted off in less than a minute and headed to the hospital.

After the heart was in and beating, they still had 15 minutes left on the clock. I got them an extra 12 minutes with a high speed approach. I might have been a little faster than 250 knots indicated when I went below 10,000 feet, but I was too busy to look (wink, wink). The people we worked with at all the hospitals in Denver were some of the best sports and greatest passengers I ever had. I think all of the IJA crews felt the same way. In my "Orchid letter" file, among the many letters I received giving me a pat on the back for some trip, the ones I treasure the most are the ones from the medical teams we flew. Quite often they included the details of what happened to the organs and the people who benefited from them. Sometimes you get paid twice for doing your job. And Kurt Tipton, thanks for your help as my first officer on that trip.

Another heart trip with C.O.R.S. gave us a different set of circumstances to work with. I was dispatched to Tucson, AZ, on a heart recovery trip one night in a Lear 24 with a four person surgical team. The weather was fine; the trip down was as standard as they come, right up to the landing. As we touched down, as soon as the nose wheel touched, we had a hell of a wicked vibration develop. I lifted the nose wheel back off and used aerodynamic braking as much as I could, but when I couldn't hold it off anymore it again set up a bad vibration—but not nearly as bad as it had been. We slowed and the vibration ceased at a slow taxi speed. We taxied into the fixed base operator's ramp and parked. There was an ambulance waiting to take the team to the hospital. I was told that they expected to be back in no more than an hour and a half. I told them to get going and I would call as soon as I found out what the situation was. As they were driving out I found the problem very quickly. The nose gear shock absorbing strut was flat, meaning that all the nitrogen gas in it had been lost during flight. There was no hydraulic fluid running all over everything, so the seals in the strut hadn't been ruptured. It had somehow lost the gas and there was no way we could take off with it flat. This was specifically forbidden by the flight manual. Long before we could get up to takeoff speed, it would vibrate so badly it could possibly tear the entire nose gear assembly out of its mounts. We had to get it filled with nitrogen again before we could leave. It was now a little after midnight. The shop was closed for the night. There was only me, my copilot and two line service attendants to fix this problem in one hour. The heart team could not get that heart back in time to save the recipient if we were delayed very long. I was really feeling the pressure.

The keys to the shop were in the office. We opened it and pulled a gear jack, some tools and a nitrogen bottle with a gauge and screw-on high pressure hose out to the aircraft. Since I was the only one who had any shop experience, I set up the jack and had them jack the nose wheel to the off ground position. I hooked up the bottle, opened the strut valve lock and started easing the nitrogen feed valve open. When we had about 200 psi in it, we lowered it back onto the ground. It had about ½ inch of strut showing. I pressured it slowly up until it had about 4 inches of strut showing, locked off the strut valve, shut off and bled the pressure off the nitrogen line and secured the bottle. While the aircraft was being fueled the copilot and I washed up. I called the hospital and told the team coordinator we were ready. I had a flight plan on file and when the ambulance raced up to the aircraft, we loaded the passengers, the Playmate cooler—with the heart in it—and flew to Denver with ample time to get the heart procedure done without panic. The report we received a few days after this indicated that the patient had a very good prognosis. I got a letter of commendation from IJA for the handling of the trip, but it really should have included the copilot and those two anonymous ramp rats. We all brought that heart home.

IJA had a variety of Lears so most of the trips were scheduled for the one that was best suited for the type of trip. We had the very basic Lear, the model 24—the original Lear was the model 23, but it had numerous things that were soon upgraded and the basic Lear then became the 24—which was shorter and lighter than the model 25. The 24 was a 7 place aircraft, and had improvements to engines and systems. The improved models were noted by having a letter attached to the model number such as 24A, B, C, or D. The 24D was a little rocket ship and was able to climb initially at 6,900 feet a minute after takeoff. Its ceiling was 45,000 feet altitude and max cruise was 545 mph (.86mach), but it was normally cruised at 490 mph (.78 mach) to get the range out of it.

The 25 was larger and heavier, was 10 place and had bigger engines, but with about the same flight profile, except it would only climb 6,000 feet a minute initially. Believe me, you couldn't tell the difference.

The 35 was slightly larger than the 25, had turbo-fan jet engines and was heavier. It was about the same speed as the 25, but had about 30 per cent more range with these new engines on the same basic amount of fuel. There are now much larger Lear models and they are a far cry from the first Lear 23 that was available. One large sized pilot had a demo flight for his company in the 23. He went back to them and described this new airplane as "an executive mailing tube" which wasn't that bad of a description, all in all.

I flew thirteen different Learjets with IJA, although two of them were customer airplanes we were providing crew service on. Each one was an individual and had its own personality. Several had modifications that changed the way they flew from when they were standard models. I used to carry a small notebook in my shirt pocket that had each of these aircraft listed with all the information I needed to set it up for flying and operating it.

Some of the passenger trips were a lot of fun, others not so much. The people involved were the key and they could be the difference between day and night to handle. John Denver was sunny, funny and always laughing or causing laughter among the passengers and crew. I had known his father in the '70's in Denver before I went to New York. John "Dutch" Deutschendorf, Sr. was an ex-Air Force officer and a hell of a good pilot. He had flown John Jr.'s airplanes, and the guys at Stapleton had a lot of respect for him. He filed his final flight plan in 1982. I always thought it took something out of John, Jr. He hadn't had any real problems that I ever heard of before this. They seemed to develop after Dutch passed on.

In my logbook I found the last two times that John chartered our Cessna 340 and saw that I had flown him to Eagle and Sheridan, WY. I was shocked to hear that John had bought the farm in 1997, in a little single seat sport airplane. He was a pretty fair pilot from what I had seen, but all I know about his crash is what I read in the Accident Report by the NTSB. John Denver might be gone, but his music and the movie *Oh God* will be around a long, long time.

We had all kinds of charters and some were pretty funny. In August 1991 we had the Monday Night Football broadcasting crew to take to Akron, OH on Tuesday, after the Monday night broadcast of the Broncos game. (*Photo #52*) They sent their luggage from the hotel in the afternoon. It consisted mainly of five golf bags full of golf clubs. After removing two seats from the middle of the airplane, we cargo strapped the golf clubs down and had just enough room left to shoehorn these broadcasters into the remaining six seats (doesn't CBS hire any small people?) and thank heavens it was a relatively short trip. No cocktails were served on this flight, believe me.

Somewhat on the same subject, we flew Brent Musburger for two days on a trip—real interesting guy. I don't think I'd care to debate him on any subject except aviation. I picked up Neil Diamond in Cheyenne and took him to Aspen. We chatted for 20 minutes and I almost forgot he was a celebrity. He was about as down to earth as show folks get. The Royal Saudi Prince Kalial was formal, but polite, when I had him on a trip to a ski resort. Dr. Steven Covey is a name well known around Utah and the intermountain West. He's from BYU, in Provo, and I had flown him in the early '70s when I was flying out of Moab. He is a motivational personality and is pretty good at it from what I've heard. I had him on one trip, during this period, and he remembered me from the Moab trips.

We also flew trips that were more serious in nature and took a lot out of us. IJA contributed the services of a Learjet (*Photo #51*) which they had painted with a rainbow color scheme for the use of the Make a Wish Foundation. Phillips Petroleum donated the fuel, IJA donated the airplane and the IJA crews volunteered their time to fly these children and their families. This was one of the most difficult tasks we had. Taking a terminally ill child on his final trip took more out of us than any harsh weather or other difficulty in normal operations. It was little enough we could do, as we all felt it was the one way we could donate our skill to something really worthwhile.

I was the lucky pilot who got to fly Mrs. Lee Iacocca from Eagle, CO, to Las Vegas one trip. It was before the divorce between her and the head of the Chrysler Motor Company. The manager of her party wanted a 24 Lear. We tried to get him to take the 25 for a very small difference in price, after our dispatcher heard what the load would be. No, it had to be the cheap one. We arrived at Eagle airport, and when the two vehicles pulled up I knew this was going to be a lot of fun. They were going to Las Vegas for the weekend and there were only five people, their luggage (about 10 varied sized bags) and the dog. Did I mention the dog? This dog was certainly no bigger than a Siberian Wolfhound. Maybe it was a Siberian Wolfhound, I didn't ask. The trip took 55 minutes, but it sure seemed a lot longer. There was the manager, the security man, the maid, the PR guy, Mrs. Iacocca and the dog. Did I mention the dog?

We filled the luggage area behind the back seat and then had to load the rest of it down the aisle after everybody sat down and got their seat belts on. That only left the dog. He was firmly ensconced between the pilots, becoming more or less the flight engineer. As we got to altitude we hit some light turbulence. The dog howled, Mrs. Iacocca screamed, the maid joined in (in Spanish) and the manager leaned over the dog and said we had to stop the turbulence immediately. It was maybe moderate for a minute or so, then tapered off to light and then was gone. I had started down early to get out of it and when we touched down at McCarren Airport, I had burned about 30 extra gallons of fuel by staying low to get out of the turbulence. I was not at all surprised to hear that Mrs. Iacocca was not happy with the trip, and it was doubtful that we would be called for the trip back. The dog was the only one who enjoyed the trip, since he left us a little wet souvenir on the carpet by way of a tip. The Iacocca's divorced two years later. I didn't hear who got custody of the dog.

Speaking of Las Vegas trips, I had another one that was a lulu. I was the "on call" pilot that mid-winter day. When I got called out to go to Grand Island, NE, to pick up a charter customer, I was ready to go. He was stranded at the airport because his charter aircraft had developed a problem and couldn't finish taking him to Las Vegas. He had to be there downtown by 9:00 PM. We could make it, but it would be tight. We landed in Grand Island in a moderate snow storm, pulled up and put a quick fueling on the Lear, got luggage switched and taxied out in snow about 8 to 10 inches deep. The runways had been cleared, so take off was no problem. We were off and starting the climb, the landing gear was retracted, but the copilot told me we still had a gear unsafe light. We checked and found that the three gears were all up and locked, the main gear doors were closed, but the nose gear doors were still open to some extent. We could hear more air noise than usual. I held the speed down to maximum gear extension speed by climbing steeper and keeping the indicated speed at 210 mph. As we went higher, we were steadily going faster over the ground. That's the way air pressure works which is what you want to keep off the gear doors. The higher you are, the thinner the air, so there is less pressure against the airframe. I radioed our office in Denver, talked to the head mechanic and we both agreed that there was no danger of damage as long as I didn't exceed 210 mph indicated at any time.

This meant we could continue our trip to Las Vegas, but we had to alter our standard operating procedures to stay at or below 210 indicated. At high altitudes this would be no problem, but we had to be alert on the descent. The gear light never changed and the hydraulic pressure was normal. We started our letdown into Las Vegas further out than standard so that we had better control of our airspeed. We also informed Las Vegas approach control that we had a minor problem and should it change we would let them know. We reached the point that the gear needed to be extended and down went the gear handle. The gear lights went to warning, showing the gear was in transit, but the nose gear light stayed red, showing the gear hadn't reached the down and locked position. I called for a recycle, slowed down as much as I could and this time the main gear showed locked and a few seconds later the green "down and locked" light came on the nose gear. That was a big relief. The rest of the landing procedure was perfectly normal.

When we taxied in to the Hughes Aviation front line, the linemen were all staring at us. We shut down and opened the door. I leaped out to see what the hell they were all looking at. It was about 50 degrees temperature on the ramp. The nose wheel was almost completely covered in snow and ice was falling out of the nose wheel well. Everybody gathered around to see snow in Vegas. And that was our problem. On taxi and takeoff at Grand Island, the nose wheel had completely filled the nose wheel well by throwing soft snow up into it. The hydraulic pressure was strong enough to force the gear into the uplock, but it couldn't close the door because the snow was too packed to let the mechanism come upwards to the closed position. Our chief mechanic and I both thought that there would be no damage from this and there wasn't any.

The cab came whistling up, we loaded our passenger and his luggage in, he shook my hand and stuck something in my shirt pocket and off they roared. He had 35 minutes to make it to the Casino where the high stakes poker game was going to be played. If he didn't show by 9:00 PM, he would forfeit the $25,000 stake he had already paid to get a seat in the game. I guess he made it, but we had no way of knowing. We went in to get a cup of coffee and pay the fuel bill. I reached into my shirt pocket, felt something, and then I remembered he had stuck something into my pocket as he was getting in the cab.

The copilot was drinking coffee when I said hold out your hand, and I put three $50 bills in it. What our passenger had put in my pocket were six $50 bills. We got tips from time to time, but as far as I can remember this was the biggest one we had ever received.

One trip to California was very interesting. We got a charter request to carry a Mr. Spanos to Santa Barbara, CA, spend the day and return late night to Denver. We met Mr. Spanos at the airport and he said that he had to attend a party, and we would return after that. On the way out I visited with him while I got him something cold to drink, and learned that he was one of the sons of Alex G. Spanos, the principal owner of the San Diego Chargers football team. It became an interesting story when we landed. We were told that our passenger wanted us to come to the resort with him. I left instructions on servicing the Lear and to have it ready to leave anytime from 9:00 PM to 2:00 AM.

The van that picked us up took us about 10 miles to a gated, secured, very posh resort on the outskirts of Santa Barbara. We, the crew, were given a courtesy room to clean up, rest if we cared to and told to be ready to go to dinner with our passenger at 6:00 PM. We met him at that time by the main ballroom where there were about two or three hundred people milling about. Mr. Spanos took us to a group and introduced us to his family. Mr. Alex Spanos shook our hands, told us how glad he was to have us with them this evening, and thanked us for bringing his son safely to this celebration.

We were herded into a line and quickly found out that we were going through a receiving line to meet the head of the Greek Orthodox Church, the "other Pope." I told the senior Mr. Spanos that we didn't want to be a bother to this celebration, but he insisted that we were his guests and we would meet his Eminence. And so we did. The pope was a tall, thin man with a two foot beard, a miter on his head, simple but ornate robes and an air of great dignity.

Everyone was introduced to the pope by his ambassador, in Greek. If they were members of this religion, he would make the sign of the cross over their bowed heads. If not, he would make the slightest bow to them, and they would bow to him. We went through the line in order, and the pope smiled slightly as he gave my copilot and me a brief nod. After our very slight bow of the head, we were led out to the Spanos family table and seated at the far end. It was a swell party and just like the ones I had seen in a dozen movies. And here are us two throttle benders right in the middle of it. There was food, music and waiters with white napkins held on their arms. I was wondering how long it was going to last, when at midnight the elder Mr. Spanos came and said how glad he had been to have us as guests and to have a safe trip home.

And just like that, the party was over—like when a soap bubble disappears. In ten minutes the van was driving through the gates, and in half an hour we were lifting off in the Lear headed east. On the way back I told Mr. Spanos that I had met Pope John Paul II when I was flying in Rome. I told him that I met him through two friends I had become acquainted with there and who lived in this quaint mountain top town, which was the Popes residence during the heat of summer. You never know whom you're going to meet in the flying business.

Tammy Wynette was a country music singer and although I'm a Claude DeBussy and Maurice Ravel kind of guy, I knew who she was when I was sent to Durango, CO, to pick her and her party up and fly them to Nashville on September 23, 1990. I had been in Durango many times, stayed at the Strater Hotel, and ridden the Rio Grande train to Silverton and back. It was a great town to feel the atmosphere of the old west and the hospitality of the new west. Earl Barker was the man in charge at the Strater and what a great host he was. That Diamond Belle Saloon in the Strater was like a time machine that took you right back to the 1880's. The prices were a little more modern, however.

Miss Wynette and her band had been doing a show at the Ignacio Casino for a few days and winter came to see it. When the dispatcher called and gave me the trip, I knew it was gonna be a lot of fun. They had had about 2 feet of snow around Durango in the past 48 hours with more to come from an early fall storm. I made sure the airport at Durango was open and the runway had been plowed. Our departure time from there was after her last show at about 8:00 PM. We didn't need fuel. We parked where we were sure we could get out with a little snow clearing by the airport truck with the snow blade on it.

I called and told her husband/manager we were there and were ready to go. He said Tammy was pretty concerned about the weather and wanted to be reassured that it would be safe to fly. I told him to tell her that this is what I do for a living and I'm as good a pilot as she is a performer. It continued to snow about two inches an hour. At 9:00 PM I had the airport manager start blading off the snow in the middle 50 feet of the runway. At 9:45 PM the big van drove up and we waved them in close enough to load the bags. Most of the band was going back in the big bus they travel in, so all we had were some suitcases, hanging bags and one guitar case. There were five passengers and, as we had a Lear 25 model, there was plenty of room. I had them all wait in the little terminal.

I helped the copilot and airport manager sweep the wings and tail and started loading the passengers. When I told Miss Wynette it was time to come out and get aboard, I saw that she was as white as a sheet. Her husband was supporting her and she looked like she might refuse to get on and was shaking her head back and forth. I went over and took her hand and said "Miss Wynette, I'm just a country boy from Ennis, Texas, and you know us Texans don't lie to people. I'll take you to Nashville in 2 hours and you'll probably nap all the way. But I can't do it if you don't walk out of here, get on that airplane and act like a star. So, let's get this show on the road."

She cocked her head and smiled a very small smile and said "You really aren't worried about this weather?" I smiled back and said "I just wish it was this good all the times I have to go fly." She said "Dang if you ain't from Texas, only a Texican could tell a lie that smooth. Well, then, let's get going." She whipped out the door and got aboard. I told her I was giving her the "Catbird" seat—the best in the house. We got everybody on and buckled down good. I told them we would hit a few bumps until we got on top of the clouds in about 10 minutes. I taxied to the north end of the runway and turned around. With about 800 feet of visibility in blowing snow, we made the takeoff, lifted off so smoothly you could hardly tell we were flying instead of rolling. I made a steep climb to get into the smoother air at higher altitudes although the turbulence wasn't that bad anyway.

We popped out on top at 17,000 feet with a half-moon shining down on this deck of white clouds as far as you could see in any direction. I leveled out at 41,000 feet, put the altitude hold of the autopilot on, and handed the cockpit over to the copilot so I could go back and see to the passengers. They were all looking pretty comfortable. I got out the catering, showed them where the ice, coffee and sodas were and knelt down on one knee beside Miss Wynette's seat. Her husband was sitting across the aisle looking as though he might be asleep. Everybody else was getting after the catering.

"Okay, Miss Wynette, I hope this eases your mind some. That book I read this morning about how to take one of these things off the ground seemed to work pretty well. Now I'd better get back and read that next chapter, about how you land one in the dark." She laughed, a sweet, husky laugh, and said "I have to say, I don't like flying much, but you've got a way of making it seem natural somehow. Is the landing going to be okay?" I told her that it would be so smooth that I'd have to bounce the plane a couple of times to make her believe we were down.

And being a man of my word, I did a lady kiss bounce. You touch on lightly, then lift up just once, about 6 inches, and then down just firm enough to feel it, but not "experience" it. We unloaded just after 1:00 AM Eastern Time. When everything was off and being loaded into their vehicle, Tammy came up to me. She hugged me, kissed my cheek and said "Thank you." I said "Look out, your husband is right behind us."

She laughed, turned around and kissed him and told him he was right, this was the only way to go anywhere. Tammy Wynette, 55 years of age, exited this world's stage on April 6, 1998. She didn't make the kind of music

I'm partial to, and I saw her exactly one time in my entire life, but I liked her. There was something beyond the stage personality, the music, the lifestyle, and I saw it because she was just another passenger that needed to be reassured that she was valuable cargo. That is one part of this job that I think has more reward to it than any good landing.

"Little" Al Unser, Jr. was a nice kid to fly. I had several trips with him, but the one I remember best was to Mansfield, OH, from his home base in Albuquerque, NM, on April 20, 1993. He and his race team were setting up the car he would race at Indy this summer, and they met him there. We spent three days at the Mansfield auto racetrack in damn cold weather with the wind blowing off Lake Erie. He would run the car several laps, then this mob of specialized mechanics would swarm all over it, do things and then run it again. My copilot and I were there most of the time, and it was interesting to see what goes on in Indy car auto racing.

Little Al was always kidding me about letting him fly the Lear sometime. The picture of us in this book is at Mansfield. (*Photo #53*) I told him he would get to fly the Lear home the same day he turned me loose with that million dollar race car to see how fast I could get it around the track. He wasn't a jet pilot, and I sure wasn't an Indy race car driver, so we broke even. I flew and he drove. This was not the year he won Indy. That was the year before this one, and the year after this. Over the years I followed his career, his divorce, his problems with alcohol, the second marriage, and now hopefully, how he is getting his life back on track. He was a star, and coming from a family of stars it had to be a tough act to follow. I hope he continues to do well.

At different times we had to relay United Airlines crews to change out with other flight crews that had run out of duty time. This would make for some interesting conversations once in a while. Many of the younger pilots were glad to get a Lear ride to see how it flew. I would usually make a max effort climb, if possible, and let them see the altimeter winding around the dial at 1,000 feet every 10 seconds for a minute. Then I would ease off to 3,000 feet a minute rate and accelerate to 300 knots indicated if ATC didn't have any restrictions for us. The older pilots would grouch about the trip sometimes when it was over saying it was not smooth enough. I always told them we were paid to get them there right away, so we just flew the airplane like a jet is supposed to be flown—fast, high, and straight.

When we flew charters for UPS to ferry a crew to an aircraft, their pilots were a lot saltier than UAL crew members. Remember, freight don't complain. We flew lots of freight flights for UPS and got along real well with everybody in their organization. The other freight operators, DHL, FedEx and a few smaller ones, all have good relationships with the charter operators and they used us a lot. We were the putty to fill in the cracks when things broke down or the freighters were swamped. Freight don't complain, that's true enough, but freight customers can be a *giant* pain in the gozanga when that freight doesn't get through. The freight operators might lose a little money hiring a charter operator to get it there if they can't, but it supports the customer base and that's what must be done, if they want to stay successful in the airplane freight business. We gave them a pretty good hourly rate and that's why they kept calling us instead of "Joe Plonk's Last Chance Freight Forwarding Service."

There is a status thing with pilots in these different disciplines, starting with the Airline pilots at the top and then the large Freight carrier pilots, large corporate flight departments, small corporate departments, personal pilots, business and company pilots, charter service pilots, agricultural pilots, flight instructors and finally Joe or Josie Privatepilot. He or she owns their little machine and basically just want to be left alone. They have no pretense of becoming Joe or Josie Awsomepilot. Some things are done without a life goal just for the enjoyment and self-fulfillment of it. Skipping flat rocks across a small pond won't put you into the Olympics or into a

Learjet cockpit either. This type of thing, however, can put an easy smile on your face. It is a conscious act of will that says "I have enough. I have what most of you want. I can't give it to you. You must earn it. It is called, serenity."

Military pilots are the only group exempted from this status scale. There is no bracket big enough to fit them in. They live in a different world of challenge with aircraft, and they will knowingly and willingly take them into harm's way when necessary. They are very well trained, motivated and aware that at some point it may be necessary to play the "Queen of Spades" card in the interest of our national security and taking the risk of having it permanently trumped by the opponent. Almost all of the ones I have met, and had the opportunity to spend some time with, have had a cutting edge that you don't get in civilian flying. I can't say how good they are at their jobs, because I have no way of evaluating their performance. The only ones who will ever know their true capabilities are the pilots on the other side of the line in the dirt. I wouldn't care to be one of those people across that line.

I did some flying with IJA for Martin Aerospace Division out of Southwest Denver. About four trips I made to Ellington Air Force Base in Houston, TX were to have conferences with NASA on certain projects in the works. After I ran into John Young and several other astronauts that I met in Orlando when I was with Disney, I was allowed to see the facilities in the Astronaut Training Division. They obtained the necessary pass and clearances for me, and for nearly a day I saw the inside of the NASA training machine, the shuttle simulator (unbelievably complex), and the classrooms where training for missions *years* in the future were being conducted. I stood at the deep swimming pool, with a mockup of a portion of the space shuttle underwater, where two trainees in white space suits were conducting tasks that could be necessary on an EVA (Extra Vehicle Activity) spacewalk while on a mission. They worked as efficiently inverted as they did upright with most of the gravitational force being cancelled out by the water. My training in aircraft was almost useless in understanding very much about these systems that have to function basically without error to make all this machinery work. I came to the conclusion that it was mostly done by black magic.

We operated a few lease-back Learjets for their owners and for our operations when we needed them if they were available. One of these was a really pretty 24D owned by Harry Combs who now lived in Wickenburg, AZ. The N number was N83HC, and I must have flown that little devil thirty or forty times. It was a trade-in on a new Lear when Harry was President of Gates Learjet, Inc., in Wichita. He bought it from the company for his own personal aircraft and we kept it at our hanger at Centennial Airport in South Denver. On the trips for Harry, we picked him up in Wickenburg, took him on his trip, dropped him back home and returned to Denver. Since I had worked for Harry at Combs Aircraft at Stapleton Airport, when I was first getting started in 1955, we knew and liked one another. I was often assigned to his trips when they came up. They were all pretty standard, except one.

The dispatcher had given me the trip schedule the night before. I went to Phoenix and picked up Harry in Lear 24, N241JA, since Harry's Lear was out on another trip, and we went back to Denver. It was February 14, 1992, and late in the afternoon. We headed for Akron, OH. The weather all over the east from Canada to Alabama was miserable with snow, ice fog, icing in clouds and not much improvement expected for the next 24 hours. Just as darkness fell, we came over Indianapolis and we were given a holding clearance there because Akron was below approach minimums. I could make an approach into Indy and get some fuel and we could wait on the ground, or go on over—250 miles, 40 min. flight time—and hold at Akron, since it was forecast to come up in about 3 hours. Harry said he really needed to get there, so our best chance was to land and fuel at Indy and then go hold at Akron. This we did and about a half hour after we got into the holding pattern, Akron put out a special airport weather report.

The weather had improved somewhat but was still below minimums. There was another aircraft also holding. He requested clearance for a "look-see" approach (to see what the pilot can actually see on the approach). If you get the runway lights in sight at 200 feet, you can go down another 50 feet. Then, if you have minimum visibility, you can continue the approach and land. Remember, all this is happening at about 130 mph, so you only have 3 or 4 seconds to make your decision. If you don't have the visibility, you slam on the power, start the missed approach, get back on the instruments and *stay* on the instruments. This approach is the standard Instrument Landing System (ILS) category I approach, for which you need to have a cloud ceiling of 200 feet above the runway and a runway visibility in the touch down zone of 2,400 feet (1/2 mile). Pilots just refer to this as "200 and a half". Other approaches have higher minimums, so the ILS category I is what most everyone trains to. The airlines and some corporate aircraft can land lower on the ILS, but it takes special equipment and training which is pretty expensive.

While we were holding, Harry told me his reason for coming to Akron. He is a member of a society that is going to sponsor a round-the-world hot air balloon trip. The board is meeting tonight and tomorrow and it's pretty important to him. Gene Cernan is one of the board members. A lot of other distinguished people in the aviation industry are here waiting for Harry. I told him we'd take a look-see after the other plane reports. This happened in just a few minutes and he told the tower he had intermittent glimpses of the runway centerline lights and about a ¼ mile variable visibility. However, he decided not to try it and is going to his alternate. I told approach we'd like to take a look. He cleared us for the approach and said to report what we found.

We set up on the localizer and glide slope, and I set the radio altimeter to 150 feet. I told Todd, my copilot, that at 200 feet above the runway to look for the lights, and I would handle everything inside. We left the landing lights off but ready, dimmed the cockpit interior lights, and I put the glide slope needle slightly above the center reference bar to keep us about 20 feet low on the glide slope after the middle marker. The runway elevation was 1,228 feet, so we could go down to 1,378 feet if we had any runway contact, and we could continue to go down if we had visibility ahead. We left the outer marker and started inbound. I slowed to minimum approach speed, 20 degrees of flap and as we came up on the middle marker and crossed it Todd said lights were dimly visible. I went down another 50 feet and Todd said they were getting better. At 100 feet above the runway, Todd said he had them in sight. I looked up and saw the center lights blinking so I knew we had snow blowing across the runway. I'd been holding 4 degrees left correction to stay on the localizer. I called for full flaps and put the landing lights on. We had about 900 feet of visibility down the runway with blowing snow from left to right. We reported down and taxiing in to the tower, and said we had a momentary hole that let us have enough visibility, but that it closed up as we were rolling out and now we had about 1,200 foot runway visibility. In reality, it was about half of that.

Harry was sitting right behind us watching the whole approach. Now, Harry Combs is a very well-known aviator and has a wide experience background from biplanes to jets as a pilot. He slapped me on the back as we were taxiing in and said "John, that was one of the best damn approaches I've ever ridden through. I enjoyed the hell out of that and now let's get down to the party." We had the line service put the Lear in the hangar and told them we'd call about the servicing tomorrow.

The party was at a large, fancy motel and it was a mob scene. I found Gene Cernan and we went around eating everything in sight and meeting lots of fairly famous aviation people and a lot of non-famous ones like Todd and me. Gene kept introducing me as the Disney Chief pilot and I kept correcting him and told everybody I was flying for Harry Combs this trip. All evening and the next morning the big planning session ran on. Finally, Harry said let's leave in an hour, so Todd and I went out and got the airplane ready. The snow storm off Lake Erie had subsided to just occasional squalls; no problems, so we got going when Harry showed up. We landed in Indy on the way so Harry could do some work at the AMR Combs fixed base operation. We then went on to Wickenburg to pick up Ginnie, his lovely wife, and dropped them off at Deer Valley Airport in Phoenix. Todd flew on the way back to Denver. He was just making reserve captain with IJA. He was a great kid and did a nice job of flying.

He asked me as we got the junk out of the airplane "Don't you really think that weather was a little too bad for an approach?" I told him the truth. "For you, yes. For me, I don't know. But I do know that Harry would have let me know if *he* had thought it wasn't good enough."

The balloon trip around the world never took off, being too expensive for the sponsors, and there was too much pushing and shoving on the different committees. In later years other people did it. One was a French team of two men. Then the only successful solo flight ever made was by the American, Steve Fosset, who circumnavigated the globe in a hot air balloon, only to die a few years later all alone in a small aircraft in the western Nevada mountains.

I had trips to the Super Bowl, to the Wounded Knee Memorial on the Rosebud Indian Reservation in Southern South Dakota, to Canada, and to most of the states comprising our country—I might have missed Rhode Island. Almost every one of them had some kind of interesting story that went with it. In general though, the highest percent of my trips have been standard and only what was expected. The ones I've culled out here are some of the more interesting ones. I wanted to give you some idea of what our "day at the office" can be like. The airline pilot bids a scheduled run depending on his seniority. He knows where he will be next Thursday afternoon. The charter pilot flying part 135 "on demand charter" knows his duty time starts and ends with a chime on his cell phone. It used to be a beeper, which meant call dispatch *now*. He has to be prepared to fly to an airport that he has never heard the name of before. This takes a well-oiled machine to do this safely, with much initial and recurrent training, but it is done efficiently and safely every day of the year. The safety factor is in the strength of the support group—the mechanics, avionic technicians, dispatchers, weather briefers, the FAA Flight Service Station staff for flight planning, filing flight plans, giving destination airport current reports … the list is a lot longer than this, but you get the idea.

This is not the John Sparks, boy wonder, super pilot story. It is, rather, John Sparks, the point of the nail that is hammered into the project, by the efforts of all of the hundreds of faceless and generally unrecognized valuable assistants who make it possible to fly the aircraft at all. Most of the positions in this support group entail much training to be effective. The men and women who work at this invisible level have just as much right to take pride in their efforts to sustain quality and a right to feel that they are as important to the finished product (i.e., safety for the user) as the operational team, the pilots.

I've tried to put you in the cockpit with me so you can get an idea of what life at the point of the nail is like. The project is to get from one place on earth to another place on earth quickly and safely. I have no right to say my job is better than your job, yet people seem to think that pilots are a special breed of cat. Good pilots are a lot like good manicurists. They have the right touch and they can do their job without causing you (much) discomfort. This analogy isn't all that close to reality when you get to the worst case scenario, however. I've never heard of anybody winding up dead as the result of a really lousy performance by a manicurist.

I went to the monthly pilot meeting at IJA one night and the Director of Operations said that we were going to institute a new procedure—one that the airlines were using. This was known as CRM (Cockpit Resource Management) and involved the captain and the copilot discussing the management of the flight and coming to a mutual decision about the different factors as they come up. When opinions were asked for on this move, mine was short and not sweet. I simply said "Not on my flights." I took the position that one of the jobs of the captains was to train the copilots to a satisfactory level to transition to the captain position. I could see no advantage in a captain with many thousands of hours of flight time asking a 1,500 hour copilot if he thought it was safe to make the flight, or approach, or do we have enough reserve fuel for the alternate and then having to make decisions based on this. My contention was that I could care less what the airlines are doing, and that they still seem to be sticking airplanes into the ground where they're not supposed to be, CRM or no CRM. We had good control with our training process anyway. Lynn Krogh, Steve Parks, Bob Resling, Brian Smith and several of our line captains (even me) had worked with our copilots and emerging captains in airmanship techniques and classroom support information. This was a bright bunch of young men and women who were willing and ready to learn. I always let them go out on the limb as far as I could, when they were flying the leg, before I jumped in. I learned one thing from the old timers who taught me. You can often learn more from one mistake than by doing it right twenty-five times in a row.

The result of this was that I had to make a choice—abide by the new company policy or do what I considered to be in the best interests of these young copilots, the company and myself. After a few days of difficult thought about it, I decided to stand by my initial decision. There were more aspects to this, however. Corporate flying is less hide bound and stringent by far than Part 135 ops. This was a public transportation business venture and tightly controlled by FAA regulations. My last three pilot positions had been in Part 141 (airline, scheduled and non-scheduled, Chief Instructor Pilot), Part 135 (Air Freight airline, scheduled and non-scheduled, Line Captain), and part 135 (On demand Charter operations, scheduled and non-scheduled, Line Captain). I was tired and I was not certain that I could continue to perform as well as I had been doing with the way we had to operate. If it had been a corporate flight position, I would probably have continued for a longer period of time. Corporate flying will always be my first love—my first prom date.

Regretfully, I told the company of my decision. They offered me a ground position which was very kind of them. But I'm not much good on the ground. I looked over my shoulder and there was the door opening. It was time to go.

I have one more chapter to write and my observations of my life on planet Earth will be fairly complete. I could write a few more books about airplanes perhaps, but I realize that once your life story is told, it's yesterday's news.

Chapter 11 — And Now a Word from our Sponsor

Years ago, when I was flying a corporate jet out of New York for Texasgulf Sulphur, a passenger on one of my trips asked me a question during that trip. "Why does it seem like all the pilots I've met are somehow different from people I know who aren't pilots? I can't put my finger on it, but I can feel it every time I'm around you guys." I had to smile because I had been asked similar questions numerous times before.

"Well, being a pilot doesn't make me an expert on what motivates us. I've always thought that most professional pilots I've known have a bond with the rule breakers, the people that push back boundaries, the men and women who went west, crossed the mountains, and had to see the next valley or the next card. The limits they set for themselves had to be extended when they were reached. It's a lot like that with pilots. We are not necessarily risk takers for excitement. It's more about defining who you are, what *your* limits are and how you see yourself. Most pilots would rather make a perfect instrument approach and landing in really abominable weather, than to just slick it on with the sun shining brightly and a calm wind. We have had to learn to live with our inner fears and doubts. There's no getting up and walking out when you get your feet in the fire. You have to learn how to put out the fire."

I thought I had given a pretty good answer. My passenger shook his head a few times. "That explains it. Now I understand. All you pilots are *weird.*" We both laughed.

Weird or not, flaky or not, dedication to a high standard of safety and performance seems to be a prime denominator in all levels of success in the flying business. This is why we test ourselves so much and so hard with check rides and training.

Training in the old days was basically all in the airplane itself. Sitting in the cockpit on the ground going through the systems, controls, switches, circuit breakers, fuses, back-up systems, emergency procedures and tips on performance. This didn't put any time on the engines and airframe. No fuel was burned and there was no wear and tear on tires and brakes. Then, being in actual flight gave you all the sensations of movement, warnings through the controls into your hands and feet, rapid "G" force variations, air and engine noise, head movements during turns, turbulence and maneuvering. All these factors were and are a vital and necessary part of your work environment in the cockpit. Each adds a quantity of information that helps set up the actions necessary to enhance, stabilize or counter the previous control inputs. This is necessary in order to maintain the desired speed, track, and performance. This is a second by second recognition and adjustment—major and minor— program; somewhat similar to driving a car in heavy traffic. However, with a car you have a course that is pre-determined, that does not have vertical factors, that leads you to mandatory course and speed changes and that gives you an adequate time frame to set up control for those changes.

This is not so in the sky. The Army Air Corps, in WW II, anticipated training losses of 10 to 15 per cent and combat losses of 25 to 40 per cent. I think the Navy/Marine Corps figures were slightly lower in their estimates, but no one in any service operating aircraft came out with an estimated loss of 5 per cent in training and actual operations for a very good reason. You can't take men with no previous experience, age 19-23; give them 180-200 hours of training, learning to operate one of the most complicated pieces of machinery ever built, in an environment that is so dangerous that a major mistake is often "strike three," and reasonably expect them to easily survive this learning experience. Then they were sent to places to use this new skill in the face of *armed resistance* so determined, so deadly, that combat losses can be 20 per cent to 30 per cent and occasionally even higher. The Japanese combined air forces loss was 70-80 per cent total, partially because of the Kamikaze suicide attacks during the last year of the war.

The modern "Jet Age" has changed the training and accident numbers to some extent. Jet engines operate for much longer time periods than piston (reciprocating) engines, and have a lower failure rate. Mandatory inspections for aircraft have become stringent, more often, more precise and *much* more expensive for all private, commercial and military operators, in terms of hours of operation, that is. In terms of miles flown (or seat miles) there is a much different picture. One Boeing 747-100 generates so many available seat miles in a year's operation (1,800,000) that it would take a fleet of 32 Douglas DC-3s to match it. If we wanted the available seat miles of the 300 or so 747s in the world, Douglas had better put on an extra shift, since we'll need 10,600 DC-3s in a hurry. That sounds like a lot of airplanes, but it really isn't. We produced 22,000 B-24 Liberator Bombers, 13,000 B-17's and about 60,000 other types for WW II. That's about 95,000 planes in less than 5 years. Today, the world almanac shows about 2,000,000 aircraft active across the world with about 400,000 in the USA.

Wow! That's a *lot* of iron in the sky at any one time. Why don't we hear of more accidents happening? If we could read all the foreign language newspapers around the world, we would read about small airplanes, helicopters, cargo planes, small airliners, military planes and others with too few fatalities to make the daily papers in Kansas, Wyoming or Alabama. However, if you get a good size airliner crash with 60-80 fatalities, it will make the Salina Journal in Salina, KS, even if the crash is in Dar-Es-Salaam.

The training we young pilots endured in the '50s, '60s and '70s was a double-edged sword. One edge was supposed to shape and refine our skills as we sought to become aviators, especially if we were going to try for the airlines. The other edge was supposed to eliminate the unfit (for a better word) or limit them to the private or minimal commercial license they could cope with. Each stratum in aviation requires the very basic skills to as high a level as possible. We then build upon this base to develop the specialty skills that define the standards for the airline pilot, agricultural pilot, training instructor pilot, military, corporate, general aviation (charter, air ambulance, maintenance flight), check pilots (FAA, designated flight examiners, etc.) and other specialty areas.

Did this training of the '50s to '80s era produce good pilots? Yes, in general it did. Did it eliminate the unfit (for a better word)? In many cases, yes, but to be quite honest, no system will eliminate the probabilities that some of these students will be processed into the system. No one can tell you how they will operate under extreme stress conditions. And you will never know this, if they have not been observed under this type of above normal stress. Our modern academic training systems have many fine points in their favor. They also have some inherent faults that will tend to protect students that should be noted for poor performance and tested further to make certain that a high level of minimum performance standards is not in question.

The modern electronic full motion simulator has changed training for the better in most cases of cockpit procedures. However, they have given an impression that this type of training is all that you need to be ready to operate (fly) medium performance aircraft. Or even high performance ones.

In all honesty, every employed pilot who does their PIC (pilot in command) annual check rides in the simulators of Flight Safety (or other similar training facilities) knows that they will fly the sim for 1 to 2 hours. Then they will get up, make a head call, get a cup of coffee, and come back for the second half in the other seat, if they fly dual captains like many corporate and other operators do. Then they go to class on systems, performance, etc. They do this for four or five days, get a check ride and go home for another year.

You always know that no matter how badly you screw up in the sim, they won't be sifting your bones out of the ashes. If you stall and dive in inverted, you say "Aw, _____! Back it up and I'll try it again" and again, if necessary. Sure there's pressure here, but it's not the mind numbing turbulence and "G" forces that shake you like a dog shaking a rat, as you're being sucked into the core of a medium sized thunderstorm— in the hail, lightning, rain in solid sheets, more turbulence, so much you can't get a lock on the instruments with your eyes, people are screaming in the cabin and all this in the full black of the night. Now, you're earning your pay.

I've been in several scenarios like that. The one I just described happened to me on June 23, 1962, on a night trip from La Guardia Airport in New York to Detroit in an Aero Commander 500. We were on instruments northeast of Allentown, PA, the center radar was on circular polarization only, and therefore, no thunderstorm avoidance vectoring was available. All thunderstorm activity was supposed to be well to the north of the airway we were navigating on.

I saw two lightning flashes in the clouds and then moderate rain began. We were at 8,000 feet and I told the four passengers to make sure their seat belts were tight, or at least very snug. The hair on my arms stood straight up from the static electric charge. St. Elmo's fire started bouncing off the props and rolling up the windshields. I turned the cockpit lights up full bright so I wouldn't be blinded by lightning. The radios were frying in static, the navigation track needles were bouncing from one side to the other. I made sure the autopilot was off. It quieted for a minute, and then *BAM!* We were in it.

I had slowed to about 130 miles per hour (no nautical miles in those days), the rate of climb showed us climbing between 1,500 feet and 1,800 feet per minute with moderate turbulence and light hail. We stopped climbing at about 14,000 feet and the bottom fell out. I brought the power back up to try and slow the descent so we wouldn't pull too many G's when we bottomed out. We made this elevator trip twice and then the lightning flashes seemed farther away and it smoothed out for about 30 seconds. Suddenly a giant hand grabbed the airplane and shook it like a dog shaking a rat. After 20 or 30 seconds, it spit us out of the thunderstorm about 15 miles from the Allentown airport. I said "Folks, we're going to land at Allentown so I can check the airplane and I think we'll spend the night and go on to Detroit in the morning." My boss (I was flying for a mining company in Utah) said that sounded like a great plan. The Commander checked out okay. It had a half a dozen hail dings, but no real damage.

The old timers I had flown with to Mexico in Lodestars and Twin Beeches had trained me to stay calm, don't fight the up and down drafts, stay level, go straight unless you see a hole out to sunshine and make only 20 degree maximum banks in the turns at most. Keep the airspeed down below maneuvering speed of the aircraft to lighten the G forces and a few other things. Of the twenty or so penetrations I made before we got the Bendix RDR-1B radar in our Howard 250 Lockheed Lodestar conversion, I never was comfortable taking passengers into this type of weather and did so only when that was the only reasonable course of action. My company, Texasgulf Sulphur Co., made a deal with United Airlines at the training center in Denver, where the first radar training courses were being taught to the United pilots. Four of us

TG pilots went through their school in 1965, and learned how to get and use the information off the radar scope. The United instructors essentially told us to do what the old timers had told me. They said go straight, don't try to turn around to get out, for if you do, you might get snapped over on your back, then you pull negative G's, the wings fold up and it's Adios, amigos.

This is what the simulator can't fully prepare you for. You get one shot at it. Fortunately, radar has pretty much solved the thunderstorm problem. Go around, if possible or above and between them.

To conclude this chapter, let me say I think any training is useful, but I also think that the student must be made aware that training alone is not enough. To make a good pilot, whether private, commercial or airline transport, you have to develop analytical skills and make good decisions. A lifetime of doing amazing things in the air doesn't give you a magical free pass when the crunch comes. I think Steve Fosset would agree with me on this, if he could.

The Flight Safety simulator at Marietta, GA for the Lockheed L-1329 Jetstar 4 engine corporate jet, will sweat about 3 or 4 pounds off of you in a week of training. The sim instructors were sharp, but also mean, if you got them riled up. I got along with them pretty well and my rides, although a long way from perfect, weren't so bad that I had to wear a dunce cap. The next to last PIC (pilot in command) check ride I had at Texasgulf was on the Jetstar. I had one of the most senior pilots in our flight department (we'll call him Blank) assigned to ride the sim with me. We both needed our bi-annual PIC check rides to be legal to fly as captains in our corporate flight operation. Blank was really behind the curve during his left seat time in the sim. We flew dual captains a lot in our flight operations, so each of us had to do the right seat (copilot) slot for the other pilot. This was a tough week. We were in the sim 3 hours in the morning, half left seat and half right seat, and classroom work in the afternoons. Friday, the last day, was our "ride," the check ride for our PIC which was a tough piece of work in a four engine jet aircraft. We each had an hour and a half to do it. Our older pilot went first. From the start, he was out of synch with the sim and the check list. I gave him all the help I could with prompts, clues and advice if he asked, until finally the sim instructor (*de boss*) said "Sparks, keep your mouth shut. Blank's got to do the command part on his own."

Well, Blank didn't pass the ride. He was scheduled back for the full training class a couple of weeks later. Now I'm ready for my ride, but since Blank busted his ride, he can't ride as copilot for me, so Flight Safety gave me one of their instructors to fill in. The guy was sharp, the ride was wild as usual, but it was going good. I had to make one last approach to minimums with an engine out on the right side. On the break from the holding pattern, the other engine on the right side quit. We cleaned it up with the checklist and got the latest weather for the ILS (Instrument Landing System) runway. It was still above minimums with a 300 foot ceiling, RVR (Runway Visual Range) of ¾ of a mile in fog and light drizzle. It's a piece of cake. I tell my copilot to declare a priority landing situation because of our having two engines out. The tower acknowledged the priority. We grooved the ILS, needles crossed, airspeed right on the airspeed bug, gear down and locked, LADs (Lift Augmentation Devices, better known as leading edge slats) extended, flaps approach (15 degrees), the anti-skid test gives good cycling lights and shows the pressure up; all checklist items are done. We nail the outer marker right on altitude, with glide slope and localizer indicator needles right on the money. We descend to cross the middle marker at 200 feet altitude. I'm waiting for the copilot to call runway in sight or centerline lights visible. At 250 feet above the runway, still on instruments, the tower calls and says, "Vehicle on runway, vehicle on runway, go around, go around, start the missed approach procedure, expect radar vectors for the localizer, call when established inbound on localizer."

I slammed the two left power levers to the stops as soon as I heard the first go around command from the tower. I called out to the copilot "Missed approach, flaps to 15 degrees. When climb rate is positive, gear up. At 140 knots, flaps and lads up, climb checklist now. At 1,500 feet, give me the in range, approach, and pre-landing checks. Get the current weather as we turn in on the localizer." We leveled at 1,500 feet AGL, and within 30 seconds the alarm bells go off again. Now what, I think to myself. I glanced at the master warning readout, it shows number 1 engine on the left side is spooling down. The copilot says "The number 1" .... I stop him. "I see it. Do the 1 engine shutdown checklist; check the fire warning test—we still have the main hydraulic system operational on number 2 engine. Call the tower and declare an emergency; tell them we will land, vehicle or no vehicle, we have only one engine running. We will hold the landing gear until 1 mile from the middle marker, extend the lads and 20 degrees flap intercepting the glide slope. When I ask for power, give me 100 per cent." The new weather comes in—Indefinite ceiling 100 feet, RVR 800 feet, wind calm, altimeter 29.92 and the vehicle has been removed from the runway—Oh, great, below minimums now, and not a chance of going around on one engine.

So I'm inbound on the localizer, below the glide slope. "Give me full power" and the number 2 engine spools up to 100 per cent. We start to intercept the glide slope. "Give me 20 degrees flap, check lads out." We catch the glide slope, 2 miles to the middle marker, "Stand by gear, gear down, check lights 3 green, anti-skid armed, hydraulic pressure up, hold landing lights until breakout or runway in sight. Tell tower we *WILL*, repeat, *WILL* land." The copilot complied. We pass the middle marker and he says "Gear coming down, gear shows down, 3 green, pressure up, anti-skids armed, pressure up." We have passed the middle marker at 200 feet and I say "Call 100 feet, full flaps at 100 feet." He does this and calls out centerline lights as we break out at 50 feet above the runway. I look up, see the runway lights, lift the nose slightly as I back the power off. We get a firm touchdown. I pull number 2 engine into soft, then full reverse. I use moderate, then full braking. We roll out, stop, and shut down on the runway. The ceiling is 50 feet, the visibility is 600 feet. I tell the copilot to clean up the checklist and secure the cockpit. The tower says we have 1,000 feet of runway left. We used 7,000 feet of the 8,000 foot runway.

The sim instructor comes into the cockpit as we are getting out of our harness and belts. "Well, it was a little sloppy. Maybe we ought to run through it again." I finish unbuckling my harness, step out and away from the left seat. I looked at the sim instructor and said "I got a better idea. Why don't you get up here and show me how it's done?"

Everybody breaks out laughing, me included. This is a Red Dog—A training procedure that is sometime given to a pilot after he has already completed his check ride and is certified for another year as a pilot in command of the airplane. I was told later by the sim instructor, while we were having coffee and getting ready for the last classroom review before we all headed for wherever we lived, that only about one pilot out of three makes it around with only one engine running and it's always very close.

The sim instructor said he understood my trying to help Blank. "The point is, if and when it ever gets really sticky, he might have a real inexperienced copilot along. Then he'll have to do most of it, maybe all of it." And, of course, he was absolutely right.

It seems that every time I speak anywhere, Chamber of Commerce, Lions Club, etc., one of the questions that is asked pertains to the safety of flying the airlines now with all the airport security measures that have been implemented. My answer is always the same. We are just as safe as we have ever been. It has never been absolutely safe to fly in powered airplanes. One of the first military passengers to fly with Orville Wright was in a crash on September 17, 1908, and died as a result. Your chances of dying on a commercial airliner are very, very slim, but somebody or a group of somebody's is going to have that honor every year somewhere in the world. You are far more likely to die in a bathtub, car wreck, house fire, tornado, or motorcycle wreck.

The thing that bothers me, and a lot of other very experienced pilots, is that we have let the computer nerds design the flight systems on our most modern aircraft. They have taken away the primary "direct" control systems and instituted computer servo driven systems that have caused the deaths of several thousand passengers in the last 20 years. I used to give flight checks in airplanes that you could turn off the entire electrical system and continue to fly and control it until you ran out of fuel. They were large, twin engine aircraft, not little single engine ones. I know that the airlines will do their best to maintain the highest degree of safety for their passengers. But take the case of Air France Flight 447, an AirBus 330 that departed Brazil for Paris in June 2009. When it lost some of its sophisticated flight management computer inputs, it went out of control. Even though the crew did their utmost to wrest control of the aircraft back from the AFCS (Automated Flight Control System), they were unable to do so. They went to their doom as helpless as any of the passengers—All 228 people, crew and passengers, died.

Many of the airlines forbid the crew to fly the aircraft without the autopilot/AFCS, even to the point of making all the instrument approaches with it. Does this really keep the crew sharp if they have to take over, and can manage to do it, if a problem develops? Oh, yeah, sure it does.

I read many of the reports of crashes and accidents of airliners and other aircraft on the Internet. There are a number of good databases that can be accessed such as AirSafety.com, AOPA.com, Airdisaster.com and many others. As a professional pilot, the information they give me allows me to evaluate the way the crash developed, how it was handled by the crew and what other factors were critical in this situation. I know, I know, hindsight is 20-20, but I always put it in focus, as if I were the pilot at the controls. Sometimes there is no evidence remaining and only suppositions can be made about the sequence of events. With airliners, having the flight data recorder and cockpit voice recorder available, pretty much allows a very accurate reconstruction of the events if they can be recovered. The NTSB (National Transportation Safety Board) investigates all fatal accidents in the public transportation system, buses, trains, etc., then determines the probable cause as closely as possible and mandates changes to improve the safety of the systems impacted. Of course, airplanes and airlines have been the "Glamour Tragedies" for many years, especially if someone of note is among the victims.

I am appalled at the reports of some of the recent crashes of the last 15 years. I find it hard to believe that a senior crew of American Airlines, flying a night trip in a Boeing 757 in Columbia, South America, mishandled it so badly that the NTSB report cited six probable causes of the crash directly attributed to the crew and their handling of the flight. One hundred and sixty people died, four survived. There are more than sixty crash reports that can hardly be believed, many of them in third world countries, which helps explain something about their training as you read these reports. Do I have any answers that will alleviate this situation? None you would want to hear. These new fly-by-wire aircraft *have* to operate at *optimum parameters* on their control systems. Their back-up systems are more of the same. Anyone who has *never* had a problem with a computer system at home or work, no problems with the apps you put on it, have a cell phone that has never given you a minutes teeth-gnashing problem, and a cable TV system that has purred like a pussycat, you are free to leave the room.

We live in a society that is just one series of high air burst, high yield neutron-pulse, nuclear devices away from becoming an 1890's type of society—Just one series of long range ICBM missiles to deliver them to the heart of our electrical grid systems. Bingo! The flight control system of every new era "fly-by-wire" aircraft in flight and in range of this neutron flux will go to sleep—permanently. The destruction of the electrical grid would be a time machine in reverse for the entire nation.

The systems we are putting in the new fly-by-wire aircraft are eroding the base for even having a well-trained crew in the cockpit. Super autopilots are okay on climb, cruise and initial letdown, but when it's time to do the honest work, that's when the pilot should roll up his sleeves and take the reins. But, it doesn't work that way anymore. I think every student pilot should have to learn the basics in a Stearman biplane (*Photo #54*), fly nothing but tail draggers for the first 100 hours and get the first 25 hours of instrument time in the old, beloved Link Trainer. Then graduate into the milk stools—tri-cycle gear aircraft, controllable pitch propellers, and work toward that 1,500 hours minimum they need to start an airline career. We are turning out a lot of very savvy game players, computer whizzes and simulator wizards. The problem is, we're calling them pilots.

Another problem is that the aeronautical schools, that these kids have been paying $75,000 a year to teach them this, have them convinced that they *are* pilots, every bit as good as the crew that dumped the de Havilland DHC-8 Regional airliner in with a load of ice at Buffalo, NY, in February 2009. None of the forty-nine human beings on the aircraft survived. It would seem that some instructor forgot to tell the crew that it's best to take the autopilot off and hand fly the bird when icing is moderate or heavy, so the autopilot won't stall it out and half snap roll it into the ground. These kids coming out of our collegiate and other flight schools *want* to be pilots and they *deserve* to have the education that will give them the ability to live to retirement age in these modern airplanes. They look awful cute in those little uniforms, but they would look a lot better to me crawling around the airplane with an instructor, greasy and oily from learning what an airplane really is. It's not just the cockpit, but the parts that can keep you alive, take you back home, or take your breath away.

The Lockheed L-1329 Jetstar has two interesting items on the interior preflight/prestart checklist. They are an 8 inch length common screwdriver, and a ¾ inch size open end wrench. These are checklist items. *You do NOT leave the ground without them!* Why is that?

Good question. From the time you walk up to this aircraft with the door key in your hand, until the trip is over and you walk away with the door locked and the key in your pocket, there are 306 items on the complete checklist covering the operation of this 4 engine jet aircraft, even if you are only going on a half hour flight. This is the normal operational checklist only, not any part of the emergency checklists. However, there are certain tools for use in the emergency checklists which are checked on before flight, just to make sure they are available, if needed. For instance, portable oxygen bottle, smoke mask/glasses, flashlights, fire axe, CO_2 fire extinguisher, first aid kit, water fire extinguisher, spare fuses, light bulbs, current limiters, the screwdriver and open end wrench.

Let's assume that you have the right main landing gear hung up in the uplock, and when you extend the gear the uplock won't release it, and the right gear stays up while the other two extend. You cycle the gear a few times, still no right gear. So (by the emergency checklist), you retract the landing gear into the up position. Then depressurize the aircraft, remove the carpet in the hallway behind the cockpit, take off the access plate that gives you room to reach in with the necessary tool, pry the uplock open from the gear lock, and the gear will drop downwards. Now, put the gear handle in the down position and the gear will extend and lock in the down position. This is possible to do for all three gear legs, but usually it will only be one that is hung up. But, without these two simple tools, you are going to scuttle a multi-million dollar aircraft.

My belief is that it takes a certain amount of time to become competent and comfortable with a complicated checklist, but it can be done. The PF (pilot flying) and the

PNF (pilot not flying) each have areas of responsibilities that change when they change roles. Complicated cockpit procedures are quite a bit like ballet dancing. Everybody knows the music and everybody knows the steps. Until you learn the other steps, you are locked into your role. After much training and preparation, you are ready to move up to the new role, in this case, from copilot to pilot.

I also believe it takes some humility adjustments from time to time, and I can say that from personal experience—I mean getting them, not giving them. If you have a very sensitive nature and can't take critiquing easily, you are going to have a problem working in very tight quarters with a seemingly overbearing critic, who points out every little mistake you make, especially when it's the third or fourth time in a row. It will be hard to convince yourself that this overbearing pilot actually has your best interests at heart. If you don't do it though, you will probably be back slicing up the French fries at McDonalds before too long. I have had perhaps a hundred copilots in my career and no two were alike. All had strong points and weak points. In nearly all of them, there was a great desire to do things the right way, but in haste, taking shortcuts, to hurry it up and get out of this menial stage.

I had some copilots on the Lear's that would get very put out when I would tell them to trim up the Lear and engage the autopilot as we went through flight level 290, climbing to 450. They wanted the hands on time and I told them it was company policy to fly on autopilot when going to altitudes above 290 to conserve time and fuel. To prove it to the really frumpy ones, I would take it up to 410 or 450 on autopilot, tell them to take the controls and fly smoothly and then I would disconnect the autopilot. They would get set, and within 30 seconds to a minute we were galloping up and down a thousand feet. The more they fought it, the worse it got, until I jumped in and took over. I told them that was why we fly with the autopilot at high altitudes. I set the airplane up again and told them to take the controls, but don't move them, just hold them completely still. I turned the autopilot off and the aircraft would start to climb a hundred feet, then descend a hundred. This cycle would go on for a minute or more and the copilot would say I'm not moving it and I would say I know, but you're breathing.

Then I would explain that at this speed, 485 mph, and the thin air at FL410 (41,000 feet), the aircraft was so sensitive, it would sense the slight movement of the controls caused by the act of breathing and would respond by climbing slightly, then descending slightly. This pretty much settled this question for them. I let them hand fly on all possible occasions. We had one Lear 25D that was rated to 51,000 feet. You could get it up to this altitude if the aircraft was fairly light in weight, and the outside air temperature was low enough. A lot of the young pilots wanted to fly 510 just so they could write it off in their logbooks. I pointed out to them that we would be in a 70 knot window at this altitude. If we got 35 knots too fast, we would lose control and dive with a "Mach tuck," technically known as an "aft center of lift deployment," producing a stall, dropping the nose, increasing the speed and compounding the situation greatly. If we slowed down 35 knots, we would stall the aircraft and dive. Either way, you are going to have the ride of your life and quite possibly it would be the last one.

Almost all of them eventually found a groove they could live in. Many of them have gone on to be captains on airlines and in corporate flight departments. Several sent me Christmas cards thanking me for getting them well prepared to go on with their career choice and that my cockpit training had them way ahead of the rest of the class. I was just glad I had made some difference for them.

IJA put on several female copilots the last years I was there. They were nice kids. Two of them were married and had small children. Everybody treated them well and they tried hard and performed quite well. I had one who had been a flight instructor. She was good with the checklists and cockpit duties. But every time I gave her a leg (freight flights) she kept doing something that I had told her to correct the first time it happened. When we were at altitude she did fine, but when Center brought us down coming into Denver, we would often be cleared down to 15,000 feet from flight level 410. She would start down, I ran the descent checklist, got the ATIS, set up the approach plates, etc. and when I looked at the air speed, she had slowed down 60 to 80 knots airspeed. Our rate of descent which should have been about 3,000 feet a minute was 1,500. She had pulled the power back about 30 per cent. The first two times this happened I just told her to increase the power and then I helped her get it down. The third time, though, I said to myself, the gloves come off here. I shoved the throttles up, trimmed the nose down and we go screaming down at about 450 knots. She's pulling back, but I told her to keep at least 400 knots and 3,000 feet a minute descent. She said this was too fast, she needed it slower so she could think better and make sure she did everything right.

"Look," I said, "this airplane costs $20 a minute to operate. We are flying on a contract rate. The company makes money when we fly the scheduled time from Phoenix to Denver, and they can pay us out of the profit. But, if you slow this little jewel down so you can think and we take 15 minutes longer than normal, you've just blown $300 of profit for IJA. That's more than you and I are going to make today. You've got it ass backward. The airplane doesn't fly the way you *want* it to; you fly it the way it *needs* to be flown. Fast and safe and when you can do that, you're on your way to being a pilot instead of a sheepherder." She caught on quickly after that and the last I heard of her she was a captain flying for Continental Airlines.

Over and over I get asked "What's going to happen in aviation in the future?" And the answer is: "Nobody knows." Depending on what type of government we wind up with, it could expand, contract or become totally nationalistic. If we wind up crashing our economy and let a totalitarian government take power, it would be a nightmare scenario for everything we know and aviation would be impacted in many different ways. If we stay with the Republic we have had since the American revolution of 1776, we should eventually work our way out of trouble and aviation will benefit from new fuel sources and designs. There are so many possible combinations that will alter the American lifestyle and the lifestyles of most of the free nations of the world that any prediction will have a low probability.

I have said over and over at meetings or across a café table talking with friends, that if I had children and grandchildren, which I don't, who wanted a career in aviation, my advice to them would be to get into an aviation program if it's available, and at the same time take courses toward a degree in agronomy or other programs to produce food of some type. In the next 20 to 50 years the production of food will become the single largest expenditure of labor and technology throughout the civilized world societies. Aviation will always be with us, but possibly so severely restricted to military, agricultural and government controlled airline work, that general aviation will only be available to the super powerful and super wealthy. Fuel stocks could be a major problem unless new types of power plant technologies are developed.

We stand at a nexus point in our world history. I won't be here to see the direction we take. I regret that in a way for I do have an inquiring mindset that has made my life fairly interesting. I have written this book mainly to leave a small shadow of my footprint as a token of how much appreciation I have for the life that I was allowed to enjoy. Herman Melville wrote "Moby Dick" in a different world and time, and as much as I have enjoyed this book, I always felt that the ending was lacking, it just didn't quite fit. Then I saw the movie of "Moby Dick" directed by John Houston, featuring Gregory Peck and Richard Basehart. The screenplay had been written by Ray Bradbury, one of the favorite authors of my youth, and John Houston. The last scene was electrifying, as the ending that I had been waiting for was finally put on the screen and the words of Richard Basehart as Ishmael were carved into my memory and not forgotten to this day.

"*The drama is done. All have departed away. The restless shroud of the sea rolls over the Pequod, her crew, and Moby Dick. I only, alone, am left to tell thee this.*" Now, it was complete.

This somehow sums up how I have felt the past years, as the fine friends of my youth and career have left on their final flight plans. At the age of seventy-nine, I still feel that there is some time for me to enjoy the beauty of this world I am soon to depart. I have tried to live by some of the rules that my grandfather laid out for me as a youngster. He said one day to me and my two cousins, "When you see a person in need of help, it is your responsibility as a decent human being to go and offer whatever help you can. If they will take the offer, do your best and feel good about it. If they will not take help, still feel good about it. You have done your part. The gift is the offer." He told us kids that we should learn that doing good is better than doing evil, no matter how attractive the evil is. He said make your word your bond, your good reputation is the only really valuable thing you will ever own. He also had many other words of wisdom for us.

I am not a poet, or a philosopher, or a person of great wisdom. For poetry, I read the works of Robert Frost, who has a gift of words beyond measuring. For philosophy, I read The Rubaiyat of Omar Khayyam, the Fitzgerald translation. For prose, I have a thousand names that have thrilled me, encouraged me, educated me, and warned me. The few movies I have bonded with are eclectic, each having struck a chord in my understanding, bringing quiet joy and the knowledge that I am not alone in the way I see the world. As I've said earlier, my short list of favorites are *Shane, Monty Walsh, To Kill A Mockingbird, Driving Miss Daisy, Places In The Heart, In The Heat Of The Night, Fried Green Tomatoes,* and, of course, the John Houston *Moby Dick.*

At the end of this book there are additional pages with only names on them. These are the friends, pilots, mechanics and ramp rats that I worked with in many different places. I know they won't mean anything to most people who read this book, but to some family members and other throttle jockeys, these names may bring back a wealth of memories. This may be the last time this name will help us return to the memory of a time and place where we were all young, money was scarce and work hard to come by. It is the only gift I have for all the hundreds of people who lived and breathed airplanes and who helped me on my way.

And I would like to say thank you, to all of you who read this book. (*Photo #55*) I don't expect or do I want to change any lives with this piece of writing, but I hope it brought a few smiles and laughs as you waded through it. The pilots will have a good chance of understanding the somewhat technical passages. I would hope that any non-pilots have a little better understanding of the airplane life than they had before reading it. The early years of my airplane life were hard, but wondrous. I wish I could live them again.

Everything has a beginning and an end. We travel this tenuous bridge of life over the bottomless pit of death, knowing that even to arrive safely at the far end is to meet death face to face. We are sentenced to death with the first breath of life. But this is an academic thing—like knowing that the sun will burn out in another 20 billion years. Who really cares? At the midpoint of our life, we cast no shadow. What has happened is a prelude. What lies in the future is unknown, including the distance to our fate and what may lie beyond that.

All we pilots know this, but in a different way than the farmer or merchant. They are solid people and can usually be found at a distinct point of reference on the earth. The pilot finds substance where the earthbound person finds only distant beauty. He or she interacts with the elements of time and space with a different understanding than is given to these earthbound pillars of our world. May we all enjoy the beauty of this time, this place, this unique opportunity we have to love family and honor dear friends, before we reach the end of the bridge. (*Photo #56*)

This ending note is to honor the memory of Shanley Sorenson and Jimmy F. Markham, flying friends of mine until the end of time. I flew with these two pilots in Texasgulf Aviation for 20 years. I brought Shan into our operation in Utah. He died in our Jetstar crash at Westchester, NY in 1981. It was not his fault, but it was his fate.

When the end came for Texasgulf, Jim Markham went on to become the Department Aviation Manager for Glaxo Pharmaceuticals, the U.S. operation. He was as skilled a pilot as you could ever find. The one thing skill cannot overcome is heredity. Jim had a cerebral stroke at the age of 54 and passed away immediately. This was exactly what happened to his father at approximately the same age. There is no check ride for this, no recurrent training, no go around procedure. Again, fate is the hunter.

My last flight plan will hopefully take me to the pilot's area of the afterlife (if there is such a thing) where all my friends will be waiting. If there isn't such a thing, then we all break even. I hope to see you at the hangar, guys. Save me a place at the coffee table. John

A LIST OF AVIATION FRIENDS AND CHARACTERS

TGS AVIATION	INT. JET CREW	NON DENVER
Jimmy Markham	Tyler Appleton	Marsh Bennett
Shanley Sorenson	Larry Arellano	Chris Carlos
John Sparks	Steve Arthur	Betty Clark
Lynne Hobson	Ryan Benine	Norm Cramer
R. C. Cooper	Bob Cunningham	Clyde Davis
Robert Baugh	Paul Francois	Les George
Robert Borden	Al Halbert	Don Hackett
Silvio Bucceri	Dan Herman	Carl Helberg
Jim Dawson	Lynn Krogh	George Hubler
Jim Edwards	Diane Magruder	Jim Hurst
Robert Gardiner	Kerry McPherson	Mickey Jackson
J. M. Gregory	Bill Milam	Ralph Johnson
Bill Hollis	Chris Pappas	Frank Kelsey
Wayne Kidd	Stephen Parks	Mark Kemp
Jim Lard	Keith Schmidt	Art Loomis
Marshall Locke	Brian Smith	E. J. Luther
Tom Lovingood	Ryan Stewart	Bill Marlman
Ray Moore	Dave Taylor	Earl Marlow
Joe Thigpen	Kurt Tipton	Jack Miller

TGS AVIATION	**INT. JET CREW**	**NON DENVER**
Billy Warren		Ira Reed
Earnest Weaver		Tom Rickert
Ron Whelan		Orlon Roberts
Rick Williams		Pete Rueck
		Keith Shelly
		Raine St. Pierre
		Jim Thayer
		Dutch Werner
		Wayne Werner
		Leon Wincus

I apologize to all my many friends whose names have dimmed over the years. I still see your faces, and I smile. You are not forgotten—ever.

DENVER

Bob Agee
Bob Ainsworth
Gordon Autrey
Jake Autry
Chris Basore
Diamond Jim Brady
Wayne Brown
Dick Bucknell
Bob Bueley
Jim Buswell
Mike Burger
Red Chambers
Gene Clements
Lew Clinton
Dick Cochran
Rick Cochran
Harry B. Combs
Terry Combs
Tony Combs
Forrest Conover
Adolph Coors, Jr.
Dexter Cox
Eric Dahlberg
John Darley
Tiger Mike Davis
Frank DeCastro
Steve Dennis
Charley Dilahunty
Jack Dougleby
Eddie Drapela
Bill Duff

Chuck Halderman
Les Hall
Sanford Hanggee
Elmer Hardy
Keith Harris
B. T. Hayes
Lee Hayes
Bill Haynes
Ken Hoffman
Jimmy Jo Jeffreys
E. B. Jeppesen
Les Jordan
Lyle Kennedy
Ron Knudsen
Jerry Krause
Pete Lambert
Byron lee
Bernie Lewis
Les Longbrook
Guy Lowder
John Maxwell
Tommy Mayson
Bud Maytag
Mac McClain
Eddie Mehlin
Duane Metzger
Tal Miller
Tom Miller
Ken Moe
Tommy Monroe
Bob Moose

Dave Prohira
Bill Rhoadarmer
Bill Roosevelt
Cindy Rozinski
Frank Rozinski
Jim Ruble
Bob Scherrer
Don Sellars
Brimmer Sherman
Gene Shocker
Fran Shoup
Bob Six
Tommy Smith
Dick Snyder
Jim Stevenson
Roy Stickney
Stan Taylor
Otto Trapp
Larry Ulrich
Gil Utterback
Bob Van Buskirk
Don Vest
Don Vest, Jr.
Bob Vorbeck
Jack Waddell
Faye White
Bill Whitehurst
Bill Wyman
Rowdy Yates
Hershey Young

DENVER

Harry Duff

Ed Dusang

Bud Dyas

Craig Dyas

Win Ekeland

Jack Eppard

Roy Fisher

Charlie Gates

Ken Gerard

George Graham

Ernie Green

Wally Greenameyer

Doyle Grout

Bud Morrison

Tommy Munz

Glen Nash

Don Neil

Mel Olsen

Harvey Pardun

Chuck Peacock

Raymond Peterson

Ernie Phillips

Nate Phluge

Lee Pope

Nick Popovitch

Wally Powell

.